Labour Law in Ireland

Labour Law in Ireland

Kevin Costello

This book was originally published as a monograph in the International Encyclopaedia of Laws/Labour Law and Industrial Relations.

General Editors: Roger Blanpain, Frank Hendrickx

Published by:
Kluwer Law International B.V.
PO Box 316
2400 AH Alphen aan den Rijn
The Netherlands
Website: www.wklawbusiness.com

Sold and distributed in North, Central and South America by:
Wolters Kluwer Legal & Regulatory U.S.
7201 McKinney Circle
Frederick, MD 21704
United States of America
Email: customer.service@wolterskluwer.com

Sold and distributed in all other countries by:
Turpin Distribution Services Ltd.
Stratton Business Park
Pegasus Drive, Biggleswade
Bedfordshire SG18 8TQ
United Kingdom
Email: kluwerlaw@turpin-distribution.com

DISCLAIMER: The material in this volume is in the nature of general comment only. It is not offered as advice on any particular matter and should not be taken as such. The editor and the contributing authors expressly disclaim all liability to any person with regard to anything done or omitted to be done, and with respect to the consequences of anything done or omitted to be done wholly or partly in reliance upon the whole or any part of the contents of this volume. No reader should act or refrain from acting on the basis of any matter contained in this volume without first obtaining professional advice regarding the particular facts and circumstances at issue. Any and all opinions expressed herein are those of the particular author and are not necessarily those of the editor or publisher of this volume.

Printed on acid-free paper

ISBN 978-90-411-6169-7

This title is available on www.kluwerlawonline.com

Printed and bound by CPI Group (UK) Ltd, Croydon, CR0 4YY

The Author

Dr Kevin Costello is a Senior Lecturer in the School of Law University College Dublin. His publications include monographs on *The Law of Habeas Corpus in Ireland* (2006) and the *Court of Admiralty of Ireland 1575–1893* (2011) as well as articles on aspects of English and Irish legal history published in English, Irish and American journals. His principal current research interest is in the history of judicial review in English law between the seventeenth and twentieth centuries. In 2014 he was one of the first recipients of the Irish National Forum for the Enhancement of Teaching and Learning 'Teaching Hero' award'.

The Author

Table of Contents

Table of Contents

Table of Contents

Chapter 4. The Common Law and Constitutional Rights and Duties of the Parties During the Employment Relationship

Chapter 5. Working Time and Holidays 88

Chapter 6. Parental Leave, Maternity Leave, *Force Majeure* Leave, and Carer's Leave 99

Table of Contents

Chapter 9. Legal Regulation of Dismissal at Common Law   123

Chapter 10. The Unfair Dismissals Acts 1977–2007   134

Table of Contents

Chapter 13. Protection against Discrimination on Grounds of Sex in Employment   166

Chapter 14. The Law on Discrimination on Grounds of Age, Disability and Race 183

Chapter 15. Non-competition Covenants 200

Table of Contents

Table of Contents

General Introduction

Chapter 1. Employment Law in Ireland in Context

§1. THE ECONOMIC AND HISTORICAL CONTEXT

I. The Legal Historical Background

A. The Legal and Constitutional History of Ireland to 1937

1. The transmission of the English common law into Ireland began with the arrival of the first Anglo Norman settlers in 1169. The process was formalized when, in 1210, King John (1167–1216) promulgated a charter requiring the observance of the common law in the lordship of Ireland, and later in the same year sent a register of writs to Ireland (and thereby the means to administer in Ireland the principal processes of the common law). A single 'king's court' functioned in Ireland in the early 13th century. That was superseded by two courts: the Dublin Bench, a court staffed by three or four justices based at Dublin for hearing civil pleas (a court equivalent to the Westminster Bench, whose existence was first recorded in the 1240s), and by the Court of the Justiciar (an analogue of the English king's bench, whose existence was first recorded in the 1280s). By end of the 13th century the Irish exchequer was also exercising a restricted common pleas jurisdiction. The Court of Chancery was a much later development, probably not coming into existence in Ireland until the late 15th century.

However, during the later medieval period the common law only operated within the geographical area under royal control: the Lordship of Ireland. Within the greater part of Ireland, Ulster, Connaught and the south west of the country, the legal system remained the native Irish system of jurisprudence, Brehon law. Indeed, the area under common law jurisdictional control contracted severely after 1300, and by 1450 consisted of just four counties around Dublin. The volume of work processed by the central common law courts shrank to a quarter of what it had been in the late 13th century.

The reach of the common law extended with the 'Tudor re-conquest of Ireland'. In the period 1570–1610 the process, of establishing the common law system and constructing in Ireland a judicature along English model, was completed. In 1571 a Court of Castle Chamber (equivalent to the court of Star Chamber) was established. Shortly thereafter, in 1575, Ireland had its own court of admiralty (and a further prerogative court was established when in 1622 the court of ward and liveries was constituted). In 1569 and 1571 Sir Henry Sidney established presidential courts of

Connaught and Munster in order to provide accessible, local common law tribunals which would 'withdraw the people from their liking or using of their accustomed Brehon laws'. Popular access to justice was increased by the institution of courts of assize which operated, from the beginning of the 17th century, throughout the country. These courts offered litigants the facility of simple civil bills (in place of complex and expensive common law pleadings drafted in Latin) for the recovery of small debts. (In 1796 this small claims' civil bill jurisdiction was transferred to the courts of quarter sessions presided over by assistant barristers.)

Legislation as a source of law in Ireland commenced in the early 13th century with some items of English legislation being sent to Ireland with instructions that they be adopted in Ireland. Later in the 13th century an Irish Parliament began to meet and issue ordinances. In 1494 the Irish Parliament, sitting in Drogheda, enacted Poynings's Act, which adopted into Irish law all public acts enacted by the English Parliament. It also significantly restricted the sovereignty of Parliament by requiring that no enactment of the Irish Parliament could become law without the approval of the king in council. This conciliar veto upon the law making capacity of the Irish Parliament remained until 1782 when Yelverton's Act deprived the British and Irish council of the power to veto Irish parliamentary legislative measures.

In 1800 the Parliament of Ireland was extinguished. The Act of Union of 1800 transferred Irish parliamentary representation, and the power to enact legislation affecting Ireland, to the United Kingdom Parliament at Westminster. The War of Independence, 1919–1921, resulted in victory for the separatist movement and the withdrawal of the United Kingdom government from the 26 counties of Ireland, a political unit which was known as the Irish Free State. The Anglo-Irish Treaty of 1921 conceded effective executive authority to the Irish Free State (although, symbolically, sovereign power rested with the Crown). Under the Irish Free State Constitution of 1922, the *Oireachtas* was established as the parliamentary organ of the Irish Free State. The *Oireachtas* was comprised of two bodies, a chamber of deputies, known as *Dáil Éireann*, and a senate, known as *Seanad Éireann* (Article 12). The pre-existing common law and statute law were re-adopted into the laws of the new state (Article 73).

In 1937 the Constitution of the Irish Free State was replaced by *Bunreacht na hÉireann*. The 1937 Constitution claimed full internal and external sovereignty, and the (largely symbolic) residues of the authority of the English Crown found in the constitution of 1922 were eliminated.

B. The Development of Labour Law in Ireland up to 1900

2. The historical development of labour law in Ireland may be divided into: (i) laws directed to the regulation of the individual employment relationship between employer and employee; and (ii) laws directed against trade unions.

Statutory regulation of the individual employment relationship may be traced to the Servants Acts of the 16th century. The Servants Act of 1542 was enacted in order to enforce compulsory wage control. The Irish Parliament, concerned at servants who 'aske and take unreasonable wages', empowered justices of the peace to set maximum wages. Servants who secured wages in excess of that prescribed wage were liable to have the excess forfeited and to be imprisoned.

A series of Master and Servant Acts, finally codified in the Master and Servant Act 1823 incriminated various forms of misconduct: '[servants who were] drunkards, idle or otherwise disorderly or waste their master's goods, or lend their master's or same without their master's or mistress's consent or knowledge or depart their master's or mistress's service without their consent'. Criminal penalties, including imprisonment, were imposed for breach of these standards. The legislation continued in force until 1875.

However, some of this early modern legislation was more benevolent: the Servants Acts of 1714, 1729 and 1743 provided for the recovery of unpaid wages. The Servants Act 1715 provided employees with an enforceable entitlement to a reference. Another unique Irish statute of 1819 provided that masters could be punished by a fine not exceeding 40 shillings for 'ill-usage of their apprentices'.

The 19th century witnessed the development of a coherent body of employment protection legislation. The payment of wages in cash and without deduction was enforced through the Truck Acts of 1836, 1887 and 1896. The safety of factory workers was regulated in the Factory and Workshop Acts of 1879, 1891 and 1901. Compensation schemes for injuries suffered while working were introduced by the Workman's Compensation Act, 1897. The issue of the exploitation of children at work was addressed through the Employment of Children Act 1903. Mechanisms for the inexpensive and informal recovery of wages were also put in place. The Summary Jurisdiction Act 1851 extended the jurisdiction of justices of the peace in cases involving unpaid wages. The power to set minimum wages was established by the Trade Boards Act of 1909.

Concurrent with the emergence of employment protection law was the liberalization of the laws against trade unions and strike activity. In Ireland, statutes outlawing trade union organization were enacted by the Irish Parliament earlier than in England.[1] The Combination Act of 1729 outlawed, under pain of imprisonment, combinations of workmen. The Act of 1729 was followed by the Act of 1731 which imposed special sanctions against a workman who assisted another to stop him working for an employer. The Combination Act of 1743 made it illegal to collect funds for the support of strikers, and provided that any house-owners who allowed unlawful meetings to take place in their houses were liable to be 'punished as those who keep common bawdy houses are by law punishable'. A final Combination Act was enacted in 1803. This incriminated participation in combinations designed to obtain an advance in wages, decreasing the amount of wages or preventing persons from employing who they wanted. Eventually, in 1825 the Combination Repeal Act was enacted: combinations of workmen meeting for the purposes of settling rates of wages or hours of work were permitted. The Act permitted collective bargaining over wages and hours (though not apparently over other subjects).

Furthermore, while combinations were legitimized, strike activity continued to be a criminal offence, and continued to be actively prosecuted into the 1840s. However, the Employers and Workmen Act of 1875, by decriminalizing the withdrawal

---

1. Patrick Park, 'The Combination Acts in Ireland, 1727–1825', *Irish Jurist* 340 (1979).

of labour in breach of contract, immunized striking from the criminal law. The Conspiracy and Protection of Property Act 1875 made strike-related picketing lawful. The Trade Disputes Act of 1906 was directed at neutralizing the civil consequences of strike activity. A notorious decision of the House of Lords, *Taff Vale* v. *Amalgamated Railway Servants*,[2] had provided that unions were quasi-corporations, and were therefore vicariously responsible for the civil wrongs committed by their members in the course of a trade dispute. This finding threatened the very existence of trade unions since trade disputes inevitably involved the commission of civil wrongs. The vicarious responsibility of trade unions for the acts of their members was cancelled. The civil wrong of inducing breach of contract, committed where a strike organizer induced another worker to break his contract of employment, was immunized where certain conditions were complied with. The practice of picketing was legitimized, providing the practice was carried on peacefully and with the sole purpose of persuading others not to work.

II. The Economic Historical Background. Irish Economic History 1922–2013

3. The history of Irish economic growth since Independence can be analysed as composed of four phases. The first of these was a period between the early 1920s and the late 1950s when, committed to a policy of protectionism, and closed to world markets by the Second World War, the economy grew slowly. The second was the period between the late 1950s and the early 1970s when, due to a change in economic policy which aimed at attracting multinational companies to Ireland, output, employment, productivity and exports grew. Between the early 1970s and the late 1980s, due to a combination of the oil crisis, and the subsequent accumulation of an excessive public debt, growth slowed and unemployment rose.

The third period occurred between the mid-1990s and 2008 when the economy expanded at an intense rate, achieving a 9 per cent growth rate in the mid-1990s, the fastest growth rate in the European Union. This was a growth fuelled both by exports but also by rising domestic consumption and the demands of internal industry, particularly the construction industry and services sector.

However, the character of Ireland's economy begun to change in the period 2002–2008. During this period growth continued but that growth was based on fragile conditions: employment, financial services and government revenue were all dependent on an unstable property boom. Employment was heavily construction based. Government revenue was based on property-based taxes: capital gains and stamp duties. The provision of credit by banks was dependent on the soundness of property investments.

The international financial crisis of 2008 particularly affected the Irish banking system; this failure in turn affected state solvency. In 2008 the banks began to suffer deposit withdrawals, while the banks' solvency was also threatened by irrecoverable property-based loans. The costs of measures taken by the government to recapitalize the banks proved beyond the capacity of the state's resources. In November

---

2. [1901] AC 426.

2010 the government was forced to agree a financial assistance package worth 85 million with the IMF and the EU. This agreement was accompanied by a Memorandum of Economic and Financial Policies and a commitment by the state to consult the European Commission the European Central Bank and the International Monetary Fund on changes to the policies described in the Memorandum.[3] These policies, and the oversight allowed to the EU/IMF, have, in turn, affected areas of employment law, particularly over matters like sick pay and the minimum wage.

§2. THE IRISH EMPLOYMENT MARKET IN CONTEXT

4. In 2012 the number of employees in Ireland was counted as 1,546,400 (roughly 85 per cent of the total workforce). On the other hand, the number of persons with self-employment status was 279,700 (roughly 15 per cent of the total workforce).[4]

Irish employees work on average 38.4 hours per week. This is the second lowest in the European Union – below the European average of 40.4 hours per week. Men work an average of 40.0 hours, closer to the European average; the average for women is 36.5 hours. The differential between the hours of work of men and the hours of work of women is one of the highest in Europe.[5]

The number of female employees (851,300) in 2011 is still slightly below the number of male employees (970,000).[6] Women work overwhelmingly in the public services sector: four out of five of workers in the health sector are women, as are three-quarters of those in education. Within these sectors women are clustered at the low and mid ranges of seniority. Two causes of concern have been identified. The first is under-representation at higher levels. The second is wages. Women's incomes are 93 per cent those of men.

There has been a steep increase over the decade in the number of those working part-time. In 2012 the number of persons working between one and nine hours stood at 86,064; ten years earlier it was 19,959. (The composition by sex of this group has changed. Ten years ago (and earlier) a preponderance of these workers were female: 8,252 men as opposed to 11,707 females.).[7] There has been no significant increase in participation by older workers. In 2012 13.8 per cent of older males are in employment; just 4.8 per cent of older females are in employment.[8]

The percentage of employees working under fixed term contracts is 9.9; this is considerably lower than the European average of 14.1.[9]

---

3. EU/IMF Programme of Financial Support for Ireland Programme Documents) 1 December 2010, http://www.finance.gov.ie/documents/publications/reports/2011/euimfrevised.pdf.
4. Central Statistics Office, *Quarterly National Household Survey. Quarter 3. 2012*, pp. 2–3.
5. *Eurostat Labour Force Survey 2011* < epp.eurostat.ec.europa.eu/cache/ITY> accessed 24 June 2013.
6. Central Statistics Office, *Men and Women in Ireland 2011* (CSO, 2012).
7. Casual and Part Time Workers on the Live Register by Sex and Month <http://www.cso.ie/px> accessed 24 June 2013.
8. Central Statistics Office, *Quarterly National Household Survey 2012* (CSO, 2012).
9. *Eurostat Labour Force Survey 2011* <epp.eurostat.ec.europa.eu/cache/ITY> accessed 24 June 2013).

The character of the labour market has been affected by a decline in trade union influence. Union membership in Ireland has been falling consistently since 2003. In 2003 union membership stood at 37.5 per cent. In 2007 it had fallen to 31.5 per cent. Membership levels vary according to economic sector and hours of work. Union membership is high in public administration (almost 70 per cent) and low (9 per cent) in sectors like hotels and agriculture. Full time employees are more likely to be trade union members (34.6 per cent) than part -time workers (19 per cent).[10]

---

10. Central Statistics Office, *Quarterly National Household Survey, Union Membership, Q2 2007* (CSO, 2008).

Chapter 2. The Irish Judicature and Employment-connected Litigation

§1. THE IRISH COURT SYSTEM AND EMPLOYMENT LAW DISPUTES

I. The District Court

5. At the bottom of the hierarchy of the ordinary court system sits the District Court. The District Court has jurisdiction in claims where the amount of damages does not exceed €6,348.69.[11] The District Court, therefore, is the appropriate court in labour law cases where the nature of the action involves breach of contract (wrongful dismissal, or unpaid wages) and where the amount claimed does to exceed the prescribed amount.

II. The Circuit Court

6. The Circuit Court has jurisdiction in cases of breach of contract or tort where the quantum of the claim does not exceed €38,092.14.[12]

The Circuit Court is also entrusted with a special jurisdiction under the Employment Equality Acts 1998 and 2004. While the conventional rule is that equality claims are submitted to the Equality Tribunal there is an exception in cases where the form of discrimination involves discrimination on grounds of sex: the claim may be initiated in the Circuit Court rather than before the Tribunal.[13] In the case of recommendations by the Tribunal, the maximum that can be ordered by way of redress is two years' wages. However, where a claim is initiated in the Circuit Court there is no limit to the sum that can be ordered by way of compensation.[14]

The Circuit Court also has appellate functions in the case of some employment tribunal matters. The most important of these is that under the Unfair Dismissals Acts, 1977–2007. Here a decision of the Employment Appeal Tribunal (EAT) may be appealed, within six weeks, to the Circuit Court.

The Circuit Court is also given an enforcement role where determinations of employment/labour tribunals are not complied with. Determinations of the Equality Tribunal in employment equality matters may, if an employer fails to comply, be enforced by the Circuit Court.[15] Similarly, where determinations of the EAT are ignored the employee may proceed to the Circuit Court to have them enforced. This applies in the case of the National Minimum Wage Act 2000;[16] the Organization of Working Time Act 1997;[17] the Maternity Protection Acts 1994 and 2004;[18] the

---

11. S. 77 Courts of Justice Act 1924 as amended by s. 4 Courts Act 1991.
12. Courts (Supplemental Provisions) Act 1961 as amended by s. 2 Courts Act 1991.
13. S. 77(3) Employment Equality Act 1998.
14. S. 82 (3) Employment Equality Act 1998.
15. S. 91 Employment Equality Act 1998.
16. S. 32.
17. S. 29.
18. S. 37 of the 1994 Act.

Adoptive Leave Acts 1995 and 2005;[19] the Carer's Leave Act 2001, the Parental Leave Acts 1998 and 2006;[20] the Protection of Employees (Part Time Work) Act 2001;[21] the Protection of Employees (Fixed Term Work Act 2003;[22] and the Protection of Employees (Temporary Agency Work) Act 2012.[23] The Circuit Court enforces a tribunal award by making it an order of court and amenable to all of the coercive procedures available to the Circuit Court for enforcing its own orders.

III. The High Court

7. The penultimate court in the curial hierarchy is the High Court. The High Court's jurisdiction in civil matters is unlimited (Article 34(3)(1) of the Constitution). Its jurisdiction is not restricted by minimum or maximum limits.[24] The High Court is able to dispense a wider range of remedies than those allowed to the other courts, and it is this which determines its use in employment law disputes. First, the quantum of damages which may be awarded by the High Court is unlimited. For this reason the High Court is commonly used in wrongful dismissal claims where the amount of damages will exceed the amount which can be awarded by the Circuit Court. The High Court may be used where the remedy sought is a declaration; the High Court alone can grant a declaration.[25] Declarations may be sought in employment law as a mechanism for resolving disputes over the nature of the contractual rights and obligations of employees.[26]

The High Court also has exclusive jurisdiction in the judicial supervision of the acts of the public administration. This it exercises through the remedy of judicial review. Employment disputes between workers and public institutions may where they have a public dimension, be reviewed by way of judicial review.[27]

The High Court also has, in certain cases, special appellate jurisdiction from the EAT. Any party may appeal on a point of law from the EAT in a determination under the Minimum Notice Act, 1973–2007.[28] An appeal on a question of law lies from the EAT in cases under the Redundancy Payments Acts 1969–2007[29] and under the Payment of Wages Act 1991;[30] the Protection of Employees (Part Time work Act

---

19. S. 39 of the 1995 Act.
20. S. 22 of the 1998 Act.
21. S. 18.
22. S. 16.
23. Schedule 2.
24. There are restrictions on the amount of costs which are recoverable where the damages award is beneath €20,000: s. 17 of the Courts Act 1981 as amended by s. 17 of the Courts and Court Officers Act 2002.
25. The declaratory remedy was instituted by the Chancery (Ireland) Act, 1867, s. 155.
26. *Kenny* v. *An Post* [1988] IR 285 (declaration sought to establish the right to a 15-minute break); *Flynn* v. *An Post* [1987] IR 68 (declaration sought to establish the illegality of suspension from work).
27. *Beirne* v. *Garda Commissioner* [1993] ILRM 1.
28. S. 11 (2).
29. S. 39(14) Redundancy Payments Act 1967.
30. S. 7.

2001;[31] the National Minimum Wage Act 2000;[32] the Protection of Young Persons (Employment) Act 2006; the Parental Leave Act 1998;[33] the Carers' Leave Act 2001;[34] the Adoptive Leave Act 1995;[35] the Maternity protection Act 1994;[36] the Organization of Working Time Act 1997;[37] the Terms of Employment Information Act 1994–2012;[38] and the Industrial Relations Act 1946–2012.[39]

§2. EMPLOYMENT TRIBUNALS

8. Alongside the formal court system established under the Constitution, a number of tribunals have been established with the function of adjudicating employment disputes. The most important of these are the Labour Court; the EAT and the Equality Tribunal.

I. The Labour Court

9. The Labour Court was established by the Industrial Relations Act 1946 as the institution charged with the resolution and settlement of industrial disputes. In the 1970s its role was extended to encompass some employment rights adjudicative functions.

The Labour Court hears appeals from the Equality Tribunal in cases under the Employment Equality Acts 1998–2011.[40] Ordinarily, claims for discrimination contrary to the Employment Equality Acts 1998 and 2011 must be brought to the Equality Tribunal. However, under Section 77 of the Employment Equality Act 1998, a person who claims to have been *dismissed* (a) in circumstances amounting to discrimination in contravention of the Act, or (b) in circumstances amounting to victimization must bring his claim for redress before the Labour Court.[41]

The Labour Court hears appeals from the recommendations of rights commissioners under the Organization of Working Time Act 1997.[42] It has a similar role as an appellate tribunal from the decisions of rights commissioners made under: the National Minimum Wage Act 2000,[43] the Protection of Employees (Part Time Work) Act 2001,[44] and the Protection of Employees (Fixed Term Work) Act 2003.[45]

---

31. S. 17.
32. S. 30.
33. S. 20.
34. S. 23
35. S. 36.
36. S. 34.
37. S. 28.
38. S. 8.
39. S. 46
40. Employment Equality Act 1998, s. 83.
41. *Ibid.*, s. 77(2).
42. Organization of Working Time Act 1997, s. 28.
43. National Minimum Wage Act 2000, s. 27.
44. Protection of Employees Part Time Work Act 2001, s. 17.
45. Protection of Employees (Fixed Term Work) Act 2003, s. 15.

The Labour Court may, under pain of a summary conviction, summon witness, administer the oath and require the production of documents.[46]

II. The Employment Appeals Tribunal (EAT)

10. The EAT is a specialist employment tribunal – originally established in 1967 as the Redundancy Appeals Tribunal and renamed the Employment Appeals Tribunal in 1977[47] – which adjudicates disputes under: the Unfair Dismissals Acts 1977–2007; the Redundancy Payments Acts 1977-2007; the Minimum Notice and Terms of Employment Acts 1973–2005; the Protection of Employees (Employers Insolvency) Acts 1984–2004; the Payment of Wages Act 1991; the Terms of Employment Act 1994–2001; the Maternity Protection Act 1994–2001; the European Communities (Protection of Employees on Transfer of Undertakings) Regulations 2003; the Carers' Leave Act 2001; the Parental Leave Act 1998–2006; the Protection of Young Persons (Employment) Act 1996; and the Adoptive Leave Acts 1995–2005.

The EAT has appellate jurisdiction under the Adoptive Leave Acts 1995–2005; the Maternity Protection Act, 1994–2004; the Parental Leave Acts 1998–2006; the Payment of Wages Act, 1991; the Protection for Young Persons Reporting Child Abuse Act 1998; the Protection of Young Persons (Employment) Act, 1996; the Terms of Employment (Information) Act, 1994; the Unfair Dismissals Acts, 1977–2007; the Carers' Leave Act 2001; the European Communities (Safeguarding of Employees' Rights on Transfer of Undertakings) (Amendment) Regulations 2000.[48]

The EAT also has original – as opposed to appellate – jurisdiction under the Minimum Notice and Terms of Employment Act, 1973; and the Protection of Employees (Employers' Insolvency) Act, 1984.

The Tribunal sits in divisions headed by a vice-chairman. The chairman is assisted by one member of the Tribunal who has been nominated by an organization representative of trade unions and another member nominated by a body representative of employers.[49] The tribunal has no power to award costs. The Tribunal may require evidence to be given under oath; it may also require persons to attend or to produce documents. Perjury before the Tribunal or refusal to give evidence or to produce material are amenable to prosecution.[50] The Tribunal has been characterized as 'extremely legalistic'[51] – though this is probably an unavoidable consequence of the functions entrusted to it.

Article 37 of the Constitution recognizes and permits adjudicative tribunals – tribunals which are outside the judicature established under the Constitution –so long as they are confined to 'limited functions'. It has been questioned whether the

---

46. Industrial Relations Act 1946, s. 21.
47. Redundancy Payments Act 1967, s. 39; Unfair Dismissals Act 1977, s. 18.
48. SI No. 487 of 2000.
49. Redundancy Payments Act 1967, s. 39(12).
50. *Ibid.*, s. 39(17).
51. Department of Jobs, Enterprise, and Innovation, *Legislating for a World Class Workplace Relations Service* (Dublin, 2012), 37.

EAT – whose jurisdiction can extend up to awarding 104 weeks' wages – really exercises 'limited functions'. If not, it is doubtful that the powers of the Tribunal are compliant with Article 37 of the Constitution.[52]

III. The Equality Tribunal

11. The Equality Tribunal established under the Employment Equality Acts 1998–2004[53] has as its central function the adjudication of complaints of discrimination on grounds of sex, race, age, marital status, membership of the travelling community, family status and disability in contravention of the Employment Equality Acts 1998–2004.

IV. The Rights Commissioner

12. The functions of the rights commissioner encompass two types of function: functions which are (a) quasi-judicial and (b) functions which are conciliatory.

The quasi-judicial functions of the rights commissioner involve the adjudication of over forty types of dispute.[54] The most important of these are disputes under: the Unfair Dismissals Acts 1977–2007; the Adoptive Leave Acts 1995 and 2005; the Maternity Protection Acts, 1994 and 2004; the Organization of Working Time Act 1997; the Parental Leave Acts 1998 and 2006; the Payment of Wages Act 1991; the Protection of Persons Reporting Child Abuse Act 1998; the Protection of Young Persons (Employment) Act 1996; the Terms of Employment (Information) Act 1994; the National Minimum Wage Act 2000; the Protection of Employment Regulations 2000 (SI, No. 488 of 2000); the Protection of Employees (Part Time Work) Act 2001; the Protection of Employees (Fixed Term Work) Act 2003; the European Communities (Protection of Employees on Transfer of Undertakings) Regulations 2003;[55] the European Communities (Organization of Working Time) (Mobile Staff in Civil Aviation) Regulations 2006; Employees (Provision of Information and Consultation) Act 2006; the Employment Permits Act 2006; the Carers' Leave Act 2001; the Protection of Employees (Temporary Agency Work) Act 2012.

Where the jurisdiction of the rights commissioner derives from one of the items of employment protection legislation described above the decision-making process is quasi-judicial in nature involving the application of facts to a prescribed legal standard. The purpose is to provide a cheap, informal institution for redress for employment disputes. An appeal lies against decisions or recommendations of the rights commissioner. The appellate institution varies. In some cases the appeal is to the Labour Court. This is the case in appeals under the Employees (Provision of

---

52. J. Casey, *Constitutional Law in Ireland*, 2nd edn (Dublin, 1992), p. 215; Unfair Dismissals Act 1977, s. 7 (1)(c).
53. Employment Equality Act 1998, s. 75 as amended by the Equality Act 2004, s. 30.
54. Department of Jobs, Enterprise, and Innovation, *Legislating for a World Class Workplace Relations Service* (Dublin, 2012), 36.
55. SI No. 131 of 2003.

Information and Consultation) Act 2006, the Employment Permits Act 2006, Protection of Employees (Part-Time Work) Act 2001.

More usually, the appeal from the rights commissioner is to the EAT (Adoptive Leave Acts 1995 and 2005; Carers' Leave Act 2001; European Communities (Protection of Employees on Transfer of Undertakings) Regulations 2003; the Carers' Leave Act 2001; Maternity Protection Acts 1994 and 2004; the Parental Leave Acts 1998 and 2006; the Payment of Wages Act 2001; the Protection of Young Persons (Employment) Act 1996; Terms of Employment (Information) Act 1994; the Unfair Dismissals Act 1977 to 2007).[56] The system of multiple institutions for the resolution of employment disputes has been heavily criticized.

By contrast with the industrial relation's officers' quasi-judicial functions are the industrial relations officer's conciliatory functions. Under the Industrial Relations Act 1969 the rights commissioner is empowered to investigate trade disputes.[57] The rights commissioner may issue a non-binding recommendation to the parties. Both parties must agree to the reference; the commissioner cannot proceed where one of the parties objects.[58] Where the Commissioner is exercising his trade disputes jurisdiction, there is also a right of appeal to the Labour Court.[59]

V. Reform of the Current Tribunal System

13. The system of multiple institutions for the resolution of employment disputes has been heavily criticized.[60] The principal objection to the current system is that it sometimes requires a single transaction to be channeled through different institutions rather than addressed to a single institution. A 2011 report has recommended the replacement of the current system with a two-stage structure.[61] The first part of this two stage structure would be a first instance body entitled the Workplace Relations Commission, amalgamating the Labour Court, the Employment Appeals Tribunal and the Rights Commissioner. The second component would be an 'Upper Tier Appellate Body' composed of an expanded Labour Court. The upper tier body 'would assume responsibility for all legal and appellate functions currently exercised by the Labour Court and the Employment Appeals Tribunal'.[62]

---

56. On the rights commissioner generally, *see* Kelly 'The Rights Commissioner: Conciliator, Mediator or Arbitrator?' in *Industrial Relations in Ireland*, Department of Industrial Relations, UCD, 1989.
57. A trade dispute is defined (s. 3 Industrial Relations Act 1946) as 'any dispute between employers and workers which is connected with the employment or non-employment, or the terms or conditions of or affecting the employment, of any person'.
58. S. 13(3) (b) (ii) of the Industrial Relations Act 1990 (as amended by s. 36 of the Industrial Relations Act 1990).
59. S. 13(8) of the Industrial Relations Act, 1969.
60. *Legislating for a World Class Workplace Relations Service* (Department of Jobs, Enterprise, and Innovation, 2012). The current procedures were criticized in the High Court in *JVC* v. *Panisi* [2011] IEHC 279.
61. *Consultation on the Reform of the State's Employment Rights and Industrial Relations Structures and Procedures* (Department of Jobs, Enterprise and Innovation, 2011).
62. *Legislating for a World Class Workplace Relations Service* (Department of Jobs, Enterprise, and Innovation, 2012).

Chapter 3. Sources of Employment Law

14. The following section provides a survey of the principal sources of employment rights in Irish law. Alongside the obvious sources, like statute and the express terms of the contract of employment, rights may be derive from more oblique sources: from the Constitution; from collective agreements; from implied contractual terms; from custom and practice; and from workplace rules.

§1. IMPLIED CONTRACTUAL TERMS

15. Latent or unexpressed promises may form part of a contract of employment, side by side with promises which have been expressly agreed. But the conditions under which such an unexpressed term may be recognized are extremely strict. There appear to be three principal techniques recognized by the courts in Ireland and England: (i) the business efficacy test and (ii) the parties 'unhesitatingly agreeing' test; and (iii) the parties' understanding as evidenced by their consistent practice.

I. The Business Efficacy Test

16. The first basis by reference to which a term may be implied in the contract is where a particular term, although unexpressed, is essential in order to make the contract workable. The concept is usually traced to *The Moorcock*.[63] It was held in that case that there was an implied term within a contract for the hire of a space for unloading a ship that the place be safe for a vessel to dock. While there was no express term, the term was implied because without it the contact would not be operable.

'Business efficacy' means workable; it means that a term is recognized as part of the contract of employment because without it the contract would be inoperable or ineffective. Thus there was held to be an implied term, recognized through the 'business efficacy doctrine', that an employee engaged as a sales manager with extensive travelling duties should have a valid driver's licence.[64] Provision of accommodation to a breakfast chef employed by a hotel was held to be implicit in the contract of employment, since without it the employee who lived 30 miles away would be unable to take up her duties every morning.[65] Otherwise, the employment arrangement would not have been capable of being accomplished.

Obviously, a term will not be admitted under the *Moorcock* doctrine where the contract would be workable without it.[66] In *Morley* v. *Heritage Plc*[67] an employee

---

63. [1889] 14 PD 64.
64. *Roberts* v. *Toyota (G.B.)* EAT 614/80, cited in Gaymer, *The Employment Relationship* (London, 2001) at 141.
65. *Walshe* v. *Royal George Hotel Ltd,* EAT [1999] UD757/1999.
66. The term was applied in *Vavasour* v. *O'Reilly* [2005] IEHC 15.
67. [1993] IRLR 400.

was dismissed without having taken his full complement of holidays. The employee argued that there was an implied term in the contract that he would be paid for holidays not taken. The court rejected this. The contention did not pass the conventional tests for identifying an implied term. In particular, the contract was quite workable without such a clause. The *Moorcock* test was not satisfied. In *Icelandic Foods* v. *Aparau*[68] the employer claimed that there was an implied term entitling it to transfer any employee from one branch of its chain of shops to another. The employer claimed the right to transfer the employee from one store (at Wood Green, London) to another store (at East Finchley, London). The EAT (UK) held that while such a clause might be very convenient, it was not so fundamental that the contract could not operate without it: 'Of course it is an advantage to employers of assistants in large chains to be able to move employees around but it is plainly not a necessity.'[69]

II. The Parties' Unhesitatingly Agreeing' Test

17. The second basis is the 'obvious beyond dispute'/'parties unhesitatingly agreeing' test. Where a particular term would have been so obvious, and accepted without dissent by both parties, then, although unexpressed, it can be implied. An example was given in *Sim* v. *Rotheram BC*.[70] There it was said that no one would dispute that it was part of a teacher's function to prepare in advance for classes. It need not be written in the contract. It is simply understood, and everyone would immediately agree to its existence as an implied term.

This general doctrine derives from the judgment of MacKinnon L.J. in *Shirlaw* v. *Southern Foundries*:[71]

> something so obvious that it goes without saying; so that, if, while the parties were making their bargain, an officious bystander were to suggest some express provision for it in their agreement, they would testily suppress him with a common 'oh, of course'.

The formula is intended to capture the notion of terms omitted through pure oversight. However, as the Supreme Court pointed out in *Tradex* v. *Irish Grain Board*[72] the basis of the test is simply to repair 'a failure of expression'. In deciding whether such a term exists the courts engage in an exercise in imaginative projection. It imaginatively recreates the origins of the contract and asks whether a particular proposition would have been greeted with decisive and immediate bilateral assent. Only if it passes this test, will the term be implied:

---

68. [1996] IRLR 119.
69. [1996] IRLR 119, 124.
70. [1987] 1 Ch 216.
71. [1939] 2 KB 206, 227.
72. [1984] IR 1.

The courts may imply a term in order to repair an intrinsic failure of expression, This jurisdiction ought to be exercised with care. The courts have no role in acting as contract makers.

This test is difficult to satisfy. A party fails the test where there can be identified some practical reason why the parties might not have agreed to a particular term. The fact that a proposed term might involve some practical difficulty, or financial burden, or be absent from a detailed contemporary account of the contract, are all contra-indications. The following is a survey of cases where the Irish and English courts have rejected claims that a clause was implicit in the contract on the application of the *Shirlaw* v. *Southern Foundries* test.

The fact that the term would be contrary to the interests of one of the parties may make it unlikely that it would have commanded joint approval. In *Royal and Sun Alliance* v. *Payne*[73] the company had altered its pension deed to provide that the pension would become payable when all employees reached the age of 62. This change was only financially viable by introducing a compulsory retirement age of 62 – a reduction from the previous age of 65. The employer argued that the employee had implicitly agreed to a reduction in the compulsory retirement age. The problem was that the employee, who wanted to stay in employment, objected to a reduction in the retirement age. The court held that 'a term will only be implied if it is one which the parties to the contract must necessarily have intended. In the present case, the claimant had made it clear to his supervisor that he objected to his retirement age being varied to the date in the pension scheme.' This was not a term to which the employee would have unhesitatingly agreed.

Second, the existence of very significant practical, or administrative, difficulties in implementing the claimed term, may constitute a counter–indicator. In *Sullivan* v. *Southern Health Board*[74] the plaintiff, a consultant, was appointed to Mallow Hospital at a time when there was a second consultant. The second consultant retired and was not replaced. This increased the workload and strain on the plaintiff. The plaintiff claimed that there was an implied term that a second consultant would always be provided to share the duties, and that non-reappointment breached this implied term. However, the Supreme Court rejected the view that the Southern Health Board would have 'unhesitatingly' promised this. The appointment of a consultant would have required the sanction of third parties: the Department of Health and of Comhairle na hOspidéal. The Board would not, knowing this, have been likely to have given a guarantee of a facility which was not within its power to give in the first place.

Third, it is less likely that a term will be regarded as implied where it is of exceptional complexity, or deals with contingencies which are extremely remote. In *Sweeney* v. *Duggan*[75] an employee (a quarry worker) had been employed by a one-man company which subsequently became insolvent. As a result, the employee was unable to recover an award made in his favour arising out of injuries sustained while working for the company. The employee sought a declaration that (alongside the

---

73. [2005] IRLR 848.
74. [1997] 3 IR 123.
75. [1997] 2 IR 531.

contract with the company) there was an implied collateral contract between the principal shareholder in his *individual capacity* and the employee: that the share-holder would take out insurance so that in the event of the company becoming insol-vent, or being unable to make good personal injury claims, the injured employee would be compensated. The Supreme Court did not accept that this exceptionally complex contention passed the test. The plaintiff was 'of modest means and edu-cation who was not represented by a trade union in any negotiations he had with the company'. It would have been such a remote contingency that it would not have been the sort of demand which an employee particularly one of 'modest means and education' would have insisted upon at the commencement of employment. Even if it were, it would have such an expensive demand that it would have been resisted by the employer.

Fourth, the existence of a highly detailed contact is often regarded as inconsistent with the coexistence of an implied term. The reasoning is that: it is more difficult to have a term recognized as an oversight when the contract has been drawn up with such detail and care. An omission from a detailed agreement is likely to be treated as deliberate rather than an oversight: *Ali* v. *Christian Salvesen*[76] is an example of this principle. Here, the employees worked in a food-processing factory. The hours of work varied seasonally. In order to provide employees with a stable wage, employees would be paid on the basis of a 40-hour week. That would mean that they would be overcompensated where they worked less than 40 hours, but that they would then balance that by working in excess of 40 hours during the peak period. But no provision was made for the employee who left or resigned during the busy part of the working year when he had worked more than 40 hours. The EAT (UK) held that the omission was pure oversight. The injustice of not providing for com-pensation for an underpaid employee was so obvious that if the problem had been put to the negotiating sides while the terms of the contract were being settled they would have unhesitatingly agreed to the proposition. The Court of Appeal reached a different conclusion. It held that, given the very detailed agreement negotiated between the parties, the only inference which could be drawn from the failure to deal with the contingency was that the parties could not agree. The more detailed the documentary agreement the less likely that terms have been omitted through oversight.

III. The Parties' Employment Practice

18. A third basis for the implication of terms in a contract of employment is the actual practice between the parties. A term is implied where it corresponds to the latent intentions of the parties. One of the best guides to the unexpressed intentions of the parties is their behaviour – particularly, their relative inactivity. Parties' behaviour may be explained by their latent understandings of their entitlements and duties. The rationale is that where the parties have acted in a particular way they

---

76. [1997] 1 All ER 721, [1997] IRLR 17.

can only have done so because they felt themselves bound so to act. Their practice corroborates the existence of an implied understanding of the original contract. In *Mears* v. *Safecar Security Ltd*[77] an employee had taken leave without sick pay for nearly seven months, and never asked for sick pay. Even after the end of his employment, it was some time before he thought of asking for sick pay. He then took legal action claiming that there was an implied contractual right to sick pay. The claim was denied.

The fact that the employee had behaved in a way which was contrary to his self-interest was best explained by the existence of an understanding that the contract did not allow him sick pay. Stephenson LJ said that 'in considering what obligations to imply into contracts of these kinds which are not complete, the actions of the parties may properly be considered'.

In *O'Brien* v. *Associated Fire Alarms*[78] the plaintiffs were instructed to work 120 miles from their home. The employer had never ordered them to work further than 60 miles from their homes in Liverpool. The question of the legality of the order arose. The employer argued that there was an implied mobility obligation, extending throughout the entire area where the company carried on business, and not just within reasonable daily commuting distance of the employees' homes. The Court of Appeal rejected this contention. The court said that 'it is permissible, if one is seeking to reconstruct the contract to look at what happened while the men were being employed'. The evidence was that the employees were never asked to work further than reasonable travelling distance from their home. This evidence of the parties' actual practice indicated: 'that what they were doing during their years of employment was all that they could be required to do in accordance with the terms of their employment'.

§2. CUSTOM AND PRACTICE

19. A further potential source of employment rights and duties is industry custom and practice. The 'custom and practice' principle works through the operation of a series of fictions: where a custom is well established all of the parties are deemed to be aware of its contents in advance of starting work. They are also deemed to have entered employment on the basis of an acceptance of the custom.[79]

There are three conditions to the recognition of a custom as generating an enforceable term of the contract: 'a custom of the trade must be reasonable, certain and notorious'.[80] In order to base a term on the basis of industry custom it must be so 'notorious, well known and acquiesced in, that in the absence of agreement in writing, it is to be taken as one of the terms of the contract between the parties'.[81]

---

77. [1982] ICR 626.
78. [1968] 1 WLR 1916.
79. *Sagar* v. *Ridehalgh* [1931] 1 Ch 310, 336 (Lawrence LJ).
80. *Bond* v. *CAV* [1983] IRLR 483.
81. *O'Reilly* v. *The Irish Press* (1937) 71 ILTR 194 (Maguire P).

In *Sagar* v. *Ridehalgh & Sons*[82] there was a practice operated in 85 per cent of textile factories in Yorkshire that a deduction from salary would be imposed where a worker produced cloth of unmerchantable quality. The evidence of this practice was held to be so 'notorious' as to justify a conclusion that there existed an implied right to make deductions from salary. However, as the Court of Appeal stated in *Henry* v. *London General Transport Services*,[83] '*clear* evidence of practice is, however, required to establish something as potentially nebulous as custom and practice'. In addition, *Henry* lays down the principle that the more serious the obligation which is said to have been incorporated by virtue of custom and practice, the more serious should be the court's scrutiny of the notoriety of the term. Claims of custom and practice commonly fail for lack of proof of usage.[84] 'Clear evidence' requires that the practice 'be followed without exception for a substantial period'.[85] In *O'Reilly* v. *The Irish Press*[86] it was argued that there was an industry custom and practice that the sub-editor of a national newspaper was entitled to six months' notice prior to dismissal. Contradictory evidence was provided as to the understanding of the practice by the editors of other newspapers. There was only one recorded case of the practice actually being observed. The evidence being equivocal, it was not sufficiently notorious and well known to support the claim of custom and practice. The High Court held that there was not such universality of acceptance in the newspaper world as would be required to establish the practice as a usage.[87]

The second condition to the recognition of a custom and practice is that it be 'reasonable'. In *Sagar* v. *Ridehalgh*[88] the court held that the custom of making one-shilling deductions for deficient work was reasonable. On the other hand, in *Solectron Scotland Ltd* v. *Roper*[89] the employer argued that custom and practice justified the following term: that employees would receive a redundancy package 'convenient to the employer'. The English EAT rejected this. Elias J said: 'The custom and practice relied upon [was not] reasonable since the entitlement would depend upon the will of the employer'.

---

82. [1931] 1 Ch. 310.
83. [2002] IRLR 472. Here the supposed custom was that a provision would be incorporated as a term in the contract of employment where the employer and trade union following collective bargaining agreed to it, and where it was accepted by a majority of the employees at a vote.
84. See *Stewart* v. *Swan Hunter* [1975] IRLR 143 (alleged custom and practice permitting employers transfer staff to other job functions failing for lack of proof of instances of usage); *Bond* v. *CAV* [1983] IRLR 483 (insufficient evidence of custom and practice permitting employer to lay off without pay).
85. Browne Wilkinson J. in *Duke* v. *Reliance Systems* [1982] IRLR 347 (insufficient evidence to establish retirement age of 65).
86. (1937) 71 ILTR 194.
87. The custom and practice rule was applied by the EAT in *McDonagh* v. *Shoreline Taverns Ltd* [2014] ELR 98 (holding that there was a national custom that workers on lay off were not entitled to be paid).
88. [1931] 1 Ch 310.
89. [2004] IRLR 4.

§3. COLLECTIVE AGREEMENTS

20. Collective agreements – agreements between a trade union and an employer – do not, as a general rule, constitute a source of employment rights and obligations.

The source of the problem is the common law doctrine of privity of contract: the doctrine that a contract is only binding on parties who are privy, or who are parties to the agreement.[90] Individual workers, however, are not parties to an agreement between a union and an employer. Therefore, they cannot rely on the agreement. One suggestion for avoiding this rule has been the argument that a union is the agent of workers. This has been definitively rejected. There is a basic rule that a trade union is not *per se* the agent of an employee. In *Goulding's Chemicals* v. *Bolger*[91] a collective agreement relating to redundancy payments was negotiated between a union and the employers (a Dublin fertilizer company). A group of militant employees refused to accept these terms. The Supreme Court rejected the contention that these terms automatically bound the workers, and that the union acted as the employee's agent. Mere membership of a union did not make a union the employees' or members' negotiating agent. Kenny J said:

> Membership of a corporate body or of an association does not have the consequence that every agreement made by that corporate body or association binds every member of it. None of the defendants are parties to the agreement and as they consistently opposed it, no question of their being bound by acquiescence can arise.

Since the union is not the agent of the workers, the workers were not parties to the contract; they are not 'privy' to the agreement.

21. Although an employee is not usually privy to a collective agreement, and, therefore, not bound by that agreement, there may be circumstances in which incorporation into the contract of employment can occur.

I. Where a Union Negotiator is Conferred with Agency Status

22. One case is where the union negotiator is deliberately conferred with agency status by the workers whom he or she represents.[92] An example of agency is

---

90. 'A contract cannot (as a general rule) confer rights, or impose obligations arising under it on any person except the parties to it.' *Chitty on Contracts* (25th edn), (2 vols, London, 1983), I, para. 1228.
91. [1977] IR 211; applied in *Reilly* v. *Drogheda Borough Council* [2008] IEHC 357.
92. In *Burton Group* v. *Smith* [1977] ILRM 351 it was said that 'there is no reason at all why, in a particular case, union representatives should not be the agents of an employee to make a contract, or to receive a notice, or otherwise effect a binding transaction on his behalf. But that agency so to do does not stem from the mere fact that they are union representatives and that he is a member of the union; it must be supported in the particular case by the creation of some specific agency, and that can arise only if the evidence supports the conclusion that there was such an agency.'

provided by *O'Rourke* v. *Talbot*.[93] In that case a group of senior foremen specifically selected a shop steward to act on their behalf in negotiations with the employer. The High Court held that the deal between the shop stewards andthe company generated rights enforceable by the employees. The foremen had made the shop steward their agent.[94]

II. Incorporation of Collective Agreement Terms in the Contract of Employment

23. A second way in which a collective agreement may become part of an employee's contract of employment is through a specific term in the contract of employment whereby an employee agrees to the terms of a collective agreement becoming part of the contract of employment.[95] This does not breach the rule against a third party being bound by an agreement to which he has not consented. Here, the employee gives advance consent to being bound by whatever terms may be negotiated between the employer and the employee's representatives. In *NCB* v *Galley*[96] mine supervisors worked under a contract which provided that 'the contract shall be regulated by such national agreements as then in force'. The union (NACODS) had entered into a collective agreement under which they agreed that 'deputies shall work such days or part days as may reasonably be required'. The employees refused to work on Saturdays as instructed. The National Coal Board succeeded in their claim for breach of contract. The requirement to work on Saturdays was binding; it was clear, the court held, that 'the defendant's personal contract of service is regulated by the NACODS agreement'.

§4. NATIONAL SOCIAL PARTNERSHIP AGREEMENTS

24. Irish employment law has been significantly affected by the influence obtained by the trade unions over the setting of governmental policies through social partnership agreements. Trade unions achieved significant influence in Ireland through their participation in these corporatist tripartite agreements with government and employers' organizations in which wage agreements are traded for tax, social welfare and employment law concessions.

The current cycle of national social agreements commences with the Programme for National Recovery 1987–1990. That was followed by the Programme for Economic and Social Progress 1991–1993. A further three-year tripartite deal, the Programme for Competitiveness and Work, was concluded in 1994 and ran until 1997. Partnership 2000 ran from 1997 to 2000; the Programme for Prosperity and

---

93. [1984] ILRM 562.
94. Agency status may also be conferred by the ostensible authority principle: *Harris* v. *Richard Lawson Autologistics* [2002] ICR 765.
95. S. 3(1) (m) of the Terms of Employment (Information) Act, 1994 obliges the employer to include in the statutory statement, reference to any collective agreements which directly affect the terms and conditions of the employee's employment.
96. [1958] 1 WLR 16.

Fairness operated between 2000 and 2003 and Sustaining Progress between 2003 and 2005. The seventh social partnership agreement, entitled Towards 2016 was concluded in June 2006 and provided for cumulative wage increases set at 10.4 per cent over a 27-month period. Towards 2016 came under severe pressure when the financial crisis erupted in 2008. By November 2009 the agreement effectively broke down when the Irish Business and Employers Conference withdrew from the agreement. In 2010 a local form of partnership agreement – the Public Service Agreement 2010–2014' – was negotiated between the government and the Public Services Committee of the Irish Congress of Trade Unions. This agreement involved an arrangement under which the government undertook not to introduce further wage reductions in the public service, or to make compulsory redundancies, in return for commitments by staff to agree to measures promoting greater economic efficiency within the public service through greater flexibility, willingness of undertake redeployment and interoperability.

However, it is unlikely that the terms of these agreements are binding at individual level. It is difficult to see how they can generate rights enforceable by employers against employees; or duties enforceable against employers by the government; or rights enforceable by employers against trade unions. The same privity of contract problem which applies in the case of ordinary collective agreements is a difficulty here as well. Neither individual employers nor employees are privy to the agreement, and may not, therefore, be legally bound by, or legally rely on, the agreement.

On occasions, the government has intervened by legislation to prohibit infringements by individual employers of terms contained in national agreements. In 1975, for example, the Regulation of Banks (Remuneration and Conditions of Employment) (Temporary Provisions) Act 1978 was enacted in order to prohibit the payment by banks of wages in excess of those authorized by the national wage agreement. In 2013 the government, as part of its policy of reducing its public spending deficit below 3 per cent, entered into a collective agreement with public service trade unions. This agreement – the Public Service Stability Agreement 2013[97] – involved the unions agreeing to wage cuts for public servants earning over €65,000. At common law this collective agreement would not be binding on individual workers who could still insist on their original wages. In order to make it binding the *Oireachtas* enacted the Financial Emergency Measures in the Public Interest Act 2013 which gave the collective agreement the force of law.

§5. REGISTERED EMPLOYMENT AGREEMENT

25. Part III of the Industrial Relations Act 1946 empowers the Labour Court to establish registered employment agreements. The legal effect of a registered employment agreement is different to that of an unregistered agreement: an unregistered agreement does not automatically modify the individual contracts of

---

97. Popularly known as the Haddington Road Agreement, http://www.lrc.ie/documents/2013/Haddington-Road-Agreement.pdf.

employment of the workers to whom it applies.[98] However, a registered agreement modifies the contract of employment of every worker to which it is expressed to apply.[99] An employer who fails to comply with the terms of a registered agreement may be directed to comply by order of the Labour Court. Where the order of the Labour Court is ignored the Circuit Court is empowered to exercise its machinery against the employer.[100] In addition, civil proceedings can be initiated: the employee may initiate proceedings; alternatively, a Labour Court inspector is given *locus standi* to institute civil proceedings on behalf of a worker for the enforcement of the registered agreement.[101]

The incentive for employers to enter into employment agreements is the existence of the criminal sanction for trade unions which breach internal peace provisions contained in the agreement. Criminal liability is activated by a union promoting or assisting out of its funds the maintenance of a dispute which is in contravention of the agreement and which has for its objective the enforcement of a demand on the employer to grant remuneration or conditions other than those fixed by the agreement.[102]

26. The conditions under which the Labour Court may exercise its power to register an employment agreement have had to be revised following the Supreme Court decision in *McGowan* v. *Labour Court*.[103] The Supreme Court held that a registered employment agreement is, because of its compulsory sectoral effect, a species of 'law'. Further, it is a 'law' made by a body other than the *Oireachtas*. Under the Irish Constitution a law may only by a body other than the *Oireachtas* if the principles controlling the content of that law have been set out in advance by the *Oireachtas*.[104] In *McGowan* v. *Labour Court*[105] the Supreme Court held that the very open conditions regulating the circumstances in which the Labour Court could register an agreement under the Industrial Relations Act 1946 were not circumscribed in sufficient detail. The effect was that the *Oireachtas* had ceded legislative power to the Labour Court; the width of that legislative power had not been constrained in advance. There had, as a result, been an unconstitutional delegation of legislative autonomy to the Labour Court. In order to remedy this unconstitutional delegation of power, the Industrial Relations (Amendment) Act 2012 was enacted. This subjects the Labour Court to detailed control over the circumstances in which it may make this form of quasi-legislative enactment. Under the 2012 Act the Labour Court is required to take into account matters like the potential impact on

---

98. *Goulding Chemicals* v. *Bolger* [1977] IR 211.
99. S. 30 of the Industrial Relations Act 1946.
100. S. 32 (4) of the 1946–2012 Acts.
101. S. 54 of the Industrial Relations Act 1990.
102. S. 32(2) of the Industrial Relations Act, 1946 (see generally, Horgan, 'The Failure of Legal Enforcement: A Review of the Registration of Agreements in the Labour Court' (1985) 4 *Journal of the Irish Society of Labour Law* 28).
103. [2013] IESC 31.
104. *Cityview Press* v. *An Chomhairle Oiliúna* [1980] IR 381; *John Grace Fried Chicken* v. *The Labour Court* [2011] 3 IR 211; *Laurentiu* v. *The Minister for Justice* [1999] 4 IR 26 *McGowan* v. *Labour Court* [2013] IESC 31.
105. [2013] IESC 31.

employment levels of registering the agreement; the desirability of maintaining competiveness in the area; and the level of wages in comparable areas.[106]

§6. THE PROPER LAW OF THE CONTRACT OF EMPLOYMENT

I. Rome 1 and the Brussels I Regulation in Irish Employment Law

27. The proper law of contract (and, therefore, of the contract of employment) is identified by the application of the following principles: (i) that the proper law is the law which is chosen by the parties; (ii) the principle that where the parties have not selected law to govern the contract 'the law which has the closest and most real connection with the contract and transaction' is the governing standard.[107]

Ireland is bound by Regulation No 593/2008 on the law applicable to contractual obligations (Rome I). Article 8 provides that:

> an individual employment contract shall be governed by the law chosen by the parties ... such a choice of law may not, however, have the result of depriving the employee of the protection afforded to him by provisions that cannot be derogated from by agreement under the law that, in the absence of choice, would have been applicable pursuant to paragraphs 2, 3 and 4 of this Article.

Article 8(2) provides that:

> To the extent that the law applicable to the individual employment contract has not been chosen by the parties, the contract shall be governed by the law of the country in which or, failing that, from which the employee habitually carries out his work in performance of the contract. The country where the work is habitually carried out shall not be deemed to have changed if he is temporarily employed in another country.

In other words: the employee – despite any alternative choice of law – is always protected by those 'laws that cannot be derogated from by agreement' which operate in the country in which 'he habitually carries out his work'. Article 8 guarantees 'the applicability of the law of the state in which he carries out his working activities rather than that of the state in which the employer is established'.[108]

28. The right to invoke 'mandatory rules of law' of Ireland is dependant on the employee proving that Ireland is the place where the employee 'habitually carried on work'. In *A Complainant* v. *A Company*[109] the complainant, who spent 60 per cent of his time working in the Republic of Ireland for a company based in Northern

---

106. This list is not exhaustive. The full list is contained in s. 27(3B) of the Industrial Relations Acts 1946–2012.
107. *Cripps Warburg Ltd* v. *Cologne Investments* [1980] IR 321.
108. *Koelzsch* v. *Luxembourg* Case C 29/10 [2011] ECR I-1595, [2011] IRLR 514.
109. [2003] 14 ELR 333.

Ireland, claimed that he had been discriminated against on grounds of sexual orientation contrary to the Employment Equality Acts 1998 and 2004. The Tribunal agreed that the Employment Equality Acts 1998 and 2004 were a 'mandatory rule'. The next question was whether the Republic of Ireland was the place where he 'habitually carried out work'. The complainant had his home in Northern Ireland, and returned there after each trip to this jurisdiction. He paid social insurance in the Northern Ireland. The Equality Tribunal, in determining where the employee habitually carried on work, applied the 'effective centre of his working activities' test devised in *Rutten* v. *Cross Medical Ltd*[110] Taking into account the fact that Northern Ireland was his home; that he paid social insurance there and that it would be less expensive for him to sue in Northern Ireland, the Tribunal identified Northern Ireland as the applicant's 'effective centre'. Accordingly, the Equality Tribunal declined jurisdiction.

29. Ireland is also bound by Council Regulation 44/2001 of 22 December 2000 (the 'Brussels I Regulation' which replaced the Convention on Jurisdiction and Enforcement of Judgments in Civil and Commercial Matters signed at Brussels on 27 September 1968).[111] Article 19 of Brussels I provides that an employer domiciled in a Member State may be sued in another Member State, if it is the place where the employee habitually carries out his work. Article 19 was considered in *A Complainant* v. *A Company*.[112] The Equality Tribunal held that it had no Article 19 jurisdiction to adjudicate a claim in the Republic of Ireland against a business located in Northern Ireland since the employee who was pursuing the claim was not 'habitually resident' in the Republic.

II. Employment Abroad and Access to Entitlements under the Unfair Dismissals Acts, 1977–2007 and the Redundancy Payments Acts, 1967–2007

30. Section 2(3) of the Unfair Dismissals Acts 1977–2007 provides that the Unfair Dismissals Acts shall not apply in relation to the dismissal of any employee, who, under the relevant contract of employment, ordinarily worked outside the state, unless: (1) the employee was ordinarily resident in the state during the term of the contract; or (2) (i) the employee was domiciled in the state during the term of the contract, and (ii) where this employer was (if a natural person) ordinarily resident in the state, or, if a corporation, had its principal place of business in the state during the term of the contract. Exception (1) was applied in *Roche* v. *Stena Sealink*[113] where claimants working for a British-registered ferry on trips across the Irish Sea were, since they lived in Dublin while ashore, found to be 'ordinarily resident' in the state, and, therefore, entitled to claim under the Unfair Dismissals Acts

---

110. C-383/95 [1997] ECR I-57, [1997] IRLR 249.
111. *Leo Laboratories Limited* v. *Crompton BV* [2005] 2 IR 225.
112. [2003] 14 ELR 333.
113. [1993] ELR 89.

1977–2001. Exception (2) was applied in *Kelly* v. *Aer Rianta International*[114] where the applicant, although working in Russia for an Irish company, was domiciled in Ireland, and, therefore, entitled to claim under the Unfair Dismissals Acts, 1977–2007.

The rule which operates under the Redundancy Payments Acts 1967–2001, is more restrictive than that which applies under the Unfair Dismissals Acts. Under Section 25(2) an employee who ordinarily works outside the state is not entitled to redundancy payment unless before he commenced to work outside the state, he was domiciled in the state and was in the employment of the employer concerned and unless (2) he was in the state in accordance with the instructions of his employer on the date of dismissal, or (b) he had not been afforded a reasonable opportunity by his employer of being in the state for that purpose.

§7. INTERNATIONAL TREATIES AS A SOURCE OF EMPLOYMENT RIGHTS

31. Ireland is a dualist system: international commitments are not binding upon the state in domestic law unless they have also been incorporated into national law. While breach of international conventions may give rise to consequences in international law, it may not be remedied in national law.[115]

Ireland has ratified the European Social Charter,[116] the European Social Charter (revised);[117] the Additional Protocol to the European Social Charter Providing for a System of Collective Complaints;[118] the International Convention on Economic and Social Rights[119] and the European Convention on Human Rights.[120] Ireland has ratified 71 ILO conventions since the state joined the ILO in 1923. These include: the Right to Organize and Collective Bargaining Convention, 1949; the Equal Remuneration Convention, 1951; Equality of Treatment (Social Security) Convention, 1962; the Holidays with Pay Convention, 1970; the Minimum Age Convention, 1973; the Occupational Cancer Convention, 1974; the Human Resources Development Convention, 1975; the Tripartite Consultation (International Labour Standards) Convention, 1976; the Occupational Safety and Health Convention, 1981; Vocational Rehabilitation and Employment Convention (Disabled Persons) Convention, 1973; the Labour Statistics Convention, 1985; the Working Conditions (Hotels and Restaurants) Conventions, 1991; the Safety and Health in Mines Convention, 1995; the Labour Inspection (Seafarers) Convention, 1996; the Home Work Convention, 1996; the Labour Inspection (Seafarers) Convention 1996; the Recruitment and Placement of Seafarers Convention 1996; the Seafarers' Hours of Work and the Manning of Ships Convention 1996; the Worst Forms of Child Labour Convention 1999.

---

114. [1998] ELR 170.
115. *Doyle* v. *Commissioner of An Garda Síochána* [1999] 1 IR 249.
116. Treaty Series 1965, No. 3.
117. Treaty Series 2007, No. 23.
118. Treaty Series 2007, No. 24.
119. Treaty Series 1990, No. 10.
120. Treaty Series 1953, No. 12.

Part I. The Individual Employment Relationship

Chapter 1. Identification of a Contract of Employment

32. The Irish law of employment generally regulates the rights and duties of 'employees'. However, the terms worker and employee are not coterminous. Not all workers are employees. The most common type of 'non-employee worker' is the self-employed worker. In 2012 the percentage of employees – as opposed to self-employed workers – was roughly 85 per cent of the total workforce.[121] A detailed jurisprudence has developed on the topic of distinguishing workers who are self-employed from workers who are employees.

§1. DISTINGUISHING THE EMPLOYEE FROM THE SELF-EMPLOYED WORKER

I. The Historical Evolution of the 'in Business on One's Account' Test

33. The self-employed worker is not an employee. One of the most challenging juristic issues has been the question of how to distinguish the employee from the self-employed. Historically, the first step in the search for a test for distinguishing employment from self-employment was a test which asked whether the subject was subject to the detailed direction – or control – of another as to the manner in which work was to be carried out. In the 19th-century case *Yewens* v. *Noakes*[122] Bramwell LJ suggested that the essence of employment was that the employee was 'subject to the command of the master as to the way in which he shall do his work'. The *Yewens* test for identifying an employee propounded in that case found its way into dictionaries of legal terms, and it soon became the governing test in employment law.[123]

The problem with that test was that it was 'based on social distinctions of that age; a state of society in which the ownership of the means of production coincided

---

121. Central Statistics Office, *Quarterly National Household Survey. Quarter 3*, 2012, pp. 2–3.
122. (1880) 6 QBD 530.
123. See e.g. *Simons* v. *Heath Laundry Co.* [1910] 1 KB 543.

with the possession of technical language and skill. The technological and economic developments of modern society nullified those assumptions.'[124] In the early 1950s the focus shifted to the question of whether the employer was able to direct the time and place where work was to be carried out. The focus shifted from technical, operational control to managerial control. In *Cassidy* v. *Minister for Health*[125] the question arose whether a hospital was vicariously liable for the acts of a consultant surgeon. The hospital did not exercise detailed operational control. Nonetheless, the hospital was held to be in a relationship of employment such as to make it vicariously responsible. The Court of Appeal held that the test was whether the employer could direct the employee as to *when* and *where* to work. Employment status was determined by subjection to managerial power rather than by subjection to technical direction. Employment was established by the integration of the worker into the wider organization of a business undertaking.[126] This was an improvement on the earlier test: it replaced the outdated control test. But it was still not sufficiently precise. The problem was that it also captured self-employed persons. It was possible to be a self-employed person who for the period of contractual engagement with a client was instructed *when* and *where* to work.[127] The integration test was over-inclusive: it caught both employees and self-employed businesses.

The United States Supreme Court can take the credit for patenting a new test. The leading case here is *United States* v. *Silk*.[128] Under this new approach the question was phrased as: is the subject *self-employed*? A self-employed person is characterized by a number of features: typically the person owns the assets; he or she is not paid a pre-determined wage. Instead, he or she runs the chance of profit, or the risk of loss according to his own efficiency in limiting his costs; he or she is often not obliged to work personally, but may delegate the carrying out of a job to a third party. The test works negatively. Where the subject is *not self-employed* according to the test, he or she is regarded as an employee. *United States* v. *Silk* involved the question of whether truck drivers in Kansas who carried out deliveries for a coal importer, and who owned the trucks used, and who were free to delegate the work to other drivers, were to be regarded as employees for the purpose of the Social Security Act 1935. Mr Justice Reed, who delivered the main judgment in the Supreme Court, characterized the drivers as follows:

> These driver owners are small businessmen. They own their own trucks. They hire their own helpers. It is the total situation, including the risk undertaken, the control exercised, the opportunity for profit from sound management, that mark these driver-owners as independent contractors … The truckers hire their own assistants, own the trucks, pay their expenses and depend on their own initiative, judgment and energy for the large part of their success.

---

124. O. Kahn Freund (1951) 14 *Modern Law Review* 504.
125. [1951] 1 All ER 574.
126. In *Bank voor Handel en Scheepvaart N.V.* v. *Slatford* [1952] 2 All ER 956 Denning LJ said: 'the test of being a servant does not rest nowadays on submission to orders. It depends on whether the person is part and parcel of the organization.'
127. This point was made by the High Court of Australia in *Queensland Property Ltd* v. *Federal Commissioner of Taxation* [1945] 70 CLR 539.
128. (1946) 331 US 704.

On the other hand, the manual workers who loaded coal to trucks were not in business on their own account. They had no independent business apparatus. 'They provided only picks and shovels. They had no opportunity to gain or lose except from the work of their hands and these simple tools.'

The test was imported into English law in the late 1960s. In *Market Investigations* v. *Minister for Social Security*[129] Cooke J applied the test and found that casual market research workers were employees. It had been argued that these short-term workers did not have the status of employee for lack of some of the most elementary characteristics of an employee: permanent integration into a business, and entitlement to employment benefits such as holiday provision. The Court of Appeal held that the 'fundamental test to be applied' is:

> is the person who has engaged himself to perform these services performing them as a person in business on his own account? If the answer to that question is yes, then the contract is a contract for services. If the answer is no then the contract is a contract for service ... factors which may be of importance [in determining self-employment] are such matters as whether the man performing the services provides his own equipment, whether he hires his own helpers, what degree of financial risk he takes, what degree of responsibility for investment and management he has, and whether and how far he has an opportunity of profiting from sound management in the performance of his task.

34. In 1998 the Irish Supreme Court confirmed that the 'in business on one's account test' was the governing test in Ireland. According to this approach, a problem case is processed through the test for identifying self-employment. Where this yields a negative, employment is established. The leading case is *Denny & Sons* v. *Minister for Social Welfare.*[130] The subject of the case, Ms Mahon, had been employed as a supermarket demonstrator. Her employer argued that she was self-employed: her contract described her as self-employed. However, the Supreme Court applied the in business test. She provided no equipment or made no investment. She had no full power of delegation. The Supreme Court reasoned:

> In general a person will be regarded as providing his or her services under a contract of employment and not as an independent contractor where he or she is performing those services for another person and not for himself or herself. The degree of control exercised over how the work is to be performed although a factor to be taken into account is not decisive. The inference that the person is engaged in business, in his or her own account can be more readily drawn where he or she provides the necessary premises or equipment or some other form of investment, where he or she employs others to assist in the business and where the profit which he or she derives from the business is dependent on the efficiency with which it is conducted by him or her.

---

129. [1969] 2 QB 173.
130. [1998] 1 IR 36.

In other words the subject was not self-employed; *ergo* she was an employee. The governing test in Irish law after *Denny* is: is the person under the control of the other party? Is the person 'in business in his/her own account'? If the answer to the first question is positive and the answer to the second is in the negative, then the status of employee is established.

The control requirement has not disappeared. It is still essential that there be control. But it is not enough. Control is a necessary, though not a sufficient, condition of employment status.[131] In *Ready Mixed Concrete* McKenna J stated: 'an obligation to do work subject to the other party's control is a necessary, though not always a sufficient, condition of a contract of service'. A complete lack of control will be inconsistent with the existence of a contract of employment. On the other hand, the existence of control will not necessarily establish a relationship of employment: the worker must not be 'in business on his or her own account'.

II. The Criteria for Determining Whether a Person Is in Business on Their Own Account

35. The principal factors used in determining whether a person is in business on his account: (i) the supply of significant capital equipment; (ii) self-insurance; (iii) the ability to subcontract; (iv) the ability to enhance profits by efficiency and economy of management of business; (v) the lack of employment benefits.

A. *The Supply of Apparatus*

36. The supply of unusual or high value apparatus can be an indicator of self-employment employment status. So, in *United States* v. *Silk*[132] drivers who supplied their own lorries – an expensive asset, particularly in the early 1930s – were held to be in business on their own account. On the other hand, the fact that the worker supplies minor assets is not by itself an indication of an independent business; ordinary employees often provide *some* equipment. In *US* v. *Silk*[133] the United States Supreme Court held that unloaders of coal who furnished their own picks and shovels were, nonetheless, employees. These were merely tools of a minor character. Again, in *Ready Mixed Concrete* v. *Minister of Pensions*[134] the English High Court emphasized that the provision of equipment of a minor character would not be sufficient to establish the existence of an autonomous business:

> it may well be that little weight can today be put on the provision of tools of a minor character, as opposed to the provision of plant and equipment on a large scale. In the latter case the real object of the contract is often the hiring

---

131. In *Ready Mixed Concrete* McKenna J stated: 'An obligation to do work subject to the other party's control is a necessary, though not always a sufficient, condition of a contract of service'.
132. (1946) 331 US 704.
133. *Ibid.*
134. [1968] 1 All ER 433.

of the plant, and the services of a workman to operate the plant are purely incidental.

In *McMahon* v. *Securicor Omega*[135] the EAT held that a relationship of employment existed between a courier and a dispatch company although the driver supplied the bike. The quality of this asset – the bike – was, presumably, not regarded as sufficiently unusual. In *The Western People* v. *A Worker*[136] a journalist who used his own laptop and mobile phone was held not to be making a capital contribution of such significance as to render him self-employed.

B. The Power of Delegation

37. A right to delegate is usually regarded as inconsistent with a contract of employment. In a business relationship a contractor pays for work to be done and is indifferent as to who does it. On the other hand in a relationship of employment the engagement is a personal one. It follows that the ability to sub-delegate work is unique to independent business status, and a high value indicator. In *Ready Mixed Concrete*[137] McKenna J said 'the servant must be obliged to provide his own work and skill. Freedom to do a job either by one's own hands or by another's is inconsistent with a contract of service.' In *US* v. *Silk*[138] reference was made to the fact that the truckers were (subject to approval by the company) in a position to hire helpers.

In *Express and Echo Publications Ltd* v. *Tanton*[139] the contract provided for an unrestricted right of substitution. The lower court held that the contract was one of employment. On appeal it was held that the lower court was incorrect in finding a contract of employment:

> it is necessary for a contract of employment to contain an obligation on the part of the employee to provide his services personally. A right to provide a substitute is inherently inconsistent with the existence of a contract of employment. Without such an irreducible minimum of obligation, it cannot be said that the contract is one of service.

C. The Receipt of Employment Benefits

38. The provision of employment benefits is consistent with the existence of a contract of employment. Most long-term employment arrangements provide for minimal employment benefits, such as time-off, sick pay and holidays. A complete absence of provision for these is unique to a business arrangement and therefore an indicator of a business/business relationship unless there is some explanation in the nature of the work explaining the absence of such provision.

---

135. [2002] 13 ELR 317.
136. Labour Court [2004] EDA047.
137. [1968] 2 QB 497, 515.
138. (1946) 331 US 705.
139. [1999] ICR 693.

However, the absence of employment benefits will not be decisive against employment status where the nature of the work is so casual or short term that provision could not be expected even in an ordinary employment relationship. In *Market Investigations* the casual nature of the work carried out by the interviewers explained the absence of provision for holidays, and rest periods:

> The fact that the contract makes no provision for time off is merely a reflection of the fact that there are no specified hours of work. The fact that there is no provision for sick pay and holidays is merely a reflection of the fact that the contract is of very short duration.

In *Castleisland* v. *Minister for Social and Family Affairs*[140] the relationship was long-term. There was no provision for employment benefits. The Supreme Court, in deciding that the veterinarians were not in insurable employment, took into account the absence or provision for pensions, for holidays, or for expenses.

D. The Manner of Payment

39. Ordinarily employees are paid a fixed, predetermined wage based on the amount of hours worked. Autonomous undertakings or the self-employed are paid according to the work completed. This leads to the argument that workers paid on a piece-rate basis should be regarded as self-employed. Piece-rate or productivity payment was, it was argued, typical of a business to business relationship. If this argument was accepted, unskilled workers paid on a piece rate basis might have been removed from employment status. The courts have, however, resisted this line of argument. A number of cases have emphasized that the fact that payment is on a fee per operation basis is not unique to a contract for services. In *Lee Tung Sang* v. *Chung Chi-Keung*[141] the plaintiff was a stone mason paid on a piece rate basis. He 'was paid either a piece-work rate or a daily rate according to the nature of the work he was doing'. The Privy Council did not think it unique to self-employment that the mason was paid according to a piece-rate system. A similar approach has been adopted in Ireland. In *Sheridan* v. *Fairco*[142] the worker, a window salesperson, was paid on a commission basis. It was argued that this was typical of self-employment. The argument was rejected by the EAT: 'the same could be said of any employee paid by piece rate'.

E. The Labelling of the Contract

40. The parties to a contract of employment cannot contrive the contract into something else simply by the label that they employ.[143] This point was reaffirmed in *Denny and Sons*. There, Clause 8 of the *Denny* contract provided: 'the demonstrator

---

140. [2004] 4 IR 150.
141. [1990] 2 AC 374
142. [2006] 17 ELR 246.
143. See e.g. *Massey* v. *Crown Life Assurance Co.* [1978] 2 WLR 576.

is and shall be deemed to be an independent contractor and nothing in this agreement shall be construed as creating the relationship of master and servant'. Nevertheless, the Supreme Court declined to pay any attention to the clause. The parties' self-description could not alter the legal reality of the relationship. Murphy J stated: 'whether Ms Mahon was retained under a contract of service depends essentially upon the actual relationship between the parties, and not their statement as to how liability should arise or be discharged'. Parties cannot circumvent the rights and obligations deriving from employment status by mere self-labelling.

III. The Sham Doctrine and the Drafting of Contracts of Employment

41. In order to avoid the burdens associated with employment status, lawyers advising businesses sometimes design workforce contracts which give the appearance of being self-employment arrangements.

One technique has been to draft clauses providing that the worker is to be deemed to be the owner or provider of the specialist equipment used. (In reality, no one expects the unskilled worker to provide the equipment.) The object of these clauses is to give the *appearance* that the contract is one of self-employment. The reality, of course, is different: the plant actually belongs to the employer. There is no expectation of substitution. An example is *Protectacoat* v. *Szilgay*[144] where the contract with an unskilled foreign worker provided that the worker was to provide the equipment and a van. In fact, no equipment was to be supplied. The contract was designed to give the deceptive appearance that the worker was running an independent business. In reality, there was no expectation that the worker would provide this equipment.

A second technique has been to insert a clause providing that the worker is entirely free to have the work carried out by a third party. The intention here is to manipulate the requirement that for a person to be an employee he must agree to carry out the work personally.[145] In *Autoclenz* the contract – between an unskilled car cleaner and his employer – was carefully designed to avoid employment status. It included the following delegation clause: 'For the avoidance of doubt, as an independent contractor, *you are entitled to engage one or more individuals to carry out the valeting on your behalf.*'

42. The 'sham' principle, first announced in the 1960s in *Snook* v. *London and West Riding Investments*,[146] holds that a contractual provision may be disregarded where it was intended to deceive. For a clause to be a 'sham': 'all the parties thereto must have a *common intention* that the acts or documents are not to create the legal rights and obligations which they give the appearance of creating'. Where a contract is a sham it can be set aside.

---

144. [2009] IRLR 365.
145. *Autoclenz* v. *Belcher* [2011] UKSC 14.
146. [1967] 2 QB 786.

The problem with the *Snook* definition of the 'sham' principle is that it requires both parties to have conspired together to deceive a third party. The parties must have a 'common intention' or common wish to deceive. This definition is not helpful in the employment context because 'the employee is usually either ignorant of the deceit or a victim of it'.[147] There is no 'common intention' or common wish because the employee does not positively *wish to deceive*; the employee's only wish is to secure employment. A division of opinion as to how to apply the sham principle in the employment context arose in *Consistent Group Ltd* v. *Kalwak*.[148] Here the contract with unskilled immigrant workers provided that the worker was to have a right of substitution. In reality there was no expectation that this would ever be the case. In the High Court (EAT) it was held that the clause be struck out and the true nature of the relationship as a relationship of employment exposed. The judgment was delivered by Elias J who said that 'if the reality of the situation is that *no one seriously expects* that a worker will seek to provide a substitute … the fact that the contract expressly provides for these unrealistic possibilities will not alter the true nature of the relationship'. Under this 'reality of the situation' test a clause may be struck out if it does not correspond to the 'realistic possibilities' or understanding of the relationship.

The case was appealed to the Court of Appeal. The Court of Appeal overturned the decision of the High Court. The Court of Appeal applied a definition faithful to the pure *Snook* doctrine. Rimer LJ said that a finding that the contract was in part a sham required a finding that 'both parties intended it to paint a false picture as to the true nature of their respective obligations'. Here there was no *common* intention. The business may have intended deception; the worker certainly did not. Therefore, the clause could not be struck out.

The judgment of the Court of Appeal in *Kalvak* stopped – for a short period – the courts using the sham doctrine to penetrate employment-evasion clauses.

It was revived in *Autoclenz* v. *Belcher*.[149] The worker was hired to take on work valeting cars. The contract provided a substitution clause, emphasizing that he was merely an employee and was entitled to have another carry on work for him: 'for the avoidance of doubt, as an independent contractor, you are entitled to engage one or more individuals to carry out the valeting on your behalf'. The employee asked that the contract be set aside. Agreeing with the more flexible approach of Elias J, the Supreme Court of the United Kingdom applied a liberal, extended version of the sham doctrine. It was not necessary that there be a common intention by both parties to deceive. This test set the standard too high. Such a test enabled employers to easily evade employment status. Instead, the test was whether the contract corresponded to the 'true agreement' of the parties. If it did not correspond to the true agreement the clause could be disregarded from the wider assessment. Lord Clarke said:

---

147. A. Davies, 'Sensible thinking about sham transactions' (2009) 38 *Industrial Law Journal* 318.
148. [2008] IRLR 505.
149. [2011] UKSC 14. This decision was approved by the Irish High Court in *Norton* v. *HSE* [2013] ELR 313.

The question in every case is, what was the true agreement between the parties … The relative bargaining power of the parties must be taken into account in deciding whether the terms of any written agreement in truth represent what was agreed and the true agreement will often have to be gleaned from all the circumstances of the case, of which the written agreement is only a part …

IV. Conclusion: Distinguishing Employment and Self-employment

43. In summary: in determining whether a subject is an employee the following questions should be asked: (i) is the worker subject to control? (ii) Is the worker allowed to delegate? (iii) Is the worker operating an enterprise? If the answer to the first question is positive, and the answer to the second and third questions is in the negative the worker is likely to be an employee.

In operating this test, clauses in the contract which contrive to give the appearance of a worker in business on his own account, but which do not represent the 'true reality', may be disregarded as a sham. Clauses which declare the relationship to be one of employment where that designation is inconsistent with the 'actual relationship' may also be disregarded.

§2. THE EMPLOYMENT STATUS OF OFFICERS

44. The officer is a further category of worker. An officer is a person who occupies some position in the constitutional instrument – statute, or deed of trust, articles of association of a company – establishing an organization. In *Glover* v. *BLN*[150] Kenny J defined the institution as follows:

The characteristic features of an office are that it is created by an Act of the national parliament, charter, statutory regulations, articles of association of a company or a body corporate formed under the authority of a statute, deed of trust, grant or by prescription; and that the holder of it may be removed if the instrument creating the office authorizes this.

The status of office-holder and employee are not necessarily mutually exclusive. It is possible to be both.[151]

A person holding the position of director of a company occupies an office. A company director may also be an employee as well as an employee.[152] In *Neenan Travel* v. *Minister for Social and Family Affairs*[153] the Irish High Court followed the decision of the English Court of Appeal in *Secretary of State* v. *Bottrill*[154] in determining whether a director who is also a shareholder may be an employee. The

---

150. [1973] IR 288.
151. *102 Social Club* v. *Bickerton* [1977] ICR 911: *Bottrill* v. *Secretary of State for Trade* [1999] IRLR 326 (secretary of workingmen's club could be employee; director could be employee).
152. *Lee* v. *Lee's Air Farming* [1960] 3 All ER 420.
153. [2011] IEHC 458.
154. [2000] 1 All ER 915.

key question is whether the party is in reality subject to the managerial control of the company: whether he or she is 'answerable only to himself' or whether operational power is entrusted in other directors or managers to whom the party is merely subordinate. In *Neenan* it was held that the worker, who was also a director with a minority sixteen per cent shareholding, was an employee. He was subject to managerial control, was told what, and when, to work, and was therefore under the control of the company.

§3. THE EMPLOYMENT STATUS OF THE PARTNER

45. A partnership is defined in the Partnership Act 1890 as the relationship between persons carrying on a business in common with a view to profit. The status of partner and of employee are mutually exclusive. There is co-determination rather than subordination. In *DPP* v. *McLoughlin*[155] it was held that fishermen who shared the profits of a fishing voyage were partners not employees. A similar conclusion was reached in *Duncan* v. *O'Driscoll*[156] and *Minister for Social Welfare* v. *Griffiths*.[157]

§4. THE EMPLOYMENT STATUS OF THE CIVIL SERVANT

46. A civil servant is not an employee: *Gilheany* v. *Minister for Finance*.[158] A civil servant is defined by section 1 of the Civil Service Regulation Act 1956 as a person holding a position in 'the Civil Service of the Government and the Civil Service of the State'. In *Gilheany* the High Court took the view that the state does not intend to enter into a contractually binding relationship with a civil servant. Accordingly, there is no contract of employment.

Although a civil servant is not usually an employee, most employment protection statutes deem civil servants to be employees. The effect of doing this is to extend these employment rights to civil servants. Civil servants are included in the Redundancy Payments Acts 1967–2007; Minimum Notice Terms of Employment Act 1973; the Unfair Dismissals Acts 1977–2007;[159] the Payment of Wages Act 1991; the Terms of Employment (Information) Act 1994; the Maternity Protection Acts 1994–2004; the Organization of Working Time Act 1997; the Adoptive Leave Acts 1995–2005; the Protection of Young Persons (Employment) Act 1996; the Parental Leave Acts 1998–2006; the National Minimum Wage Act 2000; the Protection of Employees (Part Time Work Act) 2001; the Protection of Employees (Fixed Term Work Act) 2003; the Carer's Leave Act 2001; the Employment Equality Acts 1998–2011; the Safety, Health and Welfare at Work Act 1987, and the Protection of Employees (Temporary Agency Work) Act 2012.

---

155. [1986] ILRM 493.
156. [1995] ELR 38.
157. [1992] ILRM 44.
158. [1996] ELR 25.
159. S. 2(1)(h) Unfair Dismissals Acts 1977–2007 as amended by s. 22 of the Civil Service Regulation Act 2005.

§5. THE EMPLOYMENT STATUS OF THE RELIGIOUS MINISTER

47. Originally, it was thought that there could not be an employment relationship between a minister and his or her church. In the English decision *Davies* v. *Presbyterian Church of Wales*[160] it was held that in the relationship between a minister and his church there was no intention to create legal relations. The predominantly spiritual relationship with his God transcended the prosaic, secular concerns of a routine employment relationship. The relationship with the church was only secondary: 'The duties owed by the pastor to the Church are not contractual or enforceable. A pastor is called and accepts the call. He does not devote his working life but his whole life to the Church and his religion. He is the servant of God.'[161]

Since intention to create legal relations is an essential condition to the validity of any contract the *Davies* doctrine had the effect of removing religious ministers from the status of employee. Irish courts have adopted the *Davies* principle, thereby disqualifying religious ministers in Ireland from employment protection legislation.[162]

48. However, the *Davies* principle has subsequently been modified. In *Percy* v. *Board of National Mission of the Church of Scotland*[163] the applicant was appointed to the position of minister for a period of five years; she was paid a stipend and was given a manse. The House of Lords held that 'it was time to recognise that employment arrangements between a church and its ministers should not lightly be taken as intended to have no legal effect'.[164] Here the relationship was regulated by detailed documentation in which services were provided in exchange for a specific consideration. There was obviously an intention to create a secular relationship. In a subsequent case the United Kingdom Supreme Court made the point that whether the relationship was a contract of employment or not was fact-sensitive. There was no categorical rule. In *Preston* v. *Methodist Conference*[165] the minister had been appointed to a parish in Cornwall. The question arose whether he was an employee. The Supreme Court distinguished *Percy*. The key point of difference was over the issue of agreement. In *Percy* the process of appointment was a voluntary one. There was an offer and voluntary acceptance. In *Preston*, by contrast, the process was coercive. The appointment was imposed on the Minister by the Methodist Church's 'Stationing Committee'. There was, unlike *Percy*, no offer and voluntary acceptance. In *Preston's* case 'the minister's duties are not consensual. They depend on the unilateral decisions of the Conference.'

---

160. [1986] ICR 280.
161. *Ibid.*, per Lord Templeman.
162. *Millen* v. *Presbyterian Church in Ireland* [2000] 11 ELR 292 (religious minister not entitled to the protection of the Terms of Employment Information Act 1994); *Representative Church Body* v. *Frazer* EAT [2005] PW27/2004 (religious minister not entitled to protection of the Payment of Wages Act 1991).
163. [2006] 2 AC 28.
164. *Ibid.*, per Lord Nicholls at para. 23.
165. [2013] UKSC 29.

Chapter 2. Fixed-term Workers, Part-time Workers, Agency Workers, Zero-hours Workers and non-EEA Workers

§1. Fixed-term Workers

I. The Fixed-term Contract and the Unfair Dismissals Acts 1977–2007

49. A fixed-term contract usually appears in one of two forms: (i) a contract under which the parties agree that the relationship will determine on a fixed, predetermined date, and (ii) a contract which will expire on a fixed date but which may also be determined earlier.[166]

Fixed-term workers have access to the Unfair Dismissals Acts 1977–2007; however the parties may opt out of this protection. At common law the expiry, followed by non-renewal, of a contract is not regarded as a dismissal. It is merely discharge by operation of law. Therefore, there is ordinarily no right to claim wrongful dismissal. However, the position is different in the case of workers protected by the Unfair Dismissals Acts 1977–2007. Section 1 of the Unfair Dismissals Act 1977 defines 'dismissal' as including 'the expiration of a contract of employment for a fixed term without its being renewed'. Therefore, non-renewal of a fixed-term contract *is* a dismissal, and must be justified under one of the restricted grounds by reference to which employees protected by the Unfair Dismissals Acts 1977–2001 may be dismissed.

There is one exception to the protection against unfair dismissal of non-renewal of a fixed-term contract. Section 2(2)(6) of the Unfair Dismissals Act 1977, provides that the Act shall not apply where the parties sign a written fixed-term contract, and give their consent to the non-application of the Act. In order to avoid the 1977 Act, the contract of employment must be in writing; it must be signed by or on behalf of the employee; and it must provide that 'the Act shall not apply to a dismissal consisting only of the expiry or lesser thereof'. The Employment Appeals Tribunal requires strict compliance with these provisions. In *Sheehan* v. *Dublin Tribune*[167] a contract which provided 'it is fully understood on the termination of this contractual arrangement you will have no claim on the company arising from the termination of such contract' (rather than 'the Act shall not apply to a dismissal consisting only of the expiry or lesser thereof'). This was held to be insufficient compliance with section 2(2)(6).

The employer's entitlement to avoid the Unfair Dismissals Acts 1977–2007 by fixed-term waiver contracts is limited by the provision that where a second fixed-term contract has expired, and has not been renewed, and where the court or tribunal takes the view that 'the entry by the employer into the second fixed-term contract was wholly or partly for, or was connected with, the purpose of avoidance of liability under the Act', then the non-renewal is deemed a dismissal.

---

166. *BBC* v. *Dixon* [1979] ICR 281; *O'Mahony* v. *Trinity College Dublin* [1998] 9 ELR 16.
167. [1992] ELR 239.

II. The Protection of Employees (Fixed-Term Work) Act 2003; Restrictions on Fixed-term Employment

50. The rights of fixed-term workers have been ameliorated by the Protection of Employees (Fixed Term Work) Act 2003. Clause 5 of the Framework Agreement on Fixed-term Work (annexed to Directive 99/70/EC) requires Member States to introduce one or more of the following measures for improving the security of fixed term workers: (a) requiring objective reasons justifying the renewal of fixed term contracts; (b) imposing a maximum duration of successive fixed term employment contracts. Sections 9(1) and (2) of the Protection of Employees (Fixed-term Work) Act 2003 implements (b) and (c) of Clause 5. Section 9(1) limits the number of fixed-term contracts by which an employee may be engaged: where a fixed-term employee has completed his, or her, third year of continuous employment then the contract may be renewed on one occasion only, and shall not exceed one year. Section 9(2) provides that where a fixed-term employee is employed on two or more continuous fixed term contracts, the aggregate of such contracts shall not exceed four years. Subsection (3) defines the consequences of an arrangement which infringes subsections (1) or (2): 'the term shall have no effect and the contract concerned shall be deemed to be a contract of indefinite duration'.[168]

The effect of non-compliance with the conditions in subsections (1) and (2) is prescribed in subsection (3). The duration of the contract is converted by operation of law into a contract of indefinite duration: 'that term shall have no effect and the contract deemed to be one of indefinite duration'. The conversion into a contract of indefinite duration only affects the duration of the contract. The former fixed-term worker's terms of employment continue as normal. The employee does not necessarily obtain the same terms as other workers in the same grade.[169] The post-conversion position has been elaborated by the decision of the European Court of Justice of the European Union in *Huet* v. *Université de Bretagne Occidentale*:[170] the conversion into a fixed-term contract does not mean that the contract of indefinite duration must reproduce the terms of the old agreement in identical terms.[171]

51. The application of the rights in section 9 depends upon the worker being 'a fixed-term employee'. A 'fixed term employee' is defined (section 2) as an arrangement in which 'the end of the contract of employment is determined by an objective condition'. In *Athlone Institute of Technology* v. *Holland*[172] the Labour Court held that the phrase 'determined by an objective condition' meant a contingency whose point of occurrence is predictable rather than merely possible. In that case the worker's contract as a lecturer was said to depend on the persistence of 'adequate student numbers'. It was held that this was not a fixed-term contract; it was a contract of indefinite duration. The mark of a fixed-term contract is that it ends upon an event

---

168. S. 9 (3) transforms the contract into one of indefinite duration with effect from the date on which the contract was concluded: *Minister for Finance* v. *McArdle* [2007] 2 ILRM 438; *HSE NW* v. *Ali Umar*, Labour Court [2010] FTD 109.
169. *Minister for Finance* v. *McArdle* [2007] 2 ILRM 438.
170. [2012] IRLR 703.
171. *Ibid.*, para. 44.
172. Labour Court [2011] FTD 1120.

which is expected to occur: for instance, providing cover for an employee who is on sick leave, or to work on a project of road construction. In *Irish Prison Service* v. *Morris*[173] the contract of prison chaplain was amenable to being determined at any time by the bishop. Determination was merely possible. It was not fixed. The worker did not work under a fixed-term engagement.

Section 9 of the Protection of Employees (Fixed-term Work) Act 2003 requires that the worker be 'employed on two or more *continuous* fixed term contracts, the aggregate of such contracts not [exceeding] four years'. The worker must be employed on 'continuous' fixed-term contracts. In a complicated cross-referencing the continuity rules prescribed in another piece of legislation, the First Schedule of the Minimum Notice and Terms of Employment Act 1973 are used for the purpose of determining whether the employment is continuous. The Labour Court has drawn attention to this failure to properly implement Directive 99/70/EC.[174] Article 5 of Directive 99/70/EC applies where a worker is employed under successive contracts of employment; 'continuous' is not the same as 'successive'. 'Successive' accommodates breaks in employment; 'continuous' does not. It was because 99/70/EC only requires 'successive' contracts that the European Court of Justice in *Adeneler* v. *Ellinikos*[175] held that a national law which disallowed the right to an indefinite contract to contracts with more than 20-day gaps contravened the directive. The Irish legislature has yet to address this apparently deficient compliance.

Subsection (4) of section 9 of the Protection of Employees (Fixed-term Work) Act 2003 permits the continued employment on fixed term contracts, notwithstanding the rules in subsections (1) and (2), where 'there are objective grounds justifying such a renewal'. Section 7 provides that a ground shall not be regarded as an 'objective ground' for section 9 unless (i) it is supported by a legitimate objective; (ii) is an appropriate, and (iii) a necessary means of achieving the objective.[176] Irish courts routinely rehearse the principle that fixed-term employment is exceptional and invoke the analysis propounded in *Adeneler* v. *Ellinikos Galaktos*[177] that 'contracts of indefinite duration are the general form of employment relationship' while it is 'only in certain circumstances that fixed-term employment contracts are likely to respond to the needs of both employers and workers. There must be precise and concrete circumstances … resulting from the specific nature of the tasks … or … from pursuit of a legitimate social policy objective'.[178]

---

173. Labour Court [2007] FTD073.
174. *Department of Foreign Affairs* v. *A Group of Workers* [2007] 18 ELR 332; *Revenue Commissioners* v. *Beary* Labour Court [2011] FTD112.
175. [2006] ECR 1-6057.
176. *HSE South* v. *Hamdy* Labour Court [2010] FTD 1014. The necessary condition was found to have been infringed where, a trainee was employed on an unnecessarily number of short fixed-term contracts rather than on a single definite fixed-term contract: *HSE North East Area* v. *Kahn* [2006] 17 ELR 313; *UCC* v. *O'Riordan* Labour Court [2011] FTD 1116.
177. [2006] IRLR 716.
178. *Angelidaki* v. *Organismos Nomarkhiaki Aftodiikisi Rethimnis* [2009] ECR 1-3071; *Kucuk* v. *Land Nordrhein* [2012] IRLR 697.

53. Following *Adeneler* Irish courts have regularly said that the derogation should be applied 'strictly'.[179] Nonetheless, objective justifications have been found on the grounds (i) that not renewing a fixed-term contract is allowable in order to meet 'temporary staffing requirements'[180] or a 'temporary [demand] over which [the employer] has no control';[181] (ii) that not renewing the fixed-term contract is permissible in the case of a worker holding a 'training post' which was 'clearly and unequivocally' established: *HSE North East Area* v. *Khan*;[182] *HSE Dublin* v. *Hamid*;[183] (iii) that not renewing, a fixed-term contractor is allowable where a temporary worker is engaged pending the commencement of a permanent, better-qualified employee: *HSE* v. *Ghulam.*[184]

On the other hand, future economic uncertainty is not a defence to using fixed term employment. In *Teagasc* v. *McNamara*[185] the employer argued that employing research workers as fixed-term workers was justified on the ground that the renewal of research funding was uncertain. The Labour Court rejected this: there were 'many forms of economic activity in which the viability of employment is generated by individual contracts or projects'. The Labour Court reasoned that, if future economic uncertainty was to be recognized as a defence, 'the effectiveness of the Act and the Directive would be seriously subverted'.

III. Fixed-term Workers: the Rights to Reasons and to Information

54. Two supplementary rights are created by sections 8 and 10 of the Protection of Employees (Fixed-term Work) Act 2003. Section 8(2) provides that where an employer proposes to renew a fixed-term contract he shall inform the employee of the 'objective ground justifying the renewal of the fixed term contract and the failure to offer a contract of indefinite duration'. This is to ensure that the employer does not, when subsequently challenged, retrospectively contrive a justification for not offering an indefinite contract; he is bound by the initial justification: *HSE North East* v. *Kahn*;[186] *HSE* v. *Abdel-Haq*;[187] *Dundalk Town Council* v. *Mathews.*[188]

Section 10(1) of the Protection of Employees (Fixed Term Work) Act 2003 provides that an employer shall inform a fixed-term employee 'in relation to vacancies

---

179. *HSE* v. *Khan* [2006] 17 ELR 313. *HSE South* v. *Hamdy* Labour Court [2010] FTD 1014; *O'Riordan* v. *University College Cork* Labour Court [2011] FTD 1116.
180. *Kucuk* v. *Land Nordrhein* [2012] IRLR 697, para. 29; *Revenue Commissioners* v. *Beary*; *Revenue Commissioners* v. *Beary*, Labour Court [2011] FTD 112; *Cunning* v. *Dublin Institute of Technology* [2014] ELR 85.
181. *Iarnrod Eaireann* v. *Higgins* Labour Court [2013] FTD 135; *Institute of Technology Tralee* v. *Cunningham*, Labour Court [2013] FTD 1311.
182. [2006] ELR 313.
183. Labour Court [2009] FTD 0910.
184. Labour Court [2008] FTD 089.
185. [2013] FTD 138. In *Arts Council* v. *Harte* [2013] ELR 85 it was held that public budgetary restrictions could not prevent the conversion of a fixed-term contract into an indefinite contract. The employer could use the power of redundancy in order to deal with any economic necessity.
186. [2006] ELR 313.
187. FTD 0919 17 December 2009.
188. Labour Court [2009] FTD 0914.

which become available to ensure that he or she shall have the same opportunity to secure a permanent position as other employees'.[189] 'Inform' includes a general announcement at a suitable place in the undertaking. Less targeted announcements will not suffice. The notification must either be delivered in person or be displayed in a prominent position in the workplace. In *Henderson* v. *Scoil Iosagain*[190] it was held that the mere placing of an advertisement in a newspaper was insufficient. Posting a notice when the school is on holidays is also insufficient: *Dublin Muslim National School* v. *Naughton*.[191] The objective is to ensure that the fixed term worker has 'the same opportunity to secure a permanent position as other employees'. This objective – the 'opportunity to secure a permanent position as other employees' – limits the employer's duty of notification to positions which would enable the fixed term worker to obtain *permanent* employment. It follows that there is no duty to inform a fixed-term employee of a purely temporary position since that will not enable the worker to obtain a contract of indefinite duration.[192]

IV. Fixed-term Workers: the Prohibition on Discrimination

55. Clause 4 of Directive 99/70/EC (the prohibition against the discrimination of fixed-term workers in comparison with comparable permanent employees) is implemented in Irish law by section 6(1) of the 2003 Act. Section 6(1) provides that a fixed-term employee shall not 'in respect of conditions of employment'[193] be treated in a less favourable manner than a 'comparable permanent employee'.[194]

A 'comparable permanent employee' may be one who is (a) employed by the same employer. If (a) does not apply, the comparator may be drawn from category (b): a permanent employee who works in employment specified in a collective agreement as comparable. Category (c) is the default rule. Where neither paragraph (a) or (b) applies, the comparator may be a permanent employee who is 'employed in the same industry or sector' *and* who (a) performs the same work, or (b) where, even if not identical, the differences are insignificant, or (c) where the work performed by the fixed-term worker is equal or greater in value to that of the worker concerned. In *University College Cork* v. *Bushin*[195] a fixed-term university research employee was made redundant; she had not received an ex gratia payment. No permanent employee of the University had been made redundant. Accordingly, part (c)

---

189. *Aer Lingus* v. *IMPACT* [2005] 16 ELR 261.
190. [2005] 16 ELR 271.
191. Labour Court [2008] FTD 0811.
192. *St Patrick's Classical School* v. *O'Keeffe* Labour Court [2013] FTD 1319.
193. In *University College Cork* v. *Bushin* [2012] IEHC 76 it was held that an ex gratia redundancy payment was a condition of employment'.
194. In *IMPACT* v. *Minister for Agriculture and Food* [2008] ECR 1-2843 this provision was held to be of direct effect, and therefore to have legal force in the interval between the coming into force of Directive 99/70/EC on 10 July 2001 and the enactment of Irish legislation on 14 July 2003. The *IMPACT* ruling was applied in applied in *NUI* v. *Morley*, Labour Court [2009] FTD 093 (where it was held that a lecturer on a fixed term contract was entitled from 10 July 2001 – the date when the Directive should have been implemented – to the same pension entitlements as a comparable permanent lecturer).
195. [2012] IEHC 76.

operated. She was held entitled to compare herself with an employee, not in her own university, employed in the 'higher education sector' for the purpose of comparing redundancy rights. Since there was evidence that permanent workers in other institutions had received a redundancy payment, it was held that her section 6 equality rights had been infringed.

56. The test of objective justification is prescribed in section 7. The elements of the test are: (i) the existence of a legitimate objective; (ii) the unequal treatment must be an appropriate and (iii) a necessary means of achieving the objective. The Labour Court and High Court routinely rehearse the statement of the European Court of Justice decision in *Adeneler*[196] and *Del Cerro Alonso* v. *Osakidetza-Servicio Vasco De Salud*[197] that the employer must show that the ground relied upon corresponds to a 'genuine need; is appropriate for achieving the objective; and is necessary for that purpose'.[198] The 'necessary' condition has been said to require that there be 'no alternative means, having a less discriminatory effect, by which the aim could be achieved. This would normally require the respondent to establish that alternative means of achieving the objective were considered and were not feasible.[199]

§2. PART-TIME WORKERS

57. The Protection of Employees (Part-Time Work) Act 2001 outlaws differential treatment of part-time employees. The Act defines a part-time worker as a worker whose hours of work are fewer than the normal hours of an employee who is a 'comparable employee'.

A 'comparable employee' includes a very wide range of comparators: (i) employees who carry out identical work to the part-timer (section 7(3)(a)); (ii) employees who carry out work so 'similar' to the part-timer such that 'any differences are of small importance' (section 7(3)(b));[200] and (iii) full-timers who carry out work of equal value to the part timer (section 7(3)(c)).[201]

---

196. [2006] IRLR 716.
197. Case C-307/05.
198. *O' Riordan* v. *UCC* Labour Court [2011] FTD 1116; *HSE Dublin NE* v. *Ali Umar* Labour Court [2010] FTD 109; *HSE* v. *Ghulam* Labour Court [2008] FTD 089; *Dooley* v. *Catholic University School* [2010] IEHC 496.
199. *NUI Maynooth* v. *Buckley* Labour Court [2010] FTD 1015.
200. S. 7(2)(b) was applied in *Dundalk Town Council* v. *Teather* Labour Court [2011] PTD 113 a part-time firefighter sub-officer was held to do work of a similar nature to a full-time sub-officer, despite the additional range of duties terms and conditions of employment, which were held to be marginal. Applying the decision of the House of Lords in *Matthews* v. *Kent & Midway Town Fire Authority* [2006] IRLR 367 it was held that the 'core duties' of both full-time and part-time firefighters were the same.
201. S. 7(3)(c) was applied in *Women's Aid* v. *Mulvey* Labour Court [2010] PTD 103 where, assessing the value of each party's work by reference to the criteria of skills, physical or mental requirements, responsibility and working conditions, it was held that the work of the complainant was of lesser value to the work undertaken by the comparator. In *Hillside Park Preschool* v. *Boyle*, Labour Court [2012] PTD 126 a part-time teacher employed in a pre-school was held to be doing 'like work' as a full-time primary school teacher.

The comparison may be made with a full time worker who (i) undertakes work of the types described in section 7(3)(a) to (c), *and* (ii) who *either* works for the same employer *or* who works for an associated employer. In the event of these two categories not being applicable, a comparison may be made with a worker who carries out work which is identical, or similar, or of equal value, in 'the same industry or section of employment'. This final provision greatly expands the potential liability of employers, who are prima facie guilty of discrimination where terms and conditions provided to a claimant employee are less favourable than those afforded to a full time employee in the same employment sector. This enables an employee to seek out a comparator in a very wide pool. It is, it appears, irrelevant that the employer could not even with due diligence have foreseen the less favourable treatment.

58. The 2001 Act provides for two important rights. The first is the right of eligibility to all employment protection legislation previously limited to persons who worked in excess of a specified number of hours; and the right of non-discrimination in the matter of terms and conditions of employment. Section 8 of the 2001 Act provides that all legislation for which the working of a minimum number of hours is a qualifying condition shall also apply to a part-time employee.

The second major entitlement (section 9(1)) is a ban on discrimination. Section 9 provides that a part-time employee shall not, in respect of his or her terms or conditions of employment, be treated in a less favourable manner than a comparable full-time employee.[202] Furthermore, section 10 implements the pro rata principle: the quantum of a benefit which is contingent on the number of hours worked must be calculated by reference to 'the proportion which the normal hours of work of that employee bears to the normal hours of work of the comparable full-time employee concerned'.[203]

There are three exceptions to the non-discrimination rule. (i) Less favourable treatment is justified where it can be justified on objective grounds: section 9(2). A ground is not to be treated as an objective ground unless it is based on considerations other than the status of the employee concerned as a part-time employee, and the less favourable treatment is for the purpose of achieving a legitimate objective of the employer.[204] (ii) The rule against discrimination does not apply to a pension scheme where the part-time worker's normal hours of work are 20 per cent of those of a comparable full time employee.[205] (iii) The prohibition on discrimination

---

202. S. 9(1) was held to have been infringed in *Department of Justice* v. *Ennis* Labour Court [2004] PTD 041 (amount of travelling allowance paid to the part-time worker was half that paid to the full time worker); *Diageo* v. *Rooney* Labour Court [2004] PTD 042 (part-time worker, unlike full-timer, was not paid while on sick leave).

203. *Department of Education* v. *Gallagher* Labour Court [2004] PTD 047: a part-time teacher who undertook supervision duties was paid half the amount paid to a full-time teacher. This was despite the fact that both worked the same number of hours. The Labour Court held that the pro rata principle had been infringed.

204. This was applied in *Louth CC* v. *Martin* Labour Court [2005] PTD 051. In that case the applicant was a part-time teacher who was paid less than her full-time comparator. The part-time worker was only part qualified. Her comparator was fully qualified. The Labour Court held that the difference in treatment was justified by an objective ground: to incentivize partly qualified teachers to become fully qualified.

205. S. 9(4) Protection of Employees (Part Time Work) Act 2001.

does not apply to part-time workers who work on a casual, short-time basis, i.e. to workers who are engaged to work for less than 13 weeks.[206]

§3. AGENCY WORKERS

I. The Employment Status of Agency Workers at Common Law

59. The legal status of the agency worker, and the issue of whether an agency worker is an employee, is unsettled. (i) The conventional view has been, that since a contract of employment requires an employer to exercise control and the employee to submit to that control, the relationship between a worker and an employment agency cannot be a relationship of employment.[207] (ii) It has also been held that there is no contract of employment between an agency temp and the agency's client. This is because the contractual relationship is between the worker and the agency, not the agency's client.[208] The combination of these principles had the result that the agency worker was a social orphan. It was not an employee of the agency, and it was not an employee of the end-user. It not an employee of anyone, and no one owed it employment-related legal duties.

In *Construction Industry Training Board* v. *Labour Force Ltd* [209] it was held that unskilled building workers hired by employment agencies were not in a relationship of employment with the agency. The end-user paid the wages to the agency, and had the right to control the men as to what to do, and to require the agency to remove a man at three days' notice (or in the case of misbehaviour, forthwith). The court considered it decisive against the identification of an employment relationship with the agency that no control was exercised by the agency over the worker. This approach has been consistently followed in Ireland. The conclusion that agency workers were not employees of the agency to whom they attach themselves was reached by the Employment Appeals Tribunal in *Cervi* v. *Atlas Staff Bureau*[210] relying heavily on the decision of the English High Court in the *Construction Industry Training Board* case.[211] This approach was confirmed in *Brightwater Selection* v. *Minister for Social and Family Affairs.*[212] This case began when a Social Welfare Appeals Officer had held that a worker sent by an agency to work in the administration section of a university worked under the control of the agency: 'the requirement to notify them of any changes in relation to responsibility, hours worked, pay, grievances … to produce a time sheet'. However, the High Court reversed this decision. It held that these minimal administrative obligations were not equivalent to

---

206. S. 11(4) Protection of Employees (Part Time Work) Act 2001.
207. *Construction Industry Training Board* v. *Labour Force Ltd* [1970] 3 All ER 220; *Cervi* v. *Atlas Staff Bureau* EAT [1985] UD 616/1985.
208. *Minister for Labour* v. *PMPA,* High Court, 16 April 1986.
209. [1970] 3 All ER 220.
210. EAT [1985] UD 616/1985.
211. See, however, the determination of the EAT, *Hyde* v. *Kelleher* [2004] ELR 145 holding that a sponsor paid by FAS was the employer of the worker despite the absence of a contract between the sponsor and the worker.
212. [2011] IEHC 511.

'control'. The High Court held that in determining whether control exists, the alleged employer must not only have the right to tell the individual what work to do, but also to dictate the manner in which this work was to be done. There was no control in this sense; accordingly, the worker was not an employee of the agency.

60. Assuming that the agency worker is not an employee of the agency, is the worker an employee of the end-user? In *Minister for Labour* v. *PMPA*[213] it was held that a temp was not an employee of the agency's client. There was a contract between the worker and the agency; there was a contract between the agency and the end user. But there was no contract between the worker and the agency. Since there was *no contract* there could be no contract *of employment*. However, despite the general rule, an independent, concurrent contract between the worker and the end-user may, in exceptional cases, be found to exist. This will be found to be in place where the two parties have, prior to finalizing the arrangement, entered into negotiations (a) settling terms and conditions and (b) agreeing for strategic reasons that the arrangement should be conducted through an employment agency. In this case there *is* a direct contract between the worker and the end-user. An example is *Diageo* v. *Rooney.*[214] The claimant had written a letter of application to Diageo's Occupational Health Centre. The end-user interviewed her and negotiated her hours of work, rate of pay and other particulars of her duties and benefits. Under the arrangement she was to be deemed an agency worker and was to be paid by an agency, Irish Recruitment Consultants. It was held that the reality of the relationship was a conventional contract of employment.

II. Agency Workers Deemed to be Employees for Miscellaneous Employment Statutes

61. At common law an agency worker is usually not an employee. However, statute may override common law. Most modern employment rights statutes do override the common law and deem the agency worker to be an employee for the purpose of entitlement to that particular statutory right. Thus, section 13 of the Unfair Dismissals Act 1977–2007 deems the agency worker to be an employee of the end-user:

> Where … an individual agrees with another person, who is carrying on the business of an employment agency … to do or perform personally any work or service for a third person then, for the purposes of the [Unfair Dismissals Act] as respects a dismissal occurring after such commencement—(a) the individual shall be deemed to be an employee employed by the third person under a contract of employment.

---

213. High Court, 16 April 1986.
214. Labour Court [2004] PTD 042.

This provision was applied in *West v. Governors of St Patrick's Hospital.*[215] The claimant was seconded to a hospital by an employment agency. The hospital asked that he be removed, and the claimant took proceedings under the Unfair Dismissals Act 1977. The hospital argued that he was not its employee. The EAT held that the Hospital had 'failed to recognise the implications of section 13'. He was an employee for the purpose of the Unfair Dismissals Act 1977.

Other employment protection statutes include agency workers as employees. Under the Payment of Wages Act 1991 the party liable to pay wages (in practice, the agency) is deemed to be the employer. Under section 1 of the Employment Equality Acts 1998 to 2011 the party liable to pay the wages of the agency worker is deemed to be the employer. Under the Protection of Employees on Transfer of Undertakings Regulations 2003 the agency is deemed the employer. Under section 2 of the Redundancy Payments Acts, 1967–2007 the agency worker is deemed to be in an employment relationship with the agency.

III. Protection of Employees Temporary Agency Work Act 2012

62. Further protection was given to agency workers by the Protection of Employees Temporary Agency Work Act 2012 – which implements EU Directive 2008/104/EC on temporary agency work. The most important provision in this Act is section 6. This provides:

> an agency worker shall be entitled to the same basic working and employment conditions as the basic working and employment conditions to which he or she would be entitled if he or she were employed by the hirer under a contract of employment to do work that is the same as or similar [to that undertaken by the agency worker].[216]

However, this does not mean that an agency worker is entitled to *all* of the same conditions as a direct worker. The agency worker is only entitled to the same *basic working and employment* conditions. That phrase – *basic working and employment conditions* – is defined in section 1 as

> terms and conditions that relate (a) pay, (b) working time,(c) rest periods,(d) rest breaks during the working day, (e) night work, (f) overtime, (g) annual leave, or (h) public holidays.

This is not comprehensive. Section 6 only gives agency workers the same rights in respect of pay and hours of work. It does not give agency workers *all* of the same contractual rights as direct workers in the same workplace. It does not, for instance, give agency workers the same rights over matters such as contractual grievance procedures. Another example is the implied common law right to trust and confidence.

---

215. EAT [2009] UD303/2009.
216. Evidence that directly employed employees are enjoying superior basic working conditions will usually provide the basis for a claim that the claimant would have been entitled to those working conditions if he or she had been directly employed: *Costello v. Team Obair* [2014] ELR

At common law, employees are entitled to this right. But agency workers – because they are not employees of anyone – do not possess the right to trust and confidence. Section 6 of the 2012 Act does not given this right – trust and confidence does not fall within the definition of 'basic working and employment conditions'.

§4. ZERO-HOURS WORKERS

63.   Section 18 of the Organization of Working Time Act 1997, is the source of legislative protection of zero-hours workers. Zero-hours workers who are not called to work are entitled to compensation for loss of income. Section 18 applies to workers whose contract of employment operates to require the employee to make himself or herself available to work for an employer in a week: 'as and when the employer requires'. When work of the type which the employee is required to make him, or herself, available to do has been done in that week, then the employee is entitled to be paid either as if he/she had worked 25 per cent of the hours for which work had been done, or as if he/she had worked 15 hours (whichever is less).

It is a condition to recognition as a protected zero-hours worker under the 1997 Act that the contract requires the worker 'to make himself or herself available to work for the employer in a week'. It will not apply to a contract in which the employee is free to refuse work if offered it: the contract at issue in *Contract Personnel Marketing Ireland* v. *Buckley*[217] provided that the employee was to have 'the right to refuse or accept these hours … not expected to be on call for work'. The claimant was held not to be a zero-hours worker. A contracted drafted in this manner can be used to evade section 18.

§5. TEMPORARY EMPLOYEES

64.   The main legal disadvantage attaching to a temporary, or short-term, contract is that the employee may be excluded from important items of employment protection legislation: under the Redundancy Payments Acts 1967–2007 an employee does not qualify unless he has accumulated two years' continuous service. The Unfair Dismissals Acts 1977–2007 only applies to employers with more than one year's continuous service. The Terms of Employment (Information) Act, 1994–2012, only applies in the case of employees who have been in continuous employment for more than one month.

§6. NON-EEA WORKERS

I. The Criminal and Administrative Consequences of a Foreign National Worker Working Without a Work Permit

65.   It is a criminal offence for a foreign national worker to work without a work permit. Section 2 of the Employment Permits Acts 2003–2012 provides that a 'foreign national shall not enter the service of an employer in the State, or be in

---

217. Labour Court [2011] DWT1145.

employment in the State' except in accordance with an employment permit granted under the Employment Permits Act 2006. The second clause was added to deal with the problem which had arisen when 'entering' employment alone was incriminated and which had been exposed in *Gleeson* v. *Chi Ho Cheung*.[218] There it was held that a prosecution for 'entering' employment without a permit was exhausted on the first occasion that it was prosecuted. A non-national who had been prosecuted for that offence, and then continued in employment without a permit could not be prosecuted for any further offence. The second part, 'be in employment', was enacted in order to close this gap.

A person working without a permit also runs the risk of deportation: section 3 of the Immigration Act, 1999 provides that a person who works in contravention of restrictions in respect of entering into the state, or leave to stay in the state, may be deported. Deportation is not, however, automatic: the Minister is obliged to consider circumstances like the person's connection with the state, the person's domestic circumstances and the period for which the person has been in the state.

Employers engaging immigrants who are not authorized to work are also subjected to the criminal law: section 2(2) provides that 'a person shall not employ a foreign national in the State except in accordance with an employment permit granted by the Minister under section 8 of the Employment Permits Act 2006'.

II.   The Doctrine of Contractual Unenforceability and the Illegal Non-national Worker

66.   The principle of the unenforceability of illegal contracts provides a further potential sanction for the non-EEA national who works in Ireland without a work permit. At common law a contract which is performed in breach of a statutory restriction is regarded as unenforceable. The doctrine also applies in the case of an immigrant who works, in contravention of the Employment Permits Acts 2003–2006 without a work permit. In *Hussein* v. *Labour Court*[219] the High Court held that a Pakistani chef who worked in the Poppadom Restaurant Dublin without a work permit was unable to claim under the Organization of Working Time Act 1997 (he had been forced to work 77 hours per week and not given paid holidays), or the Terms of Employment (Information) Act 1994 (he had not been given particulars of employment), or the National Minimum Wage Act 2000 (he had only been paid 50 cents per hour). The employer was the subject of a criminal investigation for his employment practices. The chef had assumed that his employer (who was also his cousin) would, or had, obtained a renewal of his work permit. Nonetheless, the High Court held that working without a permit was a criminal offence. It would not be coherent legal policy to term such conduct as criminal, and, at the same time, to enforce such a contract in civil actions:

> The Oireachtas has declared that a contract of employment involving a non-national is substantively illegal in the absence of the appropriate employment

218. [1996] 2 ILRM 515.
219. [2012] IEHC 364.

permit, so that, accordingly, a contract of this kind has been expressly prohibited by statute. It would scarcely be a sensible construction of the Act of 2003 if it is admitted that such a contract is expressly prohibited by statute and yet the courts permitted administrative bodies such as the Labour Court to give appropriate remedies to the parties as if the contract were perfectly lawful.[220]

The High Court recognized the harshness of its ruling: the chef (Mr Younis) had suffered 'the most appalling exploitation in respect of which he has no effective recourse'. This was particularly so since he had not been guilty of dishonest immigration evasion. He had assumed that his employer would obtain the permit. Hogan J sent his judgment to the Minister for Jobs, Enterprise and Innovation and to the *Dail* and *Seanad* so that they could consider the policy implications of the decision.

67. The employee may have a defence against the operation of the unenforceability doctrine where he can prove that he was unaware that the employer had not obtained a work permit. In *Dubnya* v. *Hourican*[221] the immigrant employee genuinely believed that his employer had obtained a work permit; in fact, he had not. The EAT held that his lack of subjective knowledge of the facts prevented the doctrine from applying.

The doctrine of severance provides a second potential defence. 'Severance' allows a clean period of work to be cut from the infected period. Severance allows the corrupt part to be cut out. The severance principle was applied in *Blue Chip Trading Ltd* v. *Helbawi*.[222] The immigrant employee who was a student illegally worked during academic term time in breach of terms in his employment permit (which forbade working during holidays). He was unable to claim for wages earned during that period. However, the employee was entitled to work without restriction during the holiday period. The court held that the holiday period could be cleanly 'severed' from the term period; that period could be severed. He was entitled to recover wages unpaid during that period.

III. Schemes for Obtaining Work Permits

68. Section 14 of the Employment Permits Act 2006 permits the Minister to make 'regulations' prescribing the circumstances in which work permits are granted. Three non-statutory schemes have been promulgated. The use of non-statutory schemes is legally questionable: section 14 of the 2006 Act requires that the terms under which work permits are granted should be detailed in legislative regulations.

The first of these schemes provides for a 'green card' employment permit.[223] The conditions for the grant of a green card are either that the remuneration attached to

---

220. *Ibid.*, para. 18.
221. EAT [2004] UD 781/2004.
222. [2009] IRLR 128
223. Department of Jobs, Enterprise and Innovation, *Employment Permits Arrangements; Guide to Green Card Permits* (June 2011).

the job be in excess of €60,000; or (ii) that it be between €30,000 and €60,000, and that the occupation be a strategically important occupation listed in Schedule A of the Scheme. The issue of the card is contingent on the existence of a bona fide offer from a company registered with the Companies Registration Office and the Revenue Commissioners and trading in Ireland.

The second of these schemes is the 'work permit' scheme. The conditions for obtaining a work permit are that the salary range is between €30,000 and €60,000 and that the vacancy, in respect of which an application for a work permit is being made, must have be 'advertised with the FÁS/EURES employment network for at least eight weeks and additionally in local and national newspapers for six days'. In exceptional cases a permit may be granted to an employee earning less than €30,000.

A third scheme is the Intra-Company Transfer Permit.[224] This scheme operates where an Irish company has a direct link with an overseas company by reason of common ownership. In order to constitute common ownership either one company must own the other, or both must be part of a group of companies controlled by the same parent company. The employee must fall into one of the categories of (i) senior management, (ii) key personnel or (iii) trainee.

---

224. Department of Jobs, Enterprise and Innovation, *Guide to Intra-Company Transfer Permits* (June 2011).

Chapter 3. The Form and Content of the Contract of Employment

§1. Writing Requirements and the Contract of Employment

I. The Statute of Frauds 1695

69. It is not generally a condition to the enforceability of a contract of employment that it be in writing. Usually a contract is enforceable, even where it is verbal. Most employment protection legislation expressly states that it applies to a contract of employment whether or not the contract is verbal or in writing.

There is, however, one exception to the general rule: section 2 of the Statute of Frauds Act 1695 provides that:

> no action shall be brought upon any agreement that is not to be performed within the space of one year from the making thereof unless the agreement upon which such action shall be brought, or some note or memorandum thereof shall be in writing and signed by the party to be charged therewith.

This provision only applies in the case of contracts which will not conclude before the end of one year. Most contracts of employment are of indeterminate duration. These may expire before one year, and therefore do not attract the Statute of Frauds 1695. However, the Act will apply in the case of a fixed-term contract which specifies a date of termination in excess of one year from the making of the contract.[225]

II. The Terms of Employment (Information) Act 1994

70. Although it is usually not a condition of a contract of employment that it be in writing, the Terms of Employment (Information) Act 1994, which implements Directive 91/532/EEC, requires that not later than two months after the commencement of the relationship the employee be provided with a statement in writing of the particulars of the contract of employment. The statement of particulars is not *the contract*. It merely enjoys 'such presumption as to its correctness as would attach in domestic law to any similar document drawn up by the employer and communicated to the employee'.[226] The employee may, despite the statement, establish either that the parties agreed differently or that there was no such agreement.

The directive does not make it a condition to enforceability of the contract of employment that the required particulars be supplied. This was confirmed by the European Court of Justice in *Lange* v. *Georg Schuuneman gmbH*[227] where the court pointed out that Article 8(1) of the directive requires that Member States introduce such measures as are necessary to enable employees who consider themselves wronged by failure to comply with the obligations in the directive to have an effective remedy. The issue of sanctions, the European Court of Justice said, is a matter

---

225. *Naughton* v. *Limestone Land* [1952] Ir. Jur. Rep. 18.
226. *Kamplemann* v. *Landschaftsverband Westfalen-Lippe* [1998] IRLR 332.
227. [2001] IRLR 244.

for the discretion of Member States, and while a Member State might introduce a sanction as radical as non-enforceability, it is not necessitated by the directive. Irish legislature has exercised the discretion by providing a financial sanction in the case of non-compliance. Non-compliance with the Act is, however, unlike non-compliance with the Statute of Frauds 1695. It does not render the obligations which have not been detailed in the statement unenforceable.

§2. LEGAL CAPACITY TO ENTER INTO A CONTRACT OF EMPLOYMENT

I. Minors

71. Section 2 of the Age of Majority Act 1985 provides that a person reaches full age when he attains the age of 18 years, or upon his marriage. Employees under the age of 18 years are minors, and their contracts of employment are regulated by the common law principles, which regulate the enforceability of minors' contracts. The common law rule is that a contract with a minor is unenforceable, except where it is a contract for necessaries. But since a contract of employment generally benefits an employee it is regarded as necessary. It will be binding unless it is not for the benefit of an infant. It is only where its costs outweigh its benefits, and so is not for the benefit of an infant, that a contract of employment with an infant will be unenforceable.

II. Convicted Prisoners

72. Under the Forfeiture Act 1875, prisoners sentenced to undergo the regime known as penal servitude suffered a number of disabilities, including inability to conclude a contract. In 1997 the Criminal Law Act, 1997 abolished penal servitude and repealed the Forfeiture Act 1875. All convicted prisoners may now during the duration of their sentence of imprisonment enter into enforceable contracts of employment.

§3. ILLEGALITY AND THE UNENFORCEABILITY OF THE CONTRACT OF EMPLOYMENT

73. The doctrine of illegality[228] has the effect of rendering a contract of employment unenforceable. Nearly all statutory employment rights are predicated on the existence of a 'contract of employment'. But 'contract of employment' is interpreted as meaning a *lawful* contract of employment.[229] Accordingly, where the contract is unenforceable by illegality, there is no lawful 'contract of employment' and these statutory rights will be withheld from the employee.

---

228. An early instance is *Poplett* v. *Stockdale* (1825) 2 Car & P; 171 ER 1041.
229. E.g. *Blue Chip Trading Ltd* v. *Helbawi* [2009] IRLR 128.

In employment law the forms of illegality which most often attract the unenforceability rule are cases involving breach of the immigration laws, the tax collection laws and the social welfare rules.

I. Fraud on the Revenue and the Employment Contract

74. The most usual case in which contracts of employment are held unenforceable arises where frauds of the revenue laws are practised. In *Lewis* v. *Squash Ireland*[230] the claimant received wages of £16,000 per annum. However, the parties decided that only £14,000 should be reported to the revenue. The outstanding £2,000 was officially recorded as expenses. The EAT declined jurisdiction in a subsequent unfair dismissal claim. The *Oireachtas* could not, it was held, have intended that intended that the statutory rights would be extended to those knowingly breaking the law by participating in a fraud upon the revenue. The Tribunal cited with approval this extract from the English High Court in *Newland* v. *Simons*:[231]

> If an employee wishes to be entitled to the statutory rights given him by the relevant legislation, then the contract of employment in respect of which he seeks those rights must be legal. We have no doubt that Parliament never intended to give the statutory rights provided by the relevant legislation to those knowingly breaking the law by committing or participating in a fraud on the revenue.[232]

The size of the fraud on the Revenue is not relevant. In *Salvesen* v. *Simons*[233] it was held that the fact that the illegality was a minor one which cannot have cost the Revenue a significant sum in lost tax was irrelevant. In *Salvesen's* case a salary of £12,000 was split in two: a salary of £10,000 paid to the employee; and a sum of £2,000 paid as service charges to a company established by the employee. The idea was that the employee would pay tax at the lower business rate on the £2,000. In fact, no services were provided by the company and the entire sum was payable in respect of the service provided by the employee. The return to the Inland Revenue was technically fraudulent. However, the sum lost to the Inland Revenue was negligible. It was argued by the employee that there was merely a minor and technical breach of the tax collection rules, and that the employee should not be so severely punished by having it declared that the entire contract was invalid. However, the court held that the *quantum* was irrelevant:

> The fact that the claimant did not know that what he was doing was *in law* (as opposed to fact) a fraud on the revenue is also irrelevant. Ignorance of the tax

---

230. [1983] ILRM 363.
231. [1981] ICR 521.
232. The merits of this view have been challenged; see Mogridge 'Illegal Contracts: Loss of Statutory Protection' (1981) 10 ILJ 23; but compare Redmond 'Illegality and the contract of employment' (1987) JISLL 17.
233. [1994] IRLR 52.

laws is not a defence. In *Miller* v. *Karlinski*[234] Lord du Parq said: 'in truth, it makes no difference whether or not the parties know what they are doing is illegal. Ignorance of the law cannot excuse them.'

The doctrine will not apply where the worker was in fact liable to pay greater tax but had made *no false representation* to the Revenue Commissioners. This is confirmed in *Enfield* v. *BF Components*.[235] The applicant had been employed as a catering equipment engineer. The contract was described as one of self-employment. He received no holiday or sickness pay. On the other hand, he worked exclusively for the contractor and did not supply equipment. He was taxed as self-employed. He informed the Revenue of the facts and they agreed with the classification. In fact, he was an employee, and was paying less than he was legally required to pay. It was argued that a claim for wrongful dismissal was unenforceable for breach of the illegality principle. The employer argued (i) that he had paid less tax than he was legally obliged; (ii) that was an illegal underpayment to the revenue; (iii) therefore the contract was unenforceable. However, the Court of Appeal rejected the argument. Here, there was an honest representation to the Revenue. The parties had honestly disclosed the facts to the Revenue. The mere fact that objectively the parties had under-paid tax was not enough. Errors of classification were understandable. Here there was no dishonest misrepresentation; accordingly, the punitive unenforceability doctrine should not apply.

II. Social Welfare Fraud and Enforceability of the Contract of Employment

76. A breach of the social welfare code has been held to render a contract of employment unenforceable. In *Morris* v. *Keogh*[236] an employee who received unemployment benefit while still working was held disentitled to claim unfair dismissal. The Tribunal invoked grounds of public policy: 'Public policy does not permit the person who wrongfully declares that he is unemployed during the particular period and thereby obtains monetary benefit from the State contrary to law, to found a claim of statutory or constitutional right on the fact that he was gainfully employed during the same period.'

III. Defences to the Unenforceability Doctrine: the Unfair Dismissals Acts 1977–2007

A. Section 8(11) of the Unfair Dismissals Acts 1977–2007

77. First, a statutory defence is provided by section 8(11) of the Unfair Dismissals Acts 1977–2007[237] which provide that an employee may enforce a claim under

---

234. (1945) 62 TLR 85.
235. [2008] IRLR 500.
236. EAT [1984] UD 74/1984.
237. 'Where the dismissal of an employee is an unfair dismissal and a term or condition of the contract of employment concerned contravened any provision of or made under the Income Tax Acts or the

the Unfair Dismissals Acts 1977–2007 notwithstanding that '*a term or condition of the contract of employment* concerned contravened any provision of or made under the Income Tax Acts or the Social Welfare Acts'.

However, this defence is subject to *four* major restrictions.

The defence only applies to claims under the Unfair Dismissals Acts, 1977–2007. It does not, therefore, apply to wrongful dismissal claims,[238] or to wages claims, or damages claims for breach of employee rights. The High Court has noted that the random application of the defence to one statutory employment right (the Unfair Dismissals Act, 1977–2007), but not to others gives rise to 'anomalies'.[239]

The defence only applies where the *source* of the illegality is the breach of the social welfare or revenue code. It does not excuse other types of unlawful act e.g. employment in breach of the Employment Permits Act 2003–2012.

The defence only applies where '*a term or condition of the contract of employment* concerned contravened any provision of or made under the Income Tax Acts or the Social Welfare Acts'. This seems to suggest that the defence might not apply where (as is usually the case) the contract is merely being operated in breach of the Income Tax Acts without it being a '*term … of the contract*' that the parties contravene the revenue code. An employee might make a false representation of his income without it being a term of his contract.

In a case where such an illegality is disclosed to the Tribunal, the Tribunal is directed to inform the Revenue Commissioners.[240]

B.   The Ignorance of the Facts Defence

78.   Ignorance of *the facts* (as opposed to the law) which constitute the illegal act may be a defence. In *Costelloe* v. *Crean Associates*[241] the claimant established that she did not know that a wage increase was not being mentioned in her wages slip in order to defraud the revenue. Her claim that she thought that it was being concealed so as not to make her co-employees jealous was believed. In *Dubnya* v. *Hourican*[242] an immigrant employee genuinely believed that his employer had obtained a work permit; in fact, he had not. The Tribunal held that his lack of subjective knowledge of the facts prevented the doctrine from applying.

Social Welfare Acts, 1981 to 1993, the employee shall, notwithstanding the contravention, be entitled to redress under this Act, in respect of the dismissal.'
238. *Tony Hayden* v. *Sean Quinn Properties*, High Court, 6 December 1993.
239. *Re Red Sail Frozen Foods Ltd* [2006] IEHC 328.
240. S. 8(12). 'Where, in proceedings under this Act, it is shown that a term or condition of a contract of employment contravened any such provision as aforesaid, the rights commissioner, the Tribunal or the Circuit Court, as the case may be, shall notify the Revenue Commissioners or the Minister for Social Welfare, as may be appropriate, of the matter.'
241. EAT [1985] UD 785/1985.
242. EAT [2004] UD 781/2004.

C. The Severance Defence

79. Fraud on the Revenue, or illegality in compliance with the immigration code, may last for just a few days or weeks. There may be longer periods when the employee is acting quite properly. An employee might receive an undeclared bonus at Christmas; should his entire contract of employment henceforth be rendered illegal? Here the principle of 'severance' might apply, allowing 'severance' of the clean period from the infected period. Severance allows the corrupt part to be cut out. The severance principle was applied in *Blue Chip Trading Ltd* v. *Helbawi*.[243] The immigrant employee illegally worked during term time in breach of terms in his employment permit. He was unable to claim for breaches of minimum wage rules committed during that period. However, the employee was entitled to work without restriction during the academic holiday period. The court held that the holiday period could be cleanly 'severed' from the term period. He was entitled to recover wages unpaid during that period.

D. The European Directive Rights Exception; Hall v. Woolston Hall Leisure Ltd

80. In *Hall* v. *Woolston Hall Ltd*[244] the English Court of Appeal held that an Industrial Tribunal was obliged to disapply the illegality doctrine in a sex discrimination case involving an employee who claimed that she had been discriminated on grounds of sex contrary to the United Kingdom's Sex Discrimination Act 1976. This was despite the fact that the employee was aware that the contract was being performed in breach of the Revenue code. The employee was a chef. She had asked for, and was granted, a wage increase of £250 per week. Her wage statement stated that her wages were £160 per week. She was aware that this was being done by the employer in order to depress his Revenue liability. The Sex Discrimination Act 1976 was intended to implement the Equal Treatment Directive 76/207/EEC. The directive, like all European employment directives, required Member States to provide an unqualified right of effective redress for sex discrimination.[245] The unenforceability doctrine *denied* effective access. Therefore, the unenforceability doctrine could not be applied. The doctrine would hinder access and, therefore, infringe the right of effective redress required by the directive.

E. The Mitigating Circumstances Defence

81. The germ of a further defence can be found is the English 1981 decision, *Coral Leisure* v. *Barnett*.[246] Here the applicant had been employed as a public relations executive for the entertainments business, Coral Leisure. It emerged that the

---

243. [2009] IRLR 128.
244. [2000] IRLR 578.
245. Article 6 required national legal systems to provide effective redress for breaches of the principle of equal treatment.
246. [1981] IRLR 204.

employee had occasionally procured prostitutes for some of the employer's clients. The employer argued that this unlawful conduct, occurring during the contract, rendered the contract unenforceable. Did this mean that every time an employee committed some illegal act his entire contract would be regarded as illegal? The English Employment Appeal Tribunal held that not every short act of illegality would render an entire contract prospectively and retrospectively unenforceable. The Tribunal said that 'the fact that a party has in the course of performing a contract committed an unlawful or immoral act will not by itself prevent him from further enforcing that contract'.

Building on the idea in *Coral Leisure*, that not every illegality should make a contract unenforceable, the Court of Appeal in *Hall* proposed a different approach to the previous one. The conventional approach had always been an inflexible one in which any illegality rendered the contract unenforceable. The newer view looks at the circumstances in which the illegality was committed.

Under this test illegality may be mitigated by three circumstances. The first ground of mitigation arises where the employee has not 'actively participated' in the illegality. The 'active' condition was not fulfilled in *Hall* v. *Woolston Hall*. Although the employee was aware of the illegality she did not actively participate in the fraud. When she asked about the matter she was told that was 'the way the company did business'. The fraud was forced on her. She did not ask for it or agree to it. She had not 'actively participated'. The *Hall* v. *Woolston Hall* 'active participation' requirement has been endorsed by the Irish High Court. In *Re Red Sail Frozen Foods Ltd*[247] factory workers were aware that their employer was understating their wages. None the less, they were still held entitled to statutory redundancy payments. They had not actively participated in the fraud on the revenue. They were merely passive recipients.

A second mitigating circumstance arises where the degree of illegality is minor. Conduct which is merely transient or minor may be overlooked. In *Colen* v. *Cebrian Ltd*[248] the claimant, who was paid on a commission basis, occasionally underdeclared the amount of his commission. The Court of Appeal distinguished an arrangement in which the contract was performed with the intention of defrauding the revenue, and some occasional, minor illegality. The Court held that the 'glimpse of a very short period of [unlawful conduct] is in no measure sufficient to turn a lawful contract into an illegal contract'.

A third mitigating circumstance arises where the employee's claim does not require disclosure of the illegality. The employee's defence will be strengthened if the illegality and the claim are not 'inextricably bound up'. In other words, is it possible to tell the story of the wrong committed against the employee without disclosing the illegality? For instance, in *Hall* the claim was for sex discrimination committed when the employer dismissed Hall when she disclosed that she was pregnant. The Court of Appeal was impressed by the fact that the employee could relate her story (her dismissal for being pregnant) without having to reveal the wrong (tax fraud in the manner of payment). The reason for this is that it is embarrassing for a court to have to overlook an illegality which has been explicitly disclosed to it.

---

247. [2007] 3 IR 361, 371.
248. [2004] IRLR 210.

There is no such embarrassment where the illegality is not included in the employee's complaint.

F.   The 'Affront to Public Conscience' Exception

84.   A further modification of the traditional strict rule is the 'affront to public conscience' test. In *Hewcastle Catering Ltd* v. *Ahmed*[249] the claimants were waiters in a club in which the employers operated a scheme for fraudulently evading VAT on the services provided to customers who paid cash. The waiters were involved in the operation of the scheme but derived no benefit. They were subsequently dismissed when they disclosed the scheme to the authorities. The Court of Appeal held that the basis of the unenforceability rule was that it would be 'an affront to the public conscience' to give the claimant access to the court. In cases involving calculated tax fraud it would be an affront to the public conscience to turn a blind eye and enforce the contract.

But in some cases it might be an affront to the public conscience to *not* to enforce the contract. The case at hand was one such case. (i) It would be contrary to public perceptions of justice if the employer was to benefit from an arrangement under which he was primarily to blame, and in which the employees were forced to comply. The party overwhelmingly at fault was the employer; the employee's role was, by comparison, marginal. The employees were acting under instructions. To enforce the rule would give this wrongdoing employer a windfall: he would be excused from responsibility for unfair dismissal. (ii) Furthermore, to regard the contract as unenforceable would discourage disclosure of tax fraud. Employees would be reluctant to disclose since they would know that their employers might dismiss them without their having any means of redress for such unfair dismissal. To deny access to the courts would in this case be a positive 'affront to the public conscience'.

---

249. [1991] IRLR 473.

Chapter 4. The Common Law and Constitutional Rights and Duties of the Parties During the Employment Relationship

§1. The Common Law Duties of the Employee

I. Duty to Observe Orders

85. An employee is bound to observe his employer's orders. In *Berber* v. *Dunnes Stores*[250] the Supreme Court endorsed the proposition that 'it has long been part of our law that a person repudiates the contract of service if he wilfully disobeys the lawful and reasonable orders of his master'.[251]

There are, however, three legal conditions which qualify the employer's ordinary right to have an instruction observed:

(i) The instruction must be justified by reference to the terms, express or implied, of the contract of employment. An instruction which is not authorized by the contract need not be observed. Thus, an instruction to move to a different place of employment, or to carry out a different job function, for which there is no provision in the contract of employment is not binding.

(ii) The instruction must not transgress positive law, or be illegal.[252] Thus the duty of obedience is not infringed by refusing to observe an order to submit deceptive invoices to a client.[253]

(iii) The instruction may not be positively unreasonable. The common law only requires compliance with reasonable orders. In *Berber*, the duty of obedience was formulated as a duty to observe instructions which are 'lawful and reasonable'. The duty is also conditioned by the employer's duty to observe the principle of trust and confidence.[254] In *United Bank* v. *Akhtar*[255] the employee, with just three days' notice, was instructed to relocate from Leeds to Birmingham, without being given an opportunity to organize relocation. The court held that the instruction conflicted with the overriding obligation that managerial prerogatives should not be oppressively exercised in breach of fair procedures.

II. The Duty Not to Interfere with the Employer's Customer Base

86. An employee is obliged not to interfere with or disturb his employer's customer base. This general duty has two common applications. (i) An employee may not solicit his employer's customers with a view to appropriating them to him or

---

250. [2009] IESC 10.
251. *Brewster* v. *Burke*, High Court, 8 February 1978 (Hamilton J).
252. *Ibid.*
253. *Brown* v. *McNamara Freight*, EAT [1978] UD 745/1987.
254. Para. 120 below.
255. [1989] IRLR 507.

herself. In *Wessex Dairies* v. *Smith*,[256] a milk roundsman who informed customers that he would, at the end of the week, be starting in business on his own account, and who invited customers to direct their business to him, was held to have infringed the overall duty of fidelity. (ii) An employee may not tender for a business opportunity which the employer holds: see *Adamson* v. *B & L Cleaning Ltd*.[257]

III. The Duty Not to Appropriate or Disclose Confidential Information

87. Information which is acquired during the employment relationship is regarded as confidential where (i) the information is not in the public domain, and (ii) the release of the information would be injurious to the employer's interests.[258] Except where there is some public interest justification for doing so, an employee may not use, disclose or appropriate such information. In *Marshall* v. *Guinle*[259] an employee who, during the currency of his contract of employment, went into competition with his employer, exploiting information about his employer's customer base, the prices paid to suppliers, and the company's fast-moving lines, was held to have infringed the duty not to disclose confidential information.

The duty not to appropriate an employer's confidential information may be infringed where the employee copies confidential information, or memorizes confidential information. In *Robb* v. *Green*[260] an employee who surreptitiously copied from his employer's order book a list of his employer's customers with the intention of going into business on his own account was held to have infringed the duty. Where an employee steals information, and then departs, the following remedies are available: (i) an order authorizing a search for the stolen documents;[261] (ii) an order compelling delivery of the information so that it may be destroyed; (iii) an order, known as a springboard order, compelling the ex-employee not to use such information until the end of such time as it is calculated the ex-employee would, through legitimate methods of competition, have acquired such information.

IV. The Duty to Account

88. There is a general duty on all employees to hand over to the employer all financial benefits coming into their possession by virtue of their position as employees. This duty extends from a duty to hand over commissions or inducements, to a duty to hand over valuables found by the employee on the employer's property. In *McDowell* v. *Ulster Bank*[262] a bank porter who had found a roll of bank notes on

---

256. [1935] 2 KB 80.
257. [1995] IRLR 193.
258. *Thomas Marshall* v. *Guinle* [1979] 1 Ch. 277; *House of Spring Gardens* v. *Point Blank Ltd* [1985] IR 613.
259. [1979] 1 Ch. 277.
260. [1895] 2 KB 315.
261. *Anton Piller KG* v. *Manufacturing Processes Ltd* [1976] Ch 55.
262. [1889] 33 ILTSJ 223.

the floor was held obliged by his status as an employee to hand over the money, and not entitled to retain the money.

V. The Duty to Adapt to Changed Work Practices

89. An employee is expected to adapt himself to new methods and techniques in the manner in which he carries out his work. In *Cresswell* v. *Board of Inland Revenue*[263] it was held that an employee is bound to submit to a change in the manner of doing work so long as there is no alteration in the essential job function, or in the terms or conditions of doing the work. However, in a case where the change in work practice requires the acquisition of a new skill, the employer must provide the employee with any necessary training and retraining, and the employer cannot expect the employee to acquire a skill so esoteric that it would not be reasonable to expect the employee to acquire it. These principles have been applied in Ireland: *Rafferty* v. *Bus Éireann.*[264]

VI. The Duty to Work Competently

90. Harmer v. *Cornelius*[265] in 1858 laid down the proposition that where a skilled labourer, artisan or artist is employed there is an implied warranty that he is of 'skill reasonably competent to the task that he undertakes … The public profession of an art is a representation to all the world that he possesses the requisite skill and ability'.

The degree of competence will vary according to the representation, express or implied, made by the employee as to the extent of his skills. A representation may be inferred by the fact of the employee applying for a job requiring a particular competence; the application is taken to be a representation of competence to undertake the function.

VII. The Duty of Fidelity

91. The basic sense of the duty of fidelity is the notion that an employee should never engage in conduct which seriously prejudices his employer's interests. The leading case in this area is *Hivac Ltd* v. *Park Royal Scientific.*[266] The case concerned a husband and wife who worked for a specialized technical instrument company. During their spare time on Sundays, the two employees worked for a fierce rival of the employer. In providing assistance to the rival the workers were, of course, economically harming their primary employer. The English Court of Appeal held that this infringed the employee's duty of fidelity. 'It must be engrafted on such

---

263. [1984] 2 All ER 713.
264. [1997] 2 IR 424; *Fitzgerald* v. *South Eastern Health Board* [2002] 2 IR 674.
265. (1858) 5 CB 236, 141 ER 94.
266. [1946] CH 169.

a contract [that is a contract of service] that the servant undertakes to serve his master with good faith and fidelity.' The court went on to say that:

> it would be deplorable if … a workman could consistently with his duty to his employer knowingly deliberately [do] something which would *inflict great harm* on his employer's business.

The principle is one of multiple application. One application of the doctrine is the principle that it is a breach of contract for an employee to engage in a lifestyle which seriously prejudices his employer's interests. In *Flynn* v. *Power*[267] the employee was a teacher in a Roman Catholic school who refused to terminate her relationship with a married but separated man, and who became pregnant by him. The employee's dismissal was held lawful. The employer's objectives included the promotion by example of the social principles of the Roman Catholic Church, and the employee's behaviour undermined the achievement of this objective. The High Court held that 'an employee's conduct in sexual matters outside the place of work may justify dismissal if it can be shown that it is capable of damaging the employer's business'.

The industrial tactic of the 'go-slow' has been characterized as a breach of the duty of fidelity. In *Secretary of State for Employment* v. *ASLEF (No. 2)*[268] it was held that since the purpose of a go-slow was to disrupt the functioning of the employer's business, a go-slow was a breach of the employees' duty not to damage their employer's undertaking.

A further application of the general duty is the obligation to disclose damaging behaviour of subordinate or superior co-employees. This was established in *Sybron Corporation* v. *Rochem Ltd.*[269]

§2. THE DUTIES OF THE EMPLOYER

I. The Duty to Maintain Trust and Confidence

A. *The Source and History of the Trust and Confidence Duty*

93. The trust and confidence obligation, developed by the courts and tribunals over the last thirty years is arguably the single most important judge-made contribution to civilizing the employment relationship in the modern period.[270] The general principle is that there is implied into all contracts of employment a general term that the employer will not impair the 'trust and confidence' of the employee. The classical formulation is that of Lord Stein in *Malik* v. *Bank of Credit and Commerce International* in 1997:

---

267. [1985] IR 648.
268. [1972] QB 455.
269. [1985] Ch. 299.
270. See D. Brodie, 'The Heart of the Matter; Mutual Trust and Confidence' (1996) ILJ 121; and Brodie, 'Beyond Exchange: the New Contract of Employment' (1998) 27 ILJ 79.

The implied obligation extends to any conduct by the employer likely to destroy or seriously damage the relationship of trust and confidence between employer and employee.[271]

This duty was considered in detail by the Irish Supreme Court for the first time in *Berber* v. *Dunnes Stores*.[272] The Supreme Court stated:

> There is implied in a contract of employment a mutual obligation that the employer and the employee will not without reasonable and proper cause conduct themselves in a manner likely to destroy or seriously damage the relationship of confidence and trust between them. The term is implied by law and is incident to all contracts of employment unless expressly excluded.

This means, in short, that the employer must not treat the employee oppressively. The duty is a highly flexible one of multiple application. In essence, it is a general duty of decency. Breach of this term may justify an employee (i) claiming damages, an injunction, or a declaration, for breach of contract; or (ii) as treating the employer as effectively or indirectly dismissing, and suing for constructive dismissal in a claim under the Unfair Dismissals Acts 1977–2007, or for wrongful constructive dismissal at common law.

B.   The Elements of the Duty of Trust and Confidence

1.   The 'Serious Damage' Requirement

94.   The concept of trust and confidence is a relative one. It will only be infringed where there occurs something in the nature of a serious breach. In *Malik* v. *Bank of Credit and Commerce International*[273] the duty was defined as outlawing conduct which 'destroys or seriously damages the relationship of trust and confidence between the parties'.[274] An alternative test, designed to stress the seriousness of the conduct, requires that the conduct be such that 'the employee cannot reasonably be expected to tolerate it a moment longer after he has discovered it.[275]

2.   The Reasonable Employee Standard

95.   Second, the matter is assessed by reference to the perspective of an objective reasonable employee, i.e. not an oversensitive employee. The plaintiff in *Berber* v. *Dunnes Stores* who had worked for the company for 20 years took offence at

---

271. [1997] 3 All ER 1, at p. 17.
272. [2009] 20 ELR 61.
273. [1997] 3 All ER 1.
274. [1997] 3 All ER 1, 18 (Lord Steyn).
275. *BCCI* v. *Ali* [1999] 4 All ER 83, 102.

a group email which referred to him as a 'trainee'. The reference was an innocent error and the employer corrected it. The Supreme Court emphasized that the standard is that of a *reasonable objective* employee:

> The conduct of the employer complained of must be unreasonable and without proper cause and its effect on the employee must be judged objectively, *reasonably and sensibly* in order to determine if it is such that the employee cannot be expected to put up with it.

3. The Significance of an Absence of Intention to Harm

96. It is not a defence for the employer to argue that it did not *intend* to harm the employee. In *Malik* v. *Bank of Credit and Commerce International*[276] the employer operated a bank in a fraudulent way which resulted in thousands of depositors losing their savings. The scandal meant that innocent employees were tainted by association and never found alternative work. The employee argued that the employer's criminal activity had damaged the reputation of the employees and that this infringed the duty of trust and confidence. The defendants counter-argued that they did not *intend* to injure the employees. They *intended* to defraud customers. The House of Lords rejected this defence. The crucial point of reference was *not* the employer's motive. It was the direct or indirect effect on the employee.

4. Not Necessary that the Employee Be Aware of the Employer's Conduct

97. Fourth, it is not necessary that the *employee* be aware of the employer's conduct at the time that it is committed. The House of Lords rejected this argument in *Malik*. It was not relevant that the employee was unaware of the senior management's fraud. Such a rule would mean that an employer who successfully concealed a corrupt practice would be immune from infringing the wrong, while an employer whose misconduct was exposed to the workforce would be liable. That would give an advantage to the concealing employer, and would not be a rational distinction.

5. Conduct May Be Cumulative

98. Fifth, a breach of the term may be committed cumulatively, as well as through a single act. In *Lewis* v. *Motorworld* [277] the employee had been illegally demoted. The employee was then unreasonably criticized. The court held that it was possible to add the two items of conduct, the demotion and the criticism, together in order to make a cumulative case of constructive dismissal.

---

276. [1997] 3 All ER 1.
277. [1985] IRLR 465.

6.   Trust and Confidence Does Not Regulate the Decision to Dismiss

99. Sixth, the duty of trust and confidence does not regulate a *decision to dismiss.* If the duty of trust and confidence did regulate dismissal it would mean that dismissal would have to be for a good and reasonable cause. The problem with that would be that it would conflict with a fundamental doctrine of the common law that an employer may dismiss for any reason no matter how arbitrary. The two rights (to dismiss on any ground/to trust and confidence) are in direct tension. The conflict has been resolved in favour of the employer's prerogative to dismiss on notice for any reason. In *Johnson* v. *Unisys Ltd*[278] the employee had been unreasonably dismissed. He argued that the dismissal decision was conditioned by the trust and confidence obligation. However, the House of Lords held that the employer dismissal prerogative was superior, and that trust and confidence did not operate within the dismissal zone.

A similar approach has been adopted in Ireland: *Orr* v. *Zomax Ltd.*[279] Here it was argued that the employer's decision to dismiss him was unfair (because it involved an unreasonable implementation of a client prejudice) and thereby infringed the duty of trust and confidence. The High Court rejected the suggestion that the trust and confidence operated here; trust and confidence could not undermine the primary common law freedom of the employer to dismiss on any ground:

> what the plaintiff is seeking to do is to introduce a new obligation under the common law on the employer to act reasonably and fairly in the case of dismissal. As the law stands, at common law an employer can terminate employment for any reason or no reason provided adequate notice is given.

7.   Trust and Confidence Duty May Be Excluded by Contract

100. Seventh, in *Berber* the Supreme Court stated that 'the term is implied by law and is incident to all contracts of employment *unless expressly excluded.*' This obiter assertion suggests, of course, that the term may be excluded by a contrary provision in the contact of employment.

C.   *Remedies for Infringement of the Duty of Trust and Confidence*

102. The most common remedies for breach of the duty are those of constructive dismissal under the Unfair Dismissal Acts 1977–2007, or a claim for common law constructive dismissal.[280] The Unfair Dismissals Act 1977 defines dismissal as including cases where the employer's oppressive conduct justifies the employer in treating himself as effectively dismissed:

---

278. [2001] 2 All ER 801.
279. [2004] 1 IR 486.
280. The employee is, also, free to remain in employment, affirm the contract, and to simply claim damages for loss caused by the employer's acts, or an injunction to remedy the perpetuation of the conduct.

the termination by the employee of the contract of employment with his employer … in circumstances in which, because of the conduct of the employer the employee was, or would have been entitled, or it would have been reasonable for the employee, to terminate the contract of employment without giving prior notice of the termination to the employer.

An equivalent remedy exists at common law. This may be used by persons who are not eligible to claim under the Unfair Dismissals Acts: constructive wrongful dismissal. Where an employer repudiates the contract of employment the employee may (in the terminology of the common law) 'accept' the repudiation, discharge him or herself from the contract, and claim damages. In *Butler* v. *Four Star Pizza*[281] the employee had complained of being been sexually harassed at work. Her employer failed to take the allegations seriously. She resigned and claimed that she had been (constructively) wrongfully dismissed by the employer. The Circuit Court awarded her £16,000.

In theory (though actual instances are difficult to establish) an employee may, instead of resigning from employment, seek a court order – an injunction – directing the employer to comply with its trust and confidence duty.

II. The Duty to Make an Employee Aware of Contingent Benefits

103. In *Scally* v. *Southern Health and Social Services Board*[282] the House of Lords held that there was a common law obligation on an employer to make an employee aware of his right to avail himself of contingent contractual entitlements: entitlements which are not automatic, but depend upon the employee taking some positive step. This duty might arise where the terms of the contract had been negotiated collectively (and not with the individual employee); where the benefit is contingent upon the employee taking some specific action; and where the employee could not be expected to be aware of the benefit.

III. The Duty to Observe Fair Procedures in the Dismissal Process

104. Article 40.3.2 of the Constitution provides that 'the State shall, in particular, protect the right to life, person, good name and property rights of every citizen'. In *Ryan* v. *Attorney General*[283] the High Court, placing stress on the phrase 'in particular' held that Article 40.3.2 was not exhaustive, but contained latently a series of unspecified rights. From an employee's point of view, perhaps, the most important of these unspecified rights is the unspecified constitutional right to fair procedures. At common law the right to fair procedures in the dismissal process had been restricted to those workers who could be classified as public officers. In *Gunn* v.

---

281. *Irish Times*, 22 March 1995.
282. [1991] IRLR 522.
283. [1965] IR 294.

National College of Art and Design[284] the Supreme Court condemned this discrimination against employees who were not officers as inconsistent with the Republican nature of the Irish Constitution.

IV. The Duty to Provide Work

105. It seems accepted that an employer may be required to provide an employee with work, in addition to merely paying an employee. However, the circumstances in which this duty will arise are unclear. According to one view, there is a general obligation to provide work.[285] According to a narrower view, a right to work is recognized only in the case of skilled workers, or where the contract of employment implicitly generates an obligation to provide work.[286]

V. The Duty to Exercise a Contractual Discretion in a Reasonable Manner

106. Where the contract of employment gives an employer the discretion to exercise a power the employer will act unlawfully if he exercises that discretion in a manner in which no reasonable employer would. The English Court of Appeal in *Clarke* v. *Nomura International*[287] held that the discretion of the employer could not be exercised unreasonably:

> An employer exercising a discretion which on the face of the contract of employment is unfettered or absolute, will be in breach of contract if no reasonable employer would have exercised the discretion in that way.

The threshold is a high one; it is not enough that the employee considers that the employer has acted wrongly; it must be conduct which no reasonable employer would adopt. This view has been endorsed by the Irish High Court: *Lichters* v. *DEPFA Bank.*[288]

VI. The Duty to Provide an Employee with a Safe System of Work

107. In addition to the statutory duty in section 6(1) of the Safety Health and Welfare at Work Acts 1989 ('it shall be the duty of every employer to ensure, so far as is reasonably practicable, the safety health and welfare at work of all his employees'), an employer is under a common law duty to provide his employees with a safe system of work.[289] Although originally understood as a duty to prevent an

---

284. [1990] 2 IR 168.
285. *Langston* v. *Chrysler UK Ltd* [1974] ICR 180.
286. *William Hill* v. *Tucker* [1999] ICR 180.
287. [2000] IRLR 766.
288. [2012] 23 ELR 258.
289. *McSweeney* v. *JS McCarthy Ltd*, Supreme Court, 28 July 2000; *Lynch* v. *Binnacle Ltd* [2011] IESC 8.

employee from physical injury, it is now recognized that the duty extends to preventing injury to an employee's mental health.[290] In *Quigley* v. *Complex Tooling*[291] it was held that liability may be imposed where an employer 'failing to observe the standard to be properly expected of a reasonable and prudent employer' fails to prevent 'reasonably foreseeable psychiatric injury'.

An injured employee may have a remedy in negligence. The standard of care is that of a reasonable employer. What is reasonable depends upon the magnitude of the risk; the seriousness of the consequences of the risk eventuating, and the cost and practicality of preventing the risk.[292] In determining the safety of the system of work, the court may take into account the principle that the employee is also under a duty to take care for his or her own safety.[293]

---

290. *Walker* v. *Northumberland County Council* [1995] IRLR 35.
291. [2005] IEHC 71.
292. *Bradley* v. *CIE* [1976] IR 217; *Kennedy* v. *Hughes Dairy Limited* [1989] IRLR 117.
293. *Barry* v. *Dunnes Stores* [2013] IEHC 259.

Chapter 5. Working Time and Holidays

§1. The Scope of Application of the Organization of Working Time Act 1997

108. Directive 94/107/EC on the Organization of Working Time has been implemented into Irish law by the Organization of Working Time Act 1997. The most important of the rights constituted by the directive, the daily rest period (Article 3), the weekly rest period (Article 5) and the 48-hour week (Article 6), have been implemented in sections 11, 13 and 15 of the 1997 Act.

I. Exclusions from the 1997 Act

A. Emergency and Public Defence Workers

109. Article 1.3 of Directive 93/104 (as amended by Directive 2000/34/EC) provides that: 'This Directive shall apply to all sectors of activity, both public and private, within the meaning of Article 2 of Directive 89/391/EEC ... ' The directive applies to sectors 'within the meaning of Article 2 of Directive 89/391/EEC'. This definition excludes 'the armed forces, the police, or certain activities in the civil protection services'. Implementing this, section 3(1) of the 1997 Act provides that the 1997 Act does not apply in the case of a member of the *Garda Siochana* or of the Defence Forces. In addition, the Organization of Working Time (Exemption of Civil Protection Services) Regulations 1998 and 2009 exclude prison officers, fire fighters, customs officers, harbour police, coast guard and members of the Marine Emergency service.[294]

B. Shift Workers, and Workers Whose Working Hours are Self-determined

110. Article 1(3) provides that the directive operates 'without prejudice to Article 17' of Directive 93/104 (as amended by Directive 2000/34/EC). Implementing Article 17 (1) (a), section 2(1)(c) of the 1997 Act exempts an employee 'the duration of whose working time ... is determined by himself or herself, whether or not provision for the making of such determination by that person is made by his or her contract of employment'. Implementing Article 17 (2) (3), section 4(1) of the 1997 Act provides that daily and weekly rest period provisions shall not apply to persons employed in shift work, each time he or she changes shift and cannot avail himself or herself of the rest period referred to in section 11 or 13.

---

294. SI 52 of 1998 and SI 478 of 2009.

C. The Organization of Working Time (General Exemptions) Regulations 1998

111. Section 4(3) of the 1997 Act empowers the Minister to disapply parts of the Act from particular employment sectors. This is the provision which has been used to implement the extensive exceptions in Article 17(2.1) of the directive. Section 4(3) is the source of the Organisation of Working Time (General Exemptions) Regulations 1998.[295] This provision removes (subject to provision for compensatory rest) the following categories of work from the protections in sections 11, 12, 13 and 16:

1. An activity in which the employee is regularly required by the employer to travel distances of significant length, either from his or her home to the workplace or from one workplace to another workplace.
2. An activity of a security or surveillance nature the purpose of which is to protect persons or property and which requires the continuous presence of the employee at a particular place or places, and, in particular, the activities of a security guard, caretaker or security firm.[296]
3. An activity falling within a sector of the economy or in the public service:
   (a) in which it is foreseeable that the rate at which production or the provision of services, as the case may be, takes place will vary significantly from time to time, or
   (b) the nature of which is such that employees are directly involved in ensuring the continuity of production or the provision of services, as the case may be, and, in particular, any of the following activities –
      (i) the provision of services relating to the reception, treatment or care of persons in a residential institution, hospital or similar establishment;
      (ii) the provision of services at a harbour or airport;
      (iii) production in the press, radio, television, cinematographic, postal or telecommunications industries;[297]
      (iv) the provision of ambulance, fire and civil protection services;
      (v) the production, transmission or distribution of gas, water or electricity;
      (vi) the collection of household refuse or the operation of an incineration plant;
      (vii) any industrial activity in which work cannot, by reason of considerations of a technical nature, be interrupted;
      (viii) research and development;
      (ix) agriculture;
      (x) tourism.

---

295. SI 21/1998.
296. Under Regulation 2, security guards have been held subject to the longer averaging periods: *Gold Force Security MGT* v. *Ryszard Suchowiecki* Labour Court [2009] DWT 0911.
297. *Sky Handling Partners Ltd* v. *Dariusz Mozolowicz* [2012] Labour Court DWT1299 (airport worker held not entitled to claim infringements of ss. 11, 12, 13, and 16; subject to the exemption regulations).

II. Doctors in Training

112. The position of doctors in training is regulated by the European Communities (Organization of Working Time) (Activities of Doctors in Training) Regulations 2004–2010.[298] These Regulations apply the ordinary Directive 93/104 rules as to daily rest, maximum weekly working time, and breaks to doctors in training. The rights given to doctors in training are subject to a series of exceptions: ((i) changes in shifts which make it impossible to take the daily rest period between the end of one and the start of the other; (ii) the need for continuity of services relating to the reception, treatment and/or care provided by hospitals or similar establishments; (iii) where collective agreements or agreements have been concluded between the two sides of industry at national or regional level in relation to the activities of doctors in training).[299]

III. Transport Workers

113. The combined effect of Article 17A of the 1993 Directive and Directive 2003/88/EC has been to provide modified working time rights for mobile workers. This has been implemented in Ireland by the Organization of Working Time (Inclusion of Transport Activities) Regulations 2004.[300] Irish law now distinguishes three different categories of mobile staff. The first two are completely excluded from the Act. These excluded categories are: persons performing mobile road transport activities as defined in Directive 2002/15/EC, and mobile staff in civil aviation as defined in the Annex to Council Directive 2000/79/EC. These workers are looked after by separate regimes. Workers in category (a) are subject to the EC (Road Transport) (Organization of Working Time of Persons Performing Mobile Road Transport) Regulations.[301] Workers in category (b) are protected by the EC (Organisation of Working Time) (Mobile Staff in Civil Aviation) Regulations 2006.[302]

'Mobile workers' outside these two categories – the generality of mobile workers[303] – are protected by the Organization of Working Time (Inclusion of Transport Activities) Regulations 2004.[304] These workers are not entitled to the full rights contained in sections 11, 12, 13 and 16 of the Act. However, they must be granted 'adequate' compensatory rest.[305]

---

298. SI No. 494/2004; SI No. 553/2010.
299. Regulation 4 as amended by EC (organization of Working Time) (Activities of Doctors in Training) (Amendment) Regulations 2010.
300. SI No. 817 of 2004.
301. SI No. 36 of 2012.
302. SI No. 507 of 2006.
303. *Goode Concrete* v. *58 Workers* Labour Court [2009] DWT 0934.
304. SI No. 817 of 2004.
305. Regulation 6 of SI 817 of 2004. On the definition of adequate rest, see *Goode Concrete* v. *58 Workers*, Labour Court [2009] DWT 0934.

§2. THE WORKING TIME RIGHTS CONFERRED BY THE ORGANIZATION OF WORKING TIME ACT 1997

I. Maximum Weekly Working Time

114. Section 15(1) of the 1997 Act is the basis of the right not to be obliged to work more than 48 hours per week:

> An employer shall not permit an employee to work, in each period of 7 days, more than an average of 48 hours, that is to say an average of 48 hours calculated over a period (hereafter in this section referred to as a 'reference period') that does not exceed four months.

A. *The Definitions of 'Permit' and 'Work'*

115. The word 'permit' does not expressly require that the employer 'knowingly' permit infringements of the Act. As a result it has been held by the Labour Court that the Act does not even require knowledge by the employer that its workers have worked in excess of the prescribed working time.[306]

'Work' is defined in the Act of 1997 (section 2) as 'any time that the employee is (a) at his or her place of work or at his employer's disposal, and (b) carrying on or performing the activities or duties of his or her work'. The definition in the 1997 Act is interpreted in line with the approach to the definition of the term taken by the Court of Justice in the *SIMAP*[307] case. An employee is working where he is actually carrying out his duties or where he is at his employer's place of work and available to the employer. In *An Employer* v. *A Worker*[308] it was held that an au pair who was required to respond to requests for assistance was 'carrying on the activities or duties of his or her work'. The Labour Court reasoned that 'the absence of a 'clear distinction between work and leisure time' was to be taken as equivalent to the employee carrying on the activities of his work. On the other hand, applying *SIMAP*, it was held that a hospital worker who was on call, but did not have to be on the hospital premises, was not working: *McGauley* v. *Beaumont Hospital.*[309]

B. *The Four-month Reference Period*

116. The four-month reference period, by reference to which compliance with section 15 is calculated, may be extended in three cases. First, the reference period

---

306. *IBM Ireland* v. *Svoboda*, Labour Court [2011] EDA 1116; *Keegan Quarries* v. *Tomanek*, Labour Court [2010] DWT 10183.
307. Case C-303/98, [2000] IRLR 845
308. Labour Court [2011] DWT 10163.
309. 22 October 2009.

may be extended to a period of six months in the case of the activities specified in the Organization of Working Time (General Exemptions) Regulations, 1998 (as amended).[310]

Second, a six-month averaging period applies in the case of doctors in training.[311]

Third, where the employee is (a) employed in an activity in respect of which it would not be practicable for the employer to comply with the requirement, because of considerations of a technical nature or related to the conditions under which the work concerned is organized or otherwise of a technical nature, and (b) a collective agreement has been agreed and negotiated and approved by the Labour Court under section 24 of the 1997 Act, then a reference period of more than six, but fewer than twelve, months may be agreed.[312] Twelve-month averaging periods have now become very common. They are now the most common cause of employers and unions registering collective agreements under section 24. (However, there may be doubts about the legality of this provision. Section 15(4) derives from Article 17 of the directive, which permits derogations to be made 'by collective agreements or agreements concluded between the two sides of industry at national or regional level'. The intention was to limit the extension to agreements set only at the highest level. The provision in Section 15, however, extends this power to agreements at purely local or plant level.)

II. The Daily Rest Period

117. Section 11 of the Organization of Working Time Act 1997 implements Article 3 of Directive 93/104/EC: 'An employee shall be entitled to a rest period of not less than 11 consecutive hours in each period of 24 hours during which he or she works for his or her employer.'

The daily rest provision is phrased as an entitlement, or right, of the employee. It is not phrased as a categorical prohibition on the employee's freedom to work for more than 13 hours. Therefore, while an employee may not be instructed to work for more than 13 hours, and while such an instruction is unlawful, there is, on the other hand, no prohibition on an employee volunteering to work for more than 13 hours. The daily rest period (section 11) is unlike the maximum working week provision (section 15) under which an employer is forbidden to permit an employee to work more than an average of 48 hours. There are five exceptions.

A. *Exceptions to the Daily Rest Period*

118. Section 4(1) provides that Section 11 shall not apply in respect of a person employed in shift work, each time he or she changes shift and cannot avail himself or herself of the rest period referred to in Section 11. This applies to new shift

---

310. SI No. 21 of 1998, as amended by SI No. 817 of 2004.
311. Regulation 9(1)(c) (SI 294/2004).
312. S. 15(5) Organization of Working Time Act 1997.

arrangements where there is not a sufficient gap before the start of the new shift: *Primark* v. *Preciado*.[313] Commonly, workers may work under alternating shift patterns, working an early shift from, say, 6.00 am to 2.00 pm and a late shift from 2.00 pm to 10.00 pm. Where a change in the start of the shift takes place the employee will not receive his full complement of eleven hours rest. Section 4(1) is designed to legitimize this breach of the eleven hours consecutive rest standard. Section 4(1) only applies to a worker engaged in 'shift work' which follows a pattern. The employee in *Flexsource* v. *Karaliunas*[314] was assigned by text message to either an early or late shift; the daily rest period was overlooked. The employer argued that the section 4 defence applied. The Labour Court rejected this: relying on the definition of shift work in Article 2.6 of Directive 2003/88/EC, the Labour Court held that shift work involved work in which workers 'succeed each other at the same work stations according to a certain pattern'. Here there was no 'pattern'; assignment to shifts was unpredictable. Since there was no 'shift work', section 4(1) did not apply.

Section 4(2), which derives from Article 17(2)(3)(b), deals with the issue of periods of work of short duration split up during the day: it provides that section 11 shall not apply to a person employed in an activity consisting of periods of work spread out over the day. Article 17(2)(3)(b) of the directive, which is the source of this exemption, gives cleaning staff as an example of the constituency which was in mind when this provision was drafted. (Thus, where cleaning staff work from 6.00 am to 8.00 am before the office opens, and then from 6 pm to 8 pm after the office closes, the infringement of section 11 is excused). This exemption is subject to the qualification that the employee be given compensatory rest.[315]

Workers covered by the Organization of Working Time (General Exemptions) Regulations 1998 (SI 21 of 1998) may legitimately be instructed to work in breach of their entitlements to daily rest. However, Regulation 4 of the General Exemptions Regulations makes it a condition to the non-application of sections 11–13 that the employee be given the benefit of compensatory rest: the Labour Relations Commission has issued a code of practice on the issue of compensatory rest.[316] The Code of Practice on Compensatory Rest Periods suggests that an employee is entitled to the period of rest which the worker has missed. (It is not clear whether this is always sufficient 'compensatory rest' as required by the directive, or by the safety objective underlying the legislation.)

Doctors in training may be denied daily rest: (a) in an emergency, or exceptional circumstances; (b) 'in respect of activities involving the need for continuity of services relating to the reception, treatment and/or care provided by hospitals'; or similar establishments; the activities being the activities of doctors in training; (c) where a collective agreement has been negotiated and settled between both sides of

313. Labour Court [2010] DWT1087.
314. Labour Court [2013] DWT1318.
315. *Noonan Services* v. *Saygina*, Labour Court [2013] DWT 13105.
316. SI 44 of 1998.

industry and registered under section 24 of the 1997 Act. All of these exceptions are subject to the grant of compensatory rest.[317]

Collective agreements registered with the Labour Court may dispense with the mandatory rest periods laid down in section 11.[318] However, such a collective agreement must include a provision requiring the employer concerned to ensure that the employee has a compensatory rest period. The validity of a collective agreement is contingent on its having been submitted to and approved by the Labour Court, which must ensure that the collective agreement is consistent with Directive 93/104/EC.

B. Weekly Rest Period

119. Section 13(2) of the 1997 Act provides that an employee shall, in each period of seven days, be granted a rest period of at least 24 hours, preceded by the 11 hours' daily rest constituted by section 11. Furthermore, that break must, unless the contract otherwise provides, include Sunday (section 13(4)).

An employee may, if the contract so provides, be required to take his weekly rest day on a day other than Sunday. However, by section 14 of the Organization of Working Time Act 1997, an employee who is required to work on a Sunday must be compensated by the payment either of an allowance of such an amount as is reasonable, or by otherwise increasing the employee's rate of pay in such amount as is reasonable having regard to the circumstances (or by reasonable compensatory paid time off from work). In *Ashbourne House Hotel* v. *O'Gorman*[319] the employee was paid €15.00 per hour. The same rate was paid throughout the week. None was referrable to the employee's working on Sunday. The Labour Court held that no Sunday premium was paid and awarded compensation of €3000.

The Labour Court has ruled that payment of time and a half is a reasonable allowance for Sunday work.[320] In determining the amount of the compensatory payment to which the employee is entitled for Sunday work the amount set out in a collective agreement applying to a comparable employee shall be the measure of compensation. In *Campbell Catering* v. *SIPTU*[321] part-time workers were paid time and a half for Sunday work. On the other hand, workers employed for more than 39 hours per week were entitled to double time. The Labour Court held that the agreement with the full-time workers was a collective agreement with a group of comparable workers. Accordingly, the part-time workers were entitled to compensatory pay equivalent to that paid to the full-time workers.

---

317. Regulations 4 and 5 of the European Communities (Organization of Working Time) (Activities of Doctors in Training) Regulations 2004 and 2010.
318. S. 4(4) of the Organization of Working Time Act 1997.
319. Labour Court [2006] DWT0634.
320. *Selcare Retail Ltd* v. *St. Ledger* Labour Court [1999] DWT 9924.
321. WTC/00/20.

III. Rest Periods at Work

A. Definitional Aspects of Section 12 of the Organization of Working Time Act 1997

120. Under section 12(1) of the 1997 Act 'an employer shall not require an employee to work for a period of more than 4 hours and 30 minutes without allowing him, or her, a break of at least 15 minutes'. In *Patterson v. Carlton Airport Hotel* [322] the employee started work at 3.00 pm. He was given a meal break at 6.30. He was asked to drive an airport bus but refused claiming that he was entitled to complete his break. The Labour Court held that his statutory break did not begin until four and a half hours had elapsed at 7.30; the employee's behaviour was not lawful. In *Tribune Printing & Publishing Group v. Graphical Print and Media Union* [323] the Labour Court held that there was an active obligation on employers to put in place structural measures to ensure that workers actually availed themselves of their right to a break. In that case the employer had argued that employees were free to take breaks and that they would not be stopped if they wished to do so. The Labour Court held that such abstention was not sufficient:

> The company is under a duty to ensure that the employee receives his equivalent rest period and breaks. Merely stating that the employee could take rest breaks if they wished and not putting in place proper procedures to ensure that the employee receives these breaks, thus protecting his health and safety, does not discharge that duty.

B. Shop Employees' Daily Rest Periods

121. Workers in shops are entitled to a more generous regime: the Organization of Working Time (Breaks at Work for Shop Employees) Regulations 1998 [324] provide that a shop employee whose hours of work include the hours from 11.30 am to 2.30 pm shall be entitled to a break of a minimum of one hour.

C. The Burden of Proof and Claims of Infringement of Section 12

122. A claimant who alleges that he was denied daily or weekly or at work rest periods is assisted by section 25(4) of the Act. This provides that where records are not maintained a rebuttable presumption of non-compliance will arise: where the employee shows a reasonable possibility that the Act has been infringed, the onus of proof will shift to the employer to show compliance. [325] In *Jakonis Antanas v. Nolan Transport* [326] it was said that:

---

322. Labour Court [2008] DWT 0844.
323. [2004] 15 ELR 222.
324. SI 57/1998.
325. *Keegan Quarries v. Tomanek*, Labour Court [2010] DWT 10183; *Nolan Transport v. Antanas* [2012] ELR 311.
326. [2011] 22 ELR 311.

If records in the prescribed form are not produced and the claimant has satisfied the evidential burden which or she bears it will be for the respondent to establish on credible evidence that the relevant provision was complied with … the respondent will thus be required to carry the legal burden of proving on the balance of probabilities that the Act was not contravened in the manner alleged by the claimant

§3. HOLIDAYS

I. Paid Annual Leave under the Organization of Working Time Act 1997

123. Part III of the Organization of Working Time Act 1997 details the rules regulating minimum holiday entitlements. The basic entitlement, which is laid down in section 19(1), is either:

(a) four working weeks in a leave year in which the employee works at least 1,365 hours;
(b) one-third of a working week for each month in the leave year in which the employee works at least 117 hours; or
(c) 8 per cent of the hours worked in a leave year (subject to a maximum of four working weeks).

Sections 19(1)(a) and (c) are only available to workers working for more than one year with an employer. Section 19(1)(b), on the other hand, may be availed of by a short-term worker.

The leave is paid annual leave.[327] The quantum and manner of payment for annual leave is determined in accordance with section 20(2):

> The pay in respect of an employee's annual leave shall be paid to the employee in advance of his or her taking the leave, be at the normal weekly rate or, as the case may be, at a rate which is proportionate to the normal weekly rate.

'Paid in advance' is interpreted as meaning paid 'immediately' in advance. Anticipating the ruling of the European Court of Justice in *Caulfield* v. *Hanson Clay Products*,[328] the Labour Court ruled in 2002 that the practice of distributing annual leave pay in the form of increments over the entire working year was illegal. In *Kvaerner Cementation* v. *Tracey*[329] the basic wage was set at £5.00 per hour, part of which was made up of a payment of 56p to cover paid annual leave. The employer's contention was that this satisfied the obligation to pay annual leave 'in advance'. Article 7 of the Working Time Directive requires Member States to take measures to ensure that every worker is entitled to paid annual leave of at least four weeks. Taking a purposive view of the duty, the Labour Court made the point that the objective

---

327. Section 19(1).
328. Cases C-131/04 and C-257/04 [2006] IRLR 386.
329. Labour Court [2001] DWT 107.

underlying the legislation was that workers be positively induced to take leave. The employer's wage structure frustrated this objective, since it would be inconceivable that payment in advance would be put aside by the employee, and there would be no significant inducement to take holidays. This principle has been repeatedly confirmed since *Kvaerner*.[330]

The 'leave year' is defined as a period of a year commencing on 1 April. Leave must be granted within the leave year, or, with the employee's consent, within six months thereafter.[331] 'Where there is a failure to provide the requisite leave and the absence of an agreement to extend the period, a contravention of the Act crystallizes at the end of the leave year.'[332] The exact time at which annual leave is granted to an employee is determined by the employer, having regard to work requirements, and subject to the employer taking into account: (i) the need for the employee to reconcile work and family commitments, and (ii) the rest and recreation activities available to the employee (sections 21(a) and (b)). The settling of the time of annual leave is subject to the employer consulting the employee or the employee's trade union (if any) not later than one month before the commencement of annual leave (section 21(1)(6)). In 2011 civil servants were instructed by email that part of their annual leave would take place at Christmas. There was no consultation about the measure; the Labour Court held that there had been an infringement of section 20.[333]

At common law an employee has no right to wages in lieu of unused annual leave.[334] However, section 23 of the Organization of Working Time Act 1997 provides a statutory entitlement to salary in lieu. Section 23 provides that where an employee ceases to be employed without having taken full annual leave, the employee shall be entitled to an amount equal to the pay that he would have received if he had been granted annual leave.

Labour Court awards of compensation for failure to provide holiday pay have been relatively high. The Labour Court applies the European law principle that sanctions for infringements of European law should be effective and have deterrent effect.[335]

II. Public Holidays and the Organization of Working Time Act 1997

124. Nine public holidays are currently recognized under Irish law. These days are detailed in the Second Schedule of the Organization of Working Time Act 1997. There is no right to leave on a public holiday. The employer is given a discretion as to whether the employee is to be entitled to a day's leave on that public holiday, or merely to some compensating benefit instead.

---

330. *Fasercourt* v. *O'Brien* Labour Court [2007] DWT 0703; *PB Cygon Ltd* v. *Wojtaszek*, Labour Court [2010] DWT 1039.
331. S. 21(c).This provision was considered in *Royal Liver* v. *Macken* [2002] 4 IR 427.
332. *Bagnalls Hotel* v. *D'Alton*, Labour Court [2012] DWT 21122.
333. *Office of Public Works* v. *Gallagher*, Labour Court [2012] DWT12172.
334. *Morley* v. *Heritage plc* [1993] IRLR 400.
335. *Glafy* v. *Pydo Labour Court* [2011] DWT111 (award of €7,500 for unpaid holiday pay).

Section 21(1) provides that an employee shall, in respect of a public holiday, be entitled either (a) to a paid day off; or (b) to a paid day off within a month of that day; (c) an additional day of annual leave; or (d) an additional day's pay. In *HSE* v. *Byrnes*[336] an employee on call on a bank holiday was called in to work for an hour. The question was whether he had had a paid day off. The employee argued that he had not and that he was entitled to an extra days pay or an extra day off on the basis that was working on that bank holiday. The employee's argument was rejected; he had, notwithstanding the hour when he was required to work, a paid day off.

Section 21(1) of the Organization of Working Time Act 1997 provides that 'if the day on which the public holiday falls is a day on which the employee would, apart from this subsection, be entitled to a paid day off this subsection shall have effect as if paragraph (a) [a paid day off on that day] were omitted therefrom'. This means that if the public holiday falls on a day on which the employee is entitled to paid leave the employee must be given further compensation for the public holiday. In *Thermo King* v. *Kenny*[337] the employee was on contractually paid sick leave on the day on which a public holiday fell. The Labour Court held that 'it is clear from the plain wording of the subsection that the claimant is entitled to a benefit in respect of the public holidays in addition to his entitlement to a paid day off on the day under the agreement'. The same principle has been applied to an employee on paid administrative leave.[338] On the other hand, where an employee does not have a right to be paid he is not entitled to the extra day's pay.

The right to leave, or compensation, in respect of a public holiday, only applies to an employee who has worked for the employer for at least 40 hours during the period of five weeks ending on the day before that public holiday. (Accordingly, part-time workers working fewer than eight hours in the period of four weeks before the holiday are excluded from the entitlement.)

---

336. Labour Court [2006] DWT 068.
337. Labour Court [2006] DWT 0611.
338. *County of Limerick* v. *Cotter* Labour Court [2008] EDA 0910.

Chapter 6. Parental Leave, Maternity Leave, *Force Majeure* Leave, and Carer's Leave

§1. The Parental Leave Act 1996

125. The Parental Leave Act of 1996 (as amended by the Parental Leave Act 2006) implements Directive 96/34/EC on the Framework Agreement on Parental Leave.

The basic entitlement is described in section 6: an employee who is the natural or adoptive parent of a child is entitled to 14 working weeks to enable him to look after the child (section 6(1)). The form in which parental leave is taken may either be a continuous period of fourteen weeks or be in two separate periods not exceeding six weeks.[339] With the agreement of the employer and employee, parental leave may be taken in shorter blocks of days or hours.

An employee is entitled to parental leave in respect of every child of which he or she is the natural or adoptive parent.[340] Statutory parental leave is unpaid. However, an employee is, while on parental leave, regarded for all purposes (other than his or her right to remuneration) as still in employment.[341] Therefore, for purposes other than remuneration the employee continues to be regarded as employed. Section 15 guarantees the right to return to work: the employee is entitled to be reinstated in the job which the employee held immediately before he or she left on parental leave and under the same contract of employment. Where 'it is not reasonably practicable' to reinstate the employee in the position which he held immediately before taking parental leave, the employee is entitled to suitable alternative employment.[342]

Parental leave may, however, either be postponed, refused or withdrawn. The taking of parental leave may be postponed where the taking of parental leave at the time proposed by the employee would have substantial adverse effects on the operation of the business.[343] A postponement of parental leave should be supplied in writing, must follow consultation with the employee, and must state the reasons for postponement.[344] The employer cannot exercise the power of postponement more than once in respect of a particular child. There is one case where postponement may be exercised on a second occasion: where there is a seasonal variation in the volume of work; this power of second postponement may only be exercised once.[345]

Parental leave is given solely to enable the parent to take care of the child.[346] Where an employer has reasonable grounds for believing that the employee is not

---

339. S. 7(1)(a) as amended by s. 4 of the Parental Leave (Amendment) Act 2006.
340. S. 6(4).
341. S. 14(1).
342. S. 16(1)).
343. S. 11(1).
344. S. 11(2) and (3).
345. S. 11 (4).
346. S. 12(1).

using the leave for the purpose of taking care of the child, the employer may cancel the employee's leave.[347]

Entitlement to parental leave is restricted to employees who have completed one year's continuous employment with the employer.[348] Entitlement to take parental leave concludes on the day on which the child reaches eight years of age.[349]

§2. FORCE MAJEURE LEAVE

126. The basic right is described in section 13 of the Parental Leave Act 1996 (as amended). An employee is entitled to take leave where, for urgent family reasons, owing to an illness or injury to a close family relative, the employee's return is indispensable.[350] *Force majeure* leave is paid. However, *force majeure* leave is not indefinite: it may not exceed three days in any period of 12 months, or five days in any period of 36 consecutive months.[351] Where an employee takes *force majeure* leave he or she must provide his or her employer with a notice specifying the dates on which the leave was taken and the facts entitling the employer to the leave.[352] (It has been held that a medical note is not essential. However, there must be some reasonable proof : there 'may be required to provide some reasonable proof either in the form of a doctor's statement or in the form of a formalized statement'.)[353]

For the *force majeure* entitlement to apply there must (a) be some 'urgent family reason'. In a number of determinations the EAT have applied quite broadly the urgent family reason condition. In *Tesco* v. *Hobson*[354] a husband who remained at home in order to look after his wife who was suffering from tonsillitis was held to have had an urgent family reason justifying *force majeure* leave. In *Crown Equipment* v. *Traynor*[355] the absence of a husband who was looking after his wife who was ill with flu was held to have had a ground of legitimate *force majeure* leave. However, in *McGaley* v. *Leibherr Container Cranes*[356] the High Court struck a more rigorous note when it held that the EAT had committed no error in principle in holding that an employee who remained at home in order to look after his wife who was suffering from a stomach bug could not claim an urgent family ground justifying the payment of *force majeure* leave. In *Quinn* v. *Higgins*[357] the employee had taken a day off work in order to look after his family whom he suspected might be showing symptoms of meningitis. A visit to the doctor the following day showed this to be unfounded. The employee remained with his family on the ground that they 'needed looking after'. The Tribunal held that while his presence in the stage

---

347. S. 12(1).
348. S. 6(4).
349. S. 6(2) (as amended by s. 3 of the Parental Leave (Amendment) Act 2006).
350. S. 13(1).
351. S. 13(4).
352. The form is contained in the Parental Leave (Notice of *Force Majeure* Leave) Regulations (SI No. 454 of 1998).
353. PL 2/2009.
354. PL 4/2001.
355. PL 7/2000.
356. [2001] 3 IR 563.
357. [2000] 11 ELR 102.

prior to the doctor's appraisal was indispensable, it ceased to be so after the doctor had discounted the possibility of meningitis.

The point of perspective from which 'urgent need' is judged is that of the employee at the time of the alleged crisis. In *Carey* v. *Penn Racquet Sports*[358] the employee took *force majeure* leave, extremely concerned that her child was suffering from meningitis. In fact, the symptoms were no more than a harmless rash. The EAT held that, judged objectively, there was no 'urgent need'. However, the High Court held that the matter should have been looked at from the plaintiff's point of view at the time the decision was made not to go to work.

The compelling reason must relate to 'an illness or injury' to one of the close family members prescribed in the list in section 13(2). (Since the exception only applies in the case of an 'illness or injury' it would not, for instance, apply where an employee remained at home in order to help in the search for a son or daughter who was missing. Nor would the entitlement apply where an employee was absent in order to attend the funeral of a child or spouse.) On the other hand, while the reason must relate to the illness of a relative, the presence of the employee at home need not necessarily be in order to look after the ill person. In *Wellman International* v. *Langty*[359] the employee's wife had an upset stomach and the employee had remained at home in order to look after the children. The employee was held to have had a good claim for *force majeure* leave: there was an urgent family reason (the need to look after the small children) and the reason was related to the illness of the employee's wife.

The urgent family reason must relate to an injury or illness to one of the categories of person described in section 13(2): in *Herbert* v. *Kostal Ireland Limited*[360] it was held that there was no entitlement to a *force majeure* payment in the case of an employee who absented himself in order to look after his mother-in-law.

The urgent family reason must require the presence of the employee 'at the place where the person is, whether at his or her home or elsewhere'. In *Maughan* v. *Gencorp Vehicle Sealing*[361] the employee's child had been admitted to hospital and while the applicant's wife stayed with the child in hospital, the employee stayed at home in order to look after the couple's other children. Here there may have been an urgent family reason, but it did not require the presence of the applicant *at the place* where the ill or injured family member was.

The presence of the employee must be 'indispensable': having identified the objective of the absence it must be shown that this objective could not have been accomplished other than by the employee absenting him or herself. In *Munnelly* v. *Warners*[362] the employee had remained with his mother while his father underwent an emergency hip replacement operation. The employee was unable to identify any reason which made his presence indispensable. The need to have a family member present was fulfilled by the presence of his mother.

---

358. [2001] 12 ELR 27. This was confirmed in *McGaley* v. *Leibherr Container Cranes* [2001] 3 IR 563.
359. EAT [2001] PL 1/2001.
360. EAT [1999] PL22/99.
361. EAT [2000] PL3/2000.
362. EAT [1999] PL19/99.

The EAT has required that the employee must be able to show that the claimant's presence unavoidably required his absence from work, and could not be accomplished in any other way, such as a change in shift or from holiday leave. In *Boxmore Plastics* v. *Crowe*[363] the employee had, by arrangement with her family who were taking turns to look after their father, taken leave for which she claimed a *force majeure* payment. The Tribunal, declining the application for paid leave, held that she had 'an opportunity prior to make alternative arrangements, that is leave without pay or taking a day's holiday'.

A concern that employees might abuse the entitlement underlies the rule that an employee must provide reasonable proof of the circumstances which are said to justify the absence. In *An Employer* v. *An Employee*[364] the employee claimed that he had remained at home because he feared that his child was ill. The employer resisted the claim on the ground that he had not produced a medical certificate. The EAT agreed that while a medical certificate might not be necessary in all cases, there should be some supporting proof. If a medical certificate was not provided, a 'formalized' statement might suffice.

§3. MATERNITY LEAVE

I. The Period and Timing of Maternity Leave under the Maternity Protection Acts 1994–2004

127. Section 8 of the Maternity Protection Act 1994 (as amended by the Maternity Protection (Amendment) Act 2004) created a basic entitlement to 22 weeks' maternity leave. The legislation goes on to provide that the Minister for Jobs, Enterprise, and Innovation may by order extend that period of leave.[365] That power to extend the duration of maternity leave was taken advantage of by the Maternity Protection Act, 1994 (Extension of Periods of Leave) Order, 2006[366] which extends the basic entitlement to 26 weeks. Unlike other forms of leave, like holiday leave, the timing of the leave is at the discretion of the employee (though it may not commence later than two weeks before the expected date of confinement nor conclude earlier than four weeks after the end of the expected week of confinement (section 10(1) (as amended by section 3 of the 2004 Act)). That basic 26-week period may then be extended in two cases. (i) In the event of late confinement: where the date of confinement occurs later than expected the period of maternity leave may be extended by an equivalent period (section 12 (2)). (ii) Where the employee avails herself of the opportunity to take additional maternity leave (section 14(1)): section 14 provides that an employee who has taken maternity leave shall, if she so wishes, be entitled to a further leave period, known as additional maternity leave, for a maximum period of 12 consecutive weeks.

---

363. EAT [2000] PL14/1999.
364. EAT [2009] PL2/2009.
365. S. 8(2) Maternity Protection Acts 1994–2004.
366. SI 51 of 2006.

Entitlement to the minimum period of maternity leave (and to additional maternity leave)[367] is subject to the employee supplying the employer, not later than four weeks before the commencement of maternity leave, with the notification of her intention to take maternity leave, together with a medical certificate confirming her pregnancy.[368] An employee is not entitled to maternity leave unless this condition is strictly complied with; ignorance of the condition is not an excuse.[369] It follows that maternity leave which is unilaterally taken without this condition being complied with is strictly an unlawful absence from work.

Maternity leave may be postponed if the child in connection with whose birth she is on maternity leave is hospitalized.[370] Following postponement she will be entitled to take 'resumed leave' following the child's discharge from hospital. The employer is entitled to refuse such a request. In order to submit a lawful request the employee must have already taken 14 weeks' maternity leave (and not less than 4 of those weeks after the end of the week of confinement).[371]

II. The Content of Statutory Maternity Leave

128. Maternity leave under the 1994 Act is not paid maternity leave.[372] Well-known European law holds that there is not discrimination on grounds of sex where a pregnant woman on maternity leave does not receive full pay from her employer.[373]

However, the European Court of Justice has also held that the amount of remuneration must not be so low as to undermine 'the Community-wide objective of protecting female workers, in particular before giving birth'.[374] There is no provision in Irish law that an employer provide some minimum pay so as to implement this element of the *Gillespie/McKenna* principle.

Dismissal of the employee during a period of maternity leave is void. The EAT has held that dismissal includes steps (such as meetings to consider the dismissal) preparatory to dismissal.[375]

The employee is also entitled to return to work, on the expiry of her maternity leave, with the employer with whom she was working immediately before the start

---

367. S. 14(3). Additional maternity leave may also be notified by an application made no later than four weeks before the expected date of return (s. 14(4)).
368. S. 9(1).
369. *O'Flaherty* v. *Coughlan* EAT [1983] P8/1983.
370. S. 14B.
371. The application must be in writing (s. 14 (1) and (2)) and be accompanied by documentation confirming the child's hospitalization (Maternity Protection Act 1994 (Postponement of Leave) Regulations 2004 (SI 655/2004)).
372. S. 22.
373. *Gillespie* v. *Northern Health and Social Services Board* [1996] ECR 1-7327; *North Western Health Board* v. *McKenna* [2005] ECR 1-7631.
374. *Gillespie* v. *Northern Health and Social Services Board* [1996] ECR 1-7327, para. 20; *North Western Health Board* v. *McKenna* [2005] ECR 1-7631, para. 20.
375. *Employee* v. *Employer*, EAT [2012] P5/2010.

of that period.[376] This provision restates an entitlement which the employee already enjoys under European law.[377]

The entitlement to return to work is said to be subject to the employee having given the employer, not later than four weeks before the date on which she expects to return to work, written notice of her intention to return to work.[378] (Where there are reasonable grounds for the employee's failure to give a notice, the Tribunal may extend the period for submitting the notice.)[379] The requirement to give notice is a strict condition to returning to work.[380] A failure to give notice has been regarded as bringing the contract of employment to an end by operation of law.[381]

III. Maternity-connected Rights

129. A pregnant employee is entitled to time off work without loss of pay in order to attend one set of ante-natal classes.[382] This entitlement is regulated by regulations made by the Minister for Justice: these regulations include the requirement that the employee should give two weeks' notice.[383] An expectant father is entitled to time off work in order to attend the last two ante-natal classes in a set of classes being attended by the expectant mother (section 15A(1) and (2)).

An employee who is breastfeeding is entitled either to time off from her work for the purpose of breastfeeding in the workplace, or to a reduction in hours in order to facilitate breastfeeding otherwise than at the workplace.[384] This entitlement is elaborated in the Maternity Protection (Protection of Mothers who are Breastfeeding) Regulations:[385] the essential entitlement is to one hour off work per each day. An employer is required to provide facilities for the purpose of breastfeeding, except where to do so would give rise to a cost other than a nominal cost to the employer .[386]

A further form of pregnancy-related leave is health and safety leave. The Safety, Health and Welfare Act (General Application) Regulations 2007[387] require an employer to assess any risk 'resulting from any activity at that employer's place of work' to the safety or health of pregnant employees (Regulation 149). Where, as a result of a risk assessment, it is not technically or objectively feasible either to adjust

---

376. S. 25.
377. *Webb* v. *EMO Air Cargo (UK) Ltd* [1994] ECR 1-3567.
378. S. 28(1).
379. *Grennan* v. *Carty* EAT [2004]RP161/2004: employer telling employee that he would not be taking her back; held a good reason for not giving notice of intention to return.
380. *Ivory* v. *Skyline Ltd* [1988] IR 399.
381. S. 28(2) of the Maternity Protection Act 1994. In *An Employee* v. *An Employer* EAT [2010] P4/2010 a hotel worker had failed to give any notice of return to work; the tribunal (though 'sympathetic to the respondent's situation') held that the employment had come to an end by operation of law.
382. S. 15A of the 1994 Act as inserted by the Maternity Protection Act 2004.
383. SI 653 of 2004.
384. S. 15(B).
385. SI 654/2004.
386. S. 15B(2).
387. SI 299 of 2007.

the employee's work or to move the employee, the employee must be granted leave from her employment.[388] This is a part-paid entitlement: the employee is entitled to remuneration for the first 21 days of such leave.[389]

§4. The Carer's Leave Act 2001

130. The Carer's Leave Act 2001 (as amended by section 48 of Social Welfare Law Reform and Pensions Act 2006) provides for the taking by employees of extensive leave in order to look after a person requiring full-time care. An employee may take up to 104 weeks leave in order to look after a person certified by the Department of Social Protection as a 'relevant person' (section 6(5)). The conditions for the taking of carer's leave are that the employee has been continuously employed for more than 12 months; that the person for whom the employee intends to take leave is certified by the Department of Social Protection as in need of full-time care (section 6). Notice of the employee's intention to take carer's leave must be given not less than six weeks before the date when it is proposed to commence the period of leave (section 9(1)).

I. The Rights Guaranteed to a Person on Carer's Leave

131. The contract of employment of a person on carer's leave is for all purposes – other than remuneration, superannuation benefits, annual leave, or public holiday benefits – suspended by operation of law.[390] The employee is, while on carer's leave, regarded 'as still working in the employment for all purposes relating to his or her employment and none of his or her rights or obligations shall be affected by availing of carer's leave'. Accordingly, an employee is entitled to continue to acquire service for the purpose of the service-related statutory rights; the employee is regarded as employed at the time of a business transfer for the purpose of the application of the transfer of undertakings code; is entitled to be notified of changes under the Terms of Employment (Information) Act 1994; the employee is entitled not to have the employer infringe the relationship of trust and confidence; the employee is entitled not to be unlawfully discriminated against; and the employee is entitled to consultation or electoral rights under the transfer of undertakings and collective redundancy codes. Reciprocally, the employee continues to be bound by the duty of fidelity and confidentiality to his employer while on carer's leave.

II. The Right to Return to Work on the Expiry of Carer's Leave

132. The employee is entitled on the termination of carer's leave, to return to work in the employment that the employee held immediately before the

---

388. S. 18(1) of the Maternity Protection Act 1994.
389. S. 18(4) of the Maternity Protection Act 1994.
390. S. 13(1)(a).

commencement of the carer's leave.[391] The right to return to work is, however, subject to a number of qualifications. First, section 14(1) provides that the right of return may only be availed of 'on the termination of carer's leave *in accordance with this Act*'. Accordingly, failure to supply the notice of intention to return to work required under section 9(6), may disentitle the employee. (This issue, however, has yet to be definitively decided.) Second, the employee does not necessarily have the right to return to the same job which he or she previously carried out. The employer may, if it is not reasonably practicable to permit the employee to return to the work which he previously carried out, offer suitable alternative employment.[392] Third, the employee's right to return to work may be overridden by other substantial reasons. An employee who is entitled to return to work, but is not so permitted by his employer, is deemed to have been unfairly dismissed for the purpose of the Unfair Dismissals Acts 1977–2007 and the date of dismissal (for the purpose of the six months' time limit) is the date on which he was entitled to return to work (section 16(4)). That dismissal is deemed to be an unfair dismissal unless 'having regard to all the circumstances there were substantial grounds justifying the dismissal' (section 16(4)). An employer may, therefore, justify refusal of permission to return on 'substantial grounds' such as redundancy.

---

391. S. 14(1).
392. S. 15.

Chapter 7. The Law Relating to Wages

§1. The Recovery of Unpaid Wages

I. Civil Proceedings in the District Court, Circuit Court and High Court

133. The main processes for the recovery of unpaid wages are: civil process in the District Court, or Civil Bill in the Circuit Court, or by proceedings under the Payment of Wages Act 1991.

The unpaid employee may enforce his right to payment either by an action in debt or breach of contract either, depending on the amount involved, by civil process in the District Court (where the amount does not exceed €6,348.69)[393] or by civil bill in the Circuit Court (where the amount does not exceed €38,092.14).[394]

II. Proceedings under the Payment of Wages Act 1991

134. An alternative mechanism is provided by the Payment of Wages Act 1991 under which an employee may, within six months of the deduction, present a claim to a Rights Commissioner that the employer has made an unauthorized deduction, or non-payment of wages.[395] The procedure before the rights commissioner is designed to provide a cheap informal wages recovery facility. The procedure applies to a 'deduction' of wages. In *McKenzie* v. *Minister for Finance*[396] the High Court limited the availability of the process in holding that the process under the 1991 Act does not apply to an illegal 'reduction' of wages (such as an unlawful wages cut) as opposed to an unlawful 'deduction' of wages (such as an illegal wages' penalty).

The definition of 'wages' under the Payment of Wages Act 1991 seems wider than remuneration strictly owed under contract. 'Wages' is defined as including any 'emolument, referable to his employment, whether payable under his contract of employment or otherwise'. The last phrase suggests that there is a right to recover under the 1991 Act money to which an employee has a legitimate expectation, even though (for lack of reciprocal consideration) there may be no strict contractual entitlement.

§2. The Right to a Wage Statement

135. Section 4 of the Payment of Wages Act 1991 requires that the employer give to an employee a statement in writing specifying the gross amount of wages and the nature and amount of any deduction. Compensation may be awarded for

---

393. S. 77 Courts of Justice Act 1924 as amended by s. 4 Courts Act 1991.
394. Courts (Supplemental Provisions) Act 1961 as amended by s. 2 Courts Act 1991.
395. S. 6(4) Payment of Wages Act 1991.
396. [2010] IEHC 461. This interpretation overlooks the definition of 'deduction' in s. 5(6)(a): 'where the total amount of any wages ... is less than the total amount of wages that it properly payable'. This seems to include an illegal salary reduction.

failure to provide a wage statement. In *Fagan* v. *Colonet*[397] an employee who was not provided with wage slips under section 4 was awarded €930. Under section 23 of the National Minimum Wage Act 2000 an employee may request from his or her employer a written statement of the employee's average hourly rate of pay for any pay reference period.

§3. WAGE INCREASES

136. An employee does not at common law have any enforceable right to a wage increase. In *Murco Petroleum* v. *Forge*[398] it was held that there was no enforceable entitlement to a wage increase at common law. Such a right might disrupt national pay agreements, and could be potentially inflationary. However, there are two constraints on the general right to withhold wage increases. First, the unequal application of a wage increase with some employees receiving wage increases, and other employees being denied increases might constitute a breach of the duty to respect trust and confidence.[399] Secondly, a provision in a contract of employment giving an employer a discretion to sanction wage increases must not be exercised capriciously or unreasonably. In *Clark* v. *BET*[400] the contract of employment provided that the 'salary shall be reviewed annually and be increased by such amount if any as the board in its absolute discretion may decide'. It was held that the 'absolute discretion' was not absolute, but must be exercised in good faith and not capriciously.

§4. ELIGIBILITY TO WAGES ISSUES; INDUSTRIAL ACTION AND IMPRISONMENT

137. Eligibility to wages issues arise in three areas in particular: are workers entitled to wages (a) during industrial action; or (b) when in prison; or (c) when ill?

I. Industrial Action and Wages

A. *Wages and the Full Strike*

138. The Supreme Court in *Carr* v. *Minister for Education*[401] endorsed the proposition, earlier established in English law, that the essential condition to wages is the ability of the employee to show to show that he is ready and willing to perform the services which form the basis for the consideration claimed. It follows that where an employee is engaged in a full-strike or withdrawal of labour he will,

---

397. EAT [2000] PW 3/2000.
398. [1987] IRLR 50.
399. *TRANSCO* v. *O'Brien* [2002] IRLR 444.
400. [1997] IRLR 348.
401. [2001] 2 ILRM 272.

obviously, be unable to claim that he is willing to work. In *Henthorn* v. *CEGB*[402] it was held that an employee on a work to rule is unable to prove that he was ready and willing to work; the essential conditions to wages cannot be established. Therefore, he has no right to wages.

B. *Wages and Activity Short of a Full Strike*

139. This doctrine has been extended to industrial action *short* of a full-scale withdrawal of labour, e.g. a ban on engaging in certain types of work. The courts' reasoning is that in order to demonstrate willingness to work an employee must be able to show willingness to work fully and cooperatively. Where a worker is involved in a work ban he is unable to show that he is willing to work fully and cooperatively. Therefore he is unable to show willingness and readiness to work––the first condition of wages. In *Miles* v. *Wakefield*[403] the House of Lords adopted the theory that even limited industrial action is irreconcilable with the requirement that the employee be able to show willingness and ability to work. Here, the employee, a Registrar of Births Marriages and Deaths, who was engaged in industrial action which took the form of a limited work ban (refusing to work on Saturday mornings) was held disentitled to wages. The court took the radical view that limited industrial action is indistinguishable from a full strike. Accordingly, the employee could not demonstrate readiness and willingness to work. Lord Templeman said:

> in principle, a worker who, in conjunction with his fellow workers, declines to work efficiently with the object of harming his fellow workers is no more entitled to his wages under the contract of employment than if he declines to work at all.

If the employer is prepared to tolerate partial performance the employee may be entitled to part wages for work actually done. The theory is that by reason of the employees' industrial action the original contract is suspended. However when the employees present themselves offering to provide reduced service, they are making an offer of a new contract. of employment. The employer may choose to accept this. If he does, a new contract comes into being. The employee is entitled to be paid under this new contract. In *Miles* v. *Wakefield*[404] the House of Lords laid down the proposition that an employee who offers partial performance with the object of inflicting maximum damage to the employer at minimum inconvenience to himself cannot prove that he is willing and ready to work. Therefore, he was not entitled to wages under his original contract. However, when the employees attended work on the five other days, and the employer was prepared to accept their service, a new contract came into existence. The employees were entitled to be paid for work done

---

402. [1980] IRLR 361.
403. [1987] AC 539.
404. [1987] 1 AC 539.

under that new contract. By contrast, in *Wiluszyski* v. *Tower Hamlets Borough Council*[405] local authority housing officers, as part of a campaign of industrial action, implemented a ban on answering queries submitted by political representatives on behalf of constituents. The Borough Council wrote to the officials saying that it regarded the ban as a serious dereliction of duty and informed them that they need not attend work if they were not prepared to work as normal. They were advised that if they did attend their work would be regarded as purely voluntary and that they could not expect to be paid. ('You will not be allowed to pick and choose which duties you perform and if you are not prepared to work normally, you will be sent off the premises. You will only be paid your salary if you continue to work normally in accordance with the requirements of your contract.') The workers did attend and claimed remuneration for the work that they did perform. The Court of Appeal held that they were not entitled to any payment. Here, unlike the *Miles* case, the employees' offer of reduced work had *not been implicitly accepted* by the employers. The employer was not required to physically eject the employees; it was enough that the employees were given a genuine warning. There was no new contract and the employees were entitled to nothing.

II. Employees in Custody

140. The employee in *Burns* v. *Santander*[406] was absent on remand awaiting trial. He argued that he was entitled to wages. The conventional condition to wages was, he claimed. satisfied: he was 'willing' to work. The proposition was rejected. It was not enough that the employee was ready and willing to perform his contract. There was a further condition (in addition to willingness to work). The employee must not be disabled from working by reason of some *avoidable impediment*. A remand in custody was an avoidable impediment. Accordingly here the employee was disabled by an avoidable impediment and was not entitled to wages.

§5. DEDUCTION OF WAGES

I. Section 5 Payment of Wages Act 1991; the General Scheme

141. Section 5 of the Payment of Wages Act 1991 regulates the common law rights of deduction on the ground of an 'act or omission'. It adds further conditions to the circumstances in which a deduction may be made.

Section 5(2) of the Payment of Wages Act 1991 provides:

> An employer shall not make a deduction from the wages of an employee in respect of—

---

405. [1989] ICR 493.
406. [2011] IRLR 639.

(a) any act or omission of the employee, or

(b) any goods or services supplied to or provided for the employee by the employer the supply or provision of which is necessary to the employment,

unless—

   (i) the deduction is required or authorised to be made by virtue of a term (whether express or implied and, if express, whether oral or in writing) of the contract of employment made between the employer and the employee, and

  (ii) the deduction is of an amount that is fair and reasonable having regard to all the circumstances (including the amount of the wages of the employee), and

 (iii) before the time of the act or omission or the provision of the goods or services, the employee has been furnished with—

    (I) in case the term referred to in *subparagraph* (*i*) is in writing, a copy thereof,

    (II) in any other case, notice in writing of the existence and effect of the term,

and

  (iv) in case the deduction is in respect of an act or omission of the employee, the employee has been furnished, at least one week before the making of the deduction, with particulars in writing of the act or omission and the amount of the deduction, and

  (v) in case the deduction is in respect of compensation for loss or damage sustained by the employer as a result of an act or omission of the employee, the deduction is of an amount not exceeding the amount of the loss or the cost of the damage, and

  (vi) in case the deduction is in respect of goods or services supplied or provided as aforesaid, the deduction is of an amount not exceeding the cost to the employer of the goods or services, and

 (vii) the deduction or, if the total amount payable to the employer by the employee in respect of the act or omission or the goods or services is to be so paid by means of more than one deduction from the wages of the employee, the first such deduction is made not later than 6 months after the act or omission becomes known to the employer or, as the case may be, after the provision of the goods or services.

Six conditions must, under section 5 (2), be complied with: the power to deduct must be pre-authorized in the contract; the amount must be fair and reasonable; the employee must have notice of the term; particulars of the act or omission must be supplied; the amount must be fair and reasonable; the deduction must be made within six months.

II. The 'Fair and Reasonable' Condition in Section 5

142. Section 5(2)(ii) of the 1991 Act requires that the scale of the deduction must be 'fair and reasonable'. *Lynch* v. *Clondara Wholesalers*[407] is an illustration of the requirement that the amount of the deduction must be 'fair and reasonable'. Here, the employee was a lorry driver who having been asked to bring in goods, refused and used aggressive language to the foreman. The employer wrote to the employee informing him of its decision to suspend without pay for four weeks. The sanction of suspension without pay for four weeks was held to have infringed the Payment of Wages Act 1991: the deduction was not of an amount that was 'fair and reasonable' having regard to the employee's low income.

III. Pre-authorized in the Contract; Notice of the Grounds; Implementation within Six Months

143. In *Grimes* v. *Iarnród Éireann*[408] the employee was suspended without pay in August 1992 in respect of an act occurring in August 1991. No notice of the precise act of misconduct had been furnished to the employee in writing as required by section 5(2)(iv). There was no entitlement in the contract to suspend without pay. The Tribunal found multiple breaches of section 5: the requirement that the deduction be made within six months had not been observed. The requirement that the right to deduct have been pre-authorized in the contract was ignored. The condition that the employee be informed of the details of the misconduct had been overlooked. The Tribunal rejected the argument that there was no requirement that the employee be told of the nature of the act or omission where it must have been obvious. The requirement was a mandatory one, and it would create uncertainty to dispense with this because the employer assumes that the employee knows of the ground.

IV. Deductions for Goods and Services Supplied to the Employee

144. The power to make deductions for goods and services (personal use of telephones or training expenses) is regulated by section 5 of the Payment of Wages Act 1991. Where an employer wishes to make a deduction in respect of services or goods an entitlement to do so must have been pre-authorized in the contract; the entitlement must have been brought to the notice of the employee; and the deduction must have been made within six months. An example of non-compliance with the rules is provided by *Ryanair* v. *Downey.*[409] The complainant had been required to enter into an 'engineer's training bond' requiring him to reimburse Ryanair if he left within two years of commencing employment. The training course (the service)

---

407. EAT [1998] PW 3/98.
408. EAT [1995] PW 3/95.
409. [2006] 17 ELR 347.

had been completed in 2003. The complainant did not leave until 2004. The Tribunal held that there had been an infringement of section 5: although the deduction was provided for in the contract of employment, it had not been implemented within six months.

§6. The National Minimum Wage Act 2000

I. The National Minimum Wage; the General Scheme

145. The National Minimum Wage Act 2000 introduced for the first time in Irish law a national minimum wage. The key provision is section 14: 'An employee who has attained the age of 18 years shall ... be remunerated by his employer in respect of the employee's working hours in any pay reference period at an hourly rate of pay that on average is not less than the national minimum hourly rate of pay.'

Section 11 of the National Minimum Wage Act 2000 provides that the Minister may 'taking account the impact the proposed rate may have on employment, the overall economic conditions in the State and national competitiveness, declare a national minimum hourly rate of pay'. The current rate is €8.65 per hour.[410] (Under the Financial Emergency measures in the Public Interest Act 2010 the Minister for Finance may declare a national minimum hourly rate of pay of €7.65.)[411]

The basic calculation for determining compliance with the statutory right is defined in section 20:

> For the purpose of determining under this Act whether an employee is being paid not less than the minimum hourly rate of pay to which he is entitled under this Act in a pay reference, the gross remuneration of the employee calculated in accordance with Section 19 shall be divided by the total working hours of the employee in the pay reference period calculated under Section 8.

The important terms are 'pay reference period', 'working hours' and 'pay'. The worker's 'gross remuneration' over the 'reference period' is divided by the 'total working hours'. This figure must not be less than the national minimum.[412]

II. 'Reckonable' Remuneration

146. The definition of 'remuneration' is elaborated in the Schedule to the National Minimum Wage Act 2000. The Schedule divides pay into reckonable components and non-reckonable components. Reckonable components are (1) basic salary; (2) shift premium; (3) piece and incentive rates, commission and bonuses;

---

410. National Minimum Wage Act 2000 (No. 2) (Section 11) Order 2011 (SI 331 of 2011).
411. Such an order was made in 2011 by the National Minimum Wage Act 2000 (Section 11) Order 2011 (SI 13 of 2011).
412. S. 20.

(4) the monetary value of board and lodgings;[413] (5) the amount of any service charge distributed through the pay roll; (6) any payments made under section 18 of the Organization of Working Time Act 1997;[414] (7) wages paid in a previous pay reference period which relate to the specific pay reference period; (8) wages in hand, i.e. any amount earned in the specific pay reference period, and paid in the next pay reference period.

The following are deemed non-reckonable components: (1) overtime premium; (2) call-out premium; (3) service pay; (4) unsocial hours premium; (5) public holiday premium, or Sunday premium, paid under the Organization of Working Time Act 1997; (6) allowances for special or additional duties; (7) expenses; (8) a period during which an employee is on call or on stand-by is not included in the calculation of hours worked;[415] (9) any payment for, or in relation to, a period of absence by the employee from the workplace, such as sick pay, holiday pay, payment for health and safety leave under the Maternity Protection Acts 1994–2004 or payment in lieu; (10) any payment by way of an allowance or gratuity in connection with the retirement or resignation of the employee, or as compensation for loss of office; (11) pension contributions paid by the employer; (12) any payment referable to the employee's redundancy; (13) any advance of a payment; (14) any payment to an employee other than in his or her capacity as an employee; (15) any payment representing compensation for the employee, such as for injury or loss of tools or equipment; (16) an amount of any award under a staff suggestion scheme; (17) any loan by the employer to the employee.

III. Working Hours

147. 'Working hours' are defined as the hours of work of an employee as determined in accordance with the employee's contract of employment or any collective agreement that relates to the employee or any statement of terms and conditions or the total hours during which the employee carries out or performs the activities of his or her work at the employee's place of employment, whichever is the greater.[416] Section 8(2) goes on to include the following periods: (a) overtime; (b) time spent travelling on official business and (c) time spent on training or on a training course or course of study authorized by the employer, within the workplace or elsewhere, during normal working hours.

Section 8(2)(ii) provides that 'time spent absent from work on annual leave, sick leave, protective leave, adoptive leave, parental leave, while laid off, on strike or on lock-out, or time for which the employee is paid in lieu of notice' does not count towards the calculation of 'working hours'. Hours spent on sick leave are not counted as working hours for which the national minimum wage must be paid. This

---

413. *Nathan Clare* v. *Barsteiga*, Labour Court [2011] MWD116; *Chtabbou* v. *Circus Gebola*, Labour Court [2012] DWT 12182.
414. S. 18 of the Organization of Working Time Act 1997 provides a minimum wage for zero-hour workers.
415. S. 8(2)(ii).
416. S. 8 of the National Minimum Wage Act 2000.

ensures that an employer retains the common law right not to pay for periods spent absent on sick leave.

IV. Exceptions to the Duty to Pay the National Minimum Wage

148. A series of exceptions to the general obligations to pay the national minimum wage are recognized. (1) Employees who are under 18 years may be paid not less than 70 per cent of the national minimum wage.[417] (2) Employees who enter employment for the first time after reaching 18 years may, in the first year of their employment, be paid not less than 80 per cent of the national minimum, and in the second year, not less than 90 per cent of the minimum. (3) Employees who enter employment before the age of 18 may be paid not less than 80 per cent of the minimum in the first year after their 18th birthday, and 90 per cent in the second.[418] (4) Where an employee is undergoing a course of study or training authorized by the employer,[419] the employee shall be remunerated by his or her employer at 75 per cent or the ordinary national minimum in respect of the first one-third period; at 75 per cent in respect of the second one-third period; and 90 per cent in respect of the final one-third period.[420] Abuse of this provision is controlled by the requirement that the training course must fall within the terms of 'regulations made by the Minister'.[421] (5) Finally, the Labour Court is given power to authorize payment of a wage which is of an amount lower than the national minimum wage where the employer does not have the means to pay the national minimum, and would, if forced to pay the wage, be forced to lay off or to dismiss employees.[422]

V. Enforcing the Right to Minimum Pay

149. Section 22(1) of the 2000 Act requires that an employer shall keep records to show that the Act is being complied with. An employee contesting compliance with the Act is assisted by section 22(3). Subsection (3) provides that where an employer fails to keep records under subsection (1) the onus of proving compliance with the Act, in proceedings before a Rights Commissioner or the Labour Court, shifts to the employer.[423]

---

417. S. 14(6).
418. S. 15(1)(ii).
419. In *Grefkes* v. *Lubig*, Labour Court [2011] MWD 119 a German couple working in a guesthouse in order to gain English-language experience and to resettle in Ireland were not undertaking a course of study or training authorized by the employer.
420. S. 16(1).
421. S. 16(1). National Minimum Wage Act 2010 (Prescribed Courses of Study or Training) Regulations 2000 (SI 99 of 2000). In *Enora Teoranta* v. *SIPTU*, Labour Court [2001] MWD 015 the employer's defence the employee was undergoing a course of training was rejected on the ground that the course did not correspond to the conditions prescribed in SI 99 of 2000.
422. S. 4(1).
423. *Dzumbira* v. *Nyazika*, Labour Court [2010] DWT 10172; *Execreate Inc Ltd* v. *Nazipova* Labour Court [2010] MWD 1013; *Durban House Bed and Breakfast* v. *Sereika*, Labour Court [2012] DWT 1233.

The right to a minimum wage may be enforced by ordinary civil proceedings for unpaid wages in the courts. Civil proceedings may be taken by the employee for the recovery of wages as a simple contract debt.[424] Alternatively, a breach may be remedied by a reference to a Rights Commissioner. The right to apply to a Rights Commissioner is subject to an awkward (and commonly overlooked) jurisdictional precondition. Under section 23 of the 2000 Act an employee may request his employer to provide him with a 'written statement of the employee's average hourly rate of pay for any pay reference period (other than the employee's current pay reference period) falling within the 12 month period immediately preceding the request'. The employer must furnish the statement within four weeks. Section 24 makes it a condition of an application to a rights commissioner that the applicant have first 'obtained a [section 23] statement of his or her average hourly rate of pay in respect of the relevant pay reference period' or that the employer have failed to provide such a statement within the four-week period. Where the claimant has failed to comply with this step the Commissioner is required to dismiss the claim without prejudice to the employee complying with section 23 and re-entering the claim.[425]

The Rights Commissioner has jurisdiction to award arrears of pay. The Rights Commissioner may also direct that the employee be indemnified for 'the reasonable expense of the employee in connection with the dispute'. (This is significant because the Rights Commissioner does not usually have power to order costs.)

Locus standi to pursue redress before the Rights Commissioner is also given to the employee's union. Furthermore, power to enforce the legislation is also given to the Minister in a case where it would not be reasonable to expect the employee to initiate proceedings.

VI. The Employment Regulation Order as a Source of Minimum Wages

150. The Employment Regulation Order provides an alternative form of national minimum wage. Under section 35 of the Industrial Relations Acts 1946–2012, the Labour Court is empowered to establish a joint labour committee in respect of certain classes, or types, or groups of workers. An Employment Regulation Order may fix the rates of remuneration to be paid either generally, or for any particular work. Upon the enactment of an Employment Regulation Order, the employer of a worker to whom an Employment Regulation Order applies must pay remuneration to such employee which is not less than the minimum prescribed. The process for the making of employment regulation orders has been revised following the decision of the High Court in *Grace* v. *Joint Labour Committee*[426] in 2011.

---

424. S. 50.
425. *Mansion House Ltd* v. *Izquierdo* Labour Court [2004] MWD 043.
426. [2011] IEHC 277.

A. The Factors Conditioning the Making of an Employment Regulation Order

151. In *Burke* v. *Minister for Labour*[427] the Supreme Court described the power to make an Employment Regulation Order as 'delegated power of the most fundamental, permissive and far-reaching kind'.[428] In *John Grace* v. *Catering Joint Labour Committee*[429] the High Court held that the system of employment regulation order under the Industrial Relations Act 1946 was unconstitutional on the ground that it offended the constitutional rule against the delegation of legislative power to the executive. Under Article 15.2 of the Constitution the sole and exclusive power of making laws for the state was vested in the *Oireachtas*. This provision limits the law-making competence of the *Oireachtas* to promulgate measures by means of secondary legislation: secondary legislation may only be enacted within the parameters of principles, policies and standards pre-determined in primary legislation. [430] The 1946 Act provided for the establishment of Joint Labour Committees to regulate certain employment sectors.[431] However, there was no restriction in the 1946 Act conditioning the content of the legislative orders made by this administrative agency (the Labour Court). In *John Grace* v. *Catering Joint Labour Committee* this unconfined legislative power was condemned as an infringement of Article 15.2:

> the Acts are entirely silent and leaves to the Labour Court and the Joint Labour Committees an unfettered discretion as to what to take into account and the basis upon which the rates of remuneration and terms and conditions of employment are to be determined ... the absence of any principle or policy results in a situation where the delegated body is establishing its own principles and policies and not just filling in details or making choices or decisions within principles and policies. [432]

The scheme was held to amount to a transfer of legislative power from the *Oireachtas* to an administrative agency. A declaration was granted that the system was invalid having regard to the provisions of Article 15.2.1 of the Constitution of Ireland.

Accordingly, in 2012 the Industrial Relations Act 1946 was amended so as to set out the policies and principles in which the executive was to exercise its discretion to make such employment regulation orders. A proposal for an employment regulation order is made by a Joint Labour Committee having regard to factors including the legitimate financial and commercial interests of the employers and the implications for employment and competitiveness in the sector.[433]

---

427. [1979] IR 354.
428. *Ibid.*, p. 358.
429. [2011] IEHC 277.
430. *Cityview Press Ltd* v. *ANCO* [1980] IR 381.
431. S. 35 Industrial Relations Act 1946.
432. Para. 27.
433. S. 42A of the Industrial Relations Act 1946 as inserted by the Industrial Relations Act 2012. This list is not exhaustive.

B.   The Procedure for Making an Employment Regulation Order

152.   In 1979 in *Burke* v. *Minister for Labour*[434] the Supreme Court described the power to make an Employment Regulation Order as 'delegated power of the most fundamental, permissive and far-reaching kind' (at p. 358), and held that a joint labour committee must fully observe fair procedures, and *audi alteram partem*, before making such an order. This duty is now institutionalized in the statutory machinery. Under section 42B of the Industrial Relations Act 1946 the Committee is required to advertise the proposal and then hear and consider any submissions which have been submitted. The second stage of the machinery requires the approval of the Labour Court: the Labour Court may adopt the proposal if it considers it proper to do so and if it is satisfied that the Committee has considered the relevant statutory considerations. The third stage in the procedure involves the Minister: the Minister must consider it appropriate to adopt the measure.[435] The final stage of the procedure is the laying of the measure before the Houses of the *Oireachtas*: either House of the *Oireachtas* may set aside the order.[436]

---

434. [1979] IR 354.
435. S. 42C(3) of the Industrial Relations Act 1946 as inserted by the Industrial Relations Act 2012.
436. S. 42(6) of the Industrial Relations Act 1946 as inserted by the Industrial Relations Act 2012.

Chapter 8. Incapacity to Work

§1. Illness and Dismissal from Employment

153. The conditions for a lawful dismissal on grounds of illness, where the employee is relying on the statutory remedy under the Unfair Dismissals Acts 1977–2007, include the requirement that the decision to dismiss must be proportionate to the disruption caused to the employer. Fair procedures must also be observed.[437] The employee must be afforded an opportunity to explain why he should not be dismissed. It has sometimes been suggested that the requirement of 'reasonableness' (a condition of dismissal under the Unfair Dismissals Acts, 1977–2007) requires that the employer attempt to locate alternative work within the enterprise. The principle does not apply where the provision of alternative work would impose an unreasonable burden on the employer.[438]

There is one important exception to the general principles of fair procedures, notice and proportionality which ordinarily regulate dismissal for illness. Very serious, irrecoverable illness will be regarded as frustrating the contract and as discharging the contract by operation of law.[439] Since the contract is terminated by operation of law, and not by the employer's act of dismissal, the Unfair Dismissals Acts 1977–2007 (which are activated by an act of dismissal) do not apply, and the ordinary conditions to a lawful dismissal need not be complied with.

§2. Remuneration and Illness at Common Law

I. Illness and Wages; the Presumptive Common Law Entitlement

154. There is no statutory right to be paid while ill. The issue depends on the terms of the contract. There are three possibilities: (i) the contract requires that full wages be paid; (ii) the contract denies an entitlement to any wages during illness,[440] and (iii) the contract says nothing.

The first two cases are straightforward: yes in the first case; no in the second. But what is the position in case (iii)? The common law begins with a presumption that wages are payable. However, that presumption may be expressly or implicitly displaced by the contract. The issue is usually resolved by seeing whether the presumption has been displaced in the case at hand.

The classical common law position is that an employee is (subject to contrary terms of the contract, or cases where inability is self-induced) entitled to wages once he or she is 'willing to perform his contract'.[441] An ill employee is still willing to work. It follows that, subject to a contrary agreement, the employee is entitled to

---

437. *Bolger* v. *Showering Ltd* [1990] ELR 184.
438. *Rogers* v. *Dublin Corporation* [1998] ELR 89.
439. *Boyle* v. *Marathon Petroleum* [1995] ELR 230.
440. For instance, clause 12 of the Crewlink/Ryanair flight attendant contract of employment provides: 'There are no company provisions for sick pay. It is your responsibility to claim statutory benefits for any absence.'
441. *Harvey on Industrial Relations*, Volume 1, s. B(I), para. 14(a).

wages. In *Cuckson* v. *Stones*[442] in 1858 it was held that there was a presumptive common law right to full wages during illness. The presumption would apply whenever the contract said nothing about the right to wages. Lord Campbell – in a rare example of the common law recognizing a social right – said:

The contract being in force, we think that there was no suspension of the weekly payments by reason of the plaintiff's illness and inability to work.

This view was followed in *Marrison* v. *Bell*[443] where a fruit salesman was absent due to rheumatism from December 1937 to March 1938. It was held that there was a rebuttable presumption in favour of payment. There being no evidence that the parties had agreed differently, the employee was entitled to wages: 'A long series of decisions say quite clearly, that under a contract of service, irrespective of the length of notice, wages continue through sickness and incapacity from sickness until the contract is terminated by notice.'

II. Illness and Wages; Displacing the Presumption

155. The common law presumption of full wages during illness may be displaced (i) by a provision providing for no wages during illness; by the employee's practice; or by a clause providing for partial payment only.

The presumptive right to sick pay equivalent to full wages may be displaced by the employee's practice. Contractual obligations may be unspoken or implicit, as well as express. Parties' actual practice may provide evidence of how they understand their obligations. One way of making sense of a person who consistently acts in a way which is contrary to his self-interest is to say that he is acting like that because he is *legally bound* so to act.

The plaintiff in *Mears* v. *Safecar Security Ltd*[444] was a security guard who had been absent for 7 months out of 14 months employment, and who during that entire period neither applied for, nor received any wages during these absences. The court said that evidence of an implied undertaking not to ask for sick pay might be provided by the regular practice of the employee in not seeking sick pay. In this case the employee had never asked for sick pay on the earlier occasions on which he was ill. Why did he do this? Why did he do something so obviously contrary to his self-interest? The obvious explanation is that the employee felt himself obliged to do this.

A second way of rebutting the presumption of full wages during illness is a clause providing for partial wages during illness. Many contracts of employment provide for partial pay only during illness. Such a clause will displace the presumptive common law right to full wages. In *Flynn* v. *Great Northern Ry Co*[445] the plaintiff was a railway fireman, absent between July and October 1947. The contract made

442. (1858) 1 El. & El. 248. William W. Schwarzer, 'Wages during Temporary Disability: Partial Impossibility in Employment Contracts' (1952) 5 *Stanford Law Review* 30.
443. [1939] 2 KB 157.
444. [1982] ICR 626.
445. (1950) 89 ILTR 46.

provision for an 'ex gratia' payment during illness. The High Court agreed that there was a common law entitlement to wages. That right could, however, be displaced:

assuming, though I am not expressing any final view on the point, that a servant has at common law a right to wages during illness, there can be no doubt that the master and servant can agree that wages shall not be paid during temporary illness if they wish to do so.

In this case the common law presumption was rebutted. The provision for an ex gratia payment was inconsistent with an obligation to pay remuneration. 'Otherwise both rights would exist together, which would be absurd to contemplate, since the workman would be better off in sickness, doing nothing, than he would be in health while doing work.'

Where, however, there is no rebutting evidence, the common law presumption will operate. *Rooney* v. *Ossie J. Kilkenny*[446] is an example. Here, the employee had been absent for reasons which she claimed were connected with bullying by her employer. She issued proceedings claiming a declaration that she was entitled to be paid while ill. The High Court held that there is a presumptive common law entitlement to be paid while ill, and granted an order requiring the employer to pay full wages.

§3. QUALIFICATION FOR STATUTORY EMPLOYMENT RIGHTS AND ILLNESS

156. Qualification for availability of the statutory rights to the unfair dismissal remedy, and to redundancy pay, depend upon the employee accumulating either 52 or 104 reckonable weeks respectively. The fact that the employee is absent on grounds of illness will not prevent the recognition of a week as a reckonable week so long as the week of illness does not exceed 26 weeks (First Schedule, para. 10 Minimum Notice and Terms of Employment Act, 1973). However, a week of illness subsisting after 26 weeks' absence will not be reckonable.

§4. SOCIAL WELFARE AND ILLNESS

157. Disability benefit is payable under the Social Welfare (Consolidation) Act 2005. There are three conditions to this payment.

(i) The employee must have been in insurable employment for no fewer than 52 contributory weeks since his entry into insurance.[447]
(ii) The employee must establish that he or she is 'incapable of work'.[448] The claim that he or she is incapable of work must be supported by a document in which incapacity is certified by a registered medical practitioner.

---

446. High Court, 9 March 2001.
447. S. 41(1)(a) Social Welfare (Consolidation) Act 2005.
448. S. 40(3) (a).

(iii) The employee must be under pensionable age.[449]
(iv) An employee is only entitled to benefit where the period of incapacity exceeds three days.[450]
(v) Disability pay may be withdrawn where the person has become incapable of work through his own misconduct, has not refrained from behaviour likely to hinder his or her recovery; or where the person has failed to undertake a medical examination; or has not made himself or herself available to meet with an officer of the Minister regarding his or her claim for illness benefit.[451]

---

449. S. 40 (1) (a)
450. S. 40(2) Social Welfare (Consolidation) Act 2005.
451. S. 46(1) Social Welfare (Consolidation) Act 2005 (as amended).

Chapter 9. Legal Regulation of Dismissal at Common Law

158. The protection of job security in Irish law derives from a number of sources: the common law of dismissal; the Unfair Dismissals Acts 1977–2007; the Redundancy Payments Acts 1967–2007; and the European Communities (Safeguarding of Employees' Rights on Transfer of Undertakings) Regulations 2000.[452]

§1. PROTECTION AGAINST DISMISSAL AT COMMON LAW

159. At common law an employer may dismiss an employee in one of two ways: (i) on giving the employee the period of notice required at common law, or by the contract, or (ii) summarily where employee has been guilty of serious misconduct following a process compliant with fair procedures. The corollary of these propositions is that an employer acts *illegally* where it (i) dismisses purportedly on notice but prematurely; or (ii) dismisses summarily but without proper compliance with fair procedures.

I. Summary Dismissal

160. There are exceptional cases in which the employer is not obliged to give notice of dismissal. Dismissal without notice is legitimate where the employee is guilty of repudiatory conduct. In *Carvill* v. *Irish Industrial Bank*[453] Kenny J. expressed the view that 'the grounds relied upon to justify a dismissal without notice must be acts or omissions by the employee which are inconsistent with the performance of 'the express or implied terms of the contract'. Grave incompetence[454] and misconduct involving the appropriation of the employer's assets have been recognised as justifying summary dismissal.[455] Disobedience may also justify summary dismissal. To justify dismissal the defiance must be wilful, or contemptuous, or indicate a systemic defiance of the authority of the employer. In *Laws* v. *London Chronicle*[456] the employee had defied an instruction to remain, after the senior employee to whom she acted as personal assistant had stormed out of an unpleasant appraisal meeting. The employee's dismissal was held unlawful. The employee was a highly conscientious one who had left with her immediate superior only out of a sense of loyalty. The disobedience was not explicable by reference to a pattern of anti-employer conduct, and did not justify summary dismissal.

---

452. SI 489 of 2000.
453. [1968] IR 325.
454. *Carvill* v. *Irish Industrial Bank* [1968] IR 325.
455. *Glover* v. *BLN* [1973] IR 368; *Carvill* v. *Irish Industrial Bank* [1968] IR 325.
456. [1959] 2 All ER 285.

II. Dismissal on Notice

161. At common law an employer is entitled to dismiss merely on giving notice. However, the notice required to determine a contract of employment must be of the correct temporal length. Usually, the period of notice will have been predetermined in the parties' contract of employment, and the notice must correspond to this contractual period. Where the length of notice has not been predetermined, the rule is that reasonable notice must be given. The period of required notice is viewed as increasing according to the seniority of, and extent of commitment of, the employee. Therefore, factors such as the employee's responsibilities, the grade or character of the employee's position;[457] the fact that the employee has undertaken a commitment to work abroad;[458] or the length of service with the employer,[459] or that the employee has made a sacrifice by giving up work in order to work for employer,[460] have all served to increase the period of notice to which the employee is entitled. Where the parties have overlooked setting out the period of contractual notice, the courts have used, as a guide, the period of notice set out in contracts given to employees of equivalent rank in the same organization.[461] There is no requirement that the notice be furnished in writing. Verbal notice will suffice. The notice of termination must specify the date of termination of notice.[462]

While there is no *general* right to time off in order to find alternative work during notice, section 7 of the Redundancy Payments Act 1979 provides that an employee of not less than 104 weeks' service, who had been given notice of the proposed dismissal on grounds of redundancy, 'shall be entitled to reasonable time off during the employee's working hours in order to look for new employment'.

III. Observance of Fair Procedures as a Condition of Lawful Dismissal

162. In 1990 the Supreme Court in *Gunn* v. *NCAD*[463] broke new ground – in common law terms – in establishing the proposition that it is a condition of a lawful summary dismissal that fair procedures have been complied with. The previous understanding at common law was that fair procedures were only available in two cases (1) where the contract expressly incorporated a disciplinary procedure, or (2) in a case where the person was an officer.[464]

However, in *Gunn* v. *NCAD*[465] the Supreme Court made fair procedures a general condition to legal dismissal, not just restricted to the two categories previously recognized at common law. In that case the dismissed employee had, allegedly,

---

457. *Lyons* v. *Kent* [1996] ELR 106; *McDonnell* v. *Minister for Education* [1940] IR 316.
458. *Lyons* v. *Kent* [1996] ELR 103.
459. *Hill* v. *Parsons* [1971] 1 Ch 305.
460. *Carey* v. *Independent Newspapers* [2004] 15 ELR 45.
461. *Donal McCarthy* v. *Breeo Foods Limited* [2010] 21 ELR 53.
462. *Hughes* v. *Gwynnad* [1977] ICR 436.
463. [1990] 2 IR 168.
464. *Ridge* v. *Baldwin* [1964] AC 40.
465. [1990] 2 IR 168.

received bribes from a builder. The High Court rejected the argument that the plaintiff was entitled to the benefit of a hearing prior to dismissal. The plaintiff was an ordinary employee; he was not an officer. Nor was a disciplinary machinery incorporated into the contract which provided for a right to a hearing. The Supreme Court rejected this distinction between categories of workers – elite officers and ordinary employees – as inconsistent with the republican nature of the Constitution. The application of the rules of natural justice should not, the Supreme Court held, depend on whether the person concerned is an office-holder as distinct from being an employee: 'the quality of justice does not depend on such distinctions ... the principles of natural justice, are applicable without regard to the status of the person entitled to benefit from them'.[466]

A. The Content of Fair Procedures in Dismissal: the Right to Be Informed of the Charge

163. The right to be supplied with notice of the charge is elementary. In *Mooney* v. *An Post* [467] Barrington J in the Supreme Court stated: 'certainly the minimum [the employee] is entitled to is to be informed of the charge against him and to be given an opportunity to answer it and to make submissions.' The grounds must be clearly communicated.

B. The Right of Access to Witness Statements

164. Where allegations are based on evidence collected from members of the public, or from co-employees the employee should be allowed access to those statements. In *Maher* v. *Irish Permanent (No. 1)*[468] the employee, who was the subject of an allegation of sexual harassment was held entitled to access to the witness statements.

C. The Right to Legal Representation

165. Legal representation may be essential to the capacity of an employee to conduct cross- examination of inculpating witnesses at a disciplinary hearing, or for making legal submissions. For these reasons disciplinary panels were held obliged to allow the employee legal representation: *Maher* v. *Irish Permanent (No. 1)*[469] and *Georgopolous* v. *Beaumont Hospital Board.*[470]

---

466. *Ibid.*, p. 181.
467. [1998] 4 IR 288.
468. [1998] 9 ELR 77.
469. [1998] 9 ELR 77.
470. [1998] 3 IR 132, 149.

IV. The Right to a Hearing before an Impartial, or Unbiased, Adjudicator

166. The decision maker in the disciplinary process should not have a personal animus against the employee who is the subject of the dismissal hearing. In *Cassidy v. Shannon Castle Banquets and Heritage Centre*[471] serious allegations of sexual harassment were investigated by the general manager of the defendant. There had been a history of unpleasantness between the two individuals. The High Court held that it was contrary to fair procedures that an important matter should be determined by a person who might be perceived as prejudiced.

V. The Argument that the Right of Dismissal on Notice is Legally Anachronistic

167. The superior courts, both in Canada[472] and in the United Kingdom,[473] have heard challenges in principle to the employer's prerogative right of dismissal on notice. In these cases it has been argued that the principle of dismissal on notice is anachronistic and should be replaced by a principle that dismissal, even if notice is given, should be conditioned by fair dealing and good faith. In *Johnson* v. *Unisys*[474] the plaintiff, a long-serving employee who was mentally fragile, had been dismissed without there being any sufficient ground. The plaintiff argued that there should be implied into a contract of employment a term that the power of dismissal be regulated by a duty of trust and confidence, under which the employer could not dismiss 'except for some good cause and after giving [the employee] a reasonable opportunity to demonstrate that no such cause existed'. The House of Lords rejected the argument on the basis that to create a right not to be dismissed except on reasonable grounds at common law would trespass on the statutory law of unfair dismissal. When Parliament enacted unfair dismissals legislation it had limited the entitlement to certain restricted categories of employee (those who had been in the dismissing employer's employment for a minimum period of one year); it had restricted the amount that could be paid by compensation to an amount lower than that available at common law; it had restricted the period within which a claim could be initiated; it had restricted the courts competent to hear the claim to specialist tribunals. Parliament's intention was that this protection should be a limited one. If a general common law right of reasonable cause dismissal were not recognized, Parliament's intention – that the right to be protected from unfair dismissal should be a limited one – would be evaded.

The *UNISYS* principle has, subsequently, been repeatedly approved in Irish law. In *Orr* v. *Zomax Ltd*[475] the plaintiff was dismissed on notice but on grounds which were, it was suggested, did not warrant dismissal. The plaintiff argued that the

---

471. [2000] ELR 245.
472. *Wallace* v. *United Grain Growers* [1997] 3 SCR 701.
473. *Johnson* v. *Unisys* [2003] 1 AC 518.
474. [2003] 1 AC 518.
475. [2004] 1 IR 486.

power of dismissal should be regulated by a standard of reasonableness and fairness in administering dismissal. Carroll J in the High Court rejected the submission:

> what the plaintiff is seeking to do is to introduce a new obligation under the common law on the employer to act reasonably and fairly in the case of dismissal. As the law stands, at common law an employer can terminate employment for any reason, or no reason, provided adequate notice is given.

In *Nolan* v. *EMO*[476] the High Court advanced a justification similar to that in *UNISYS:*

> the Oireachtas in enacting the Unfair Dismissal Acts 1977 to 2007, and in introducing the concept of unfair dismissal, provided for specific remedies for unfair dismissal and specific procedures for obtaining such remedies in specific forums, before a Rights Commissioner or the Employment Appeals Tribunal. For the courts to expand its common law jurisdiction in parallel to the statutory code in relation to unfair dismissal and redundancy would … end up supplanting part of the code.

VI. Exceptions to the Prerogative to Dismiss for Any Reason on Notice

168. There are however a number of qualifications upon the employer's traditional common law prerogative of dismissal for any reason merely on notice.

A. Cases Where the Contract Displaces the Right of Dismissal on Notice

169. It has long been recognized that, where there exists a detailed contract of employment which exhaustively sets out the circumstances in which an employee may be dismissed, the dismissal on grounds other than those grounds identified in the contract will be unlawful. The two leading cases are *McClelland* v. *NE General Health Services Board*[477] and *Grehan* v. *North Eastern Health Board.*[478] In the *McClelland* case the plaintiff entered into a contract which contained a clause providing for the dismissal of officers for 'gross misconduct', or if they proved 'inefficient and unfit to merit continued employment'. There was also a provision for dismissal on failure to take or honour the oath of allegiance. There was no provision for dismissal in other circumstances. The Board dismissed the employee on six months' notice on grounds of alleged redundancy. The House of Lords held that on the 'true construction of condition 12, the board debarred themselves from giving notice apart from the reasons specified therein'; and that the comprehensive condition of dismissal superseded the employer's ordinary right of dismissal on notice.

---

476. [2009] 20 ELR 122.
477. [1957] NI 100.
478. [1989] IR 422.

In *Grehan* v. *North Eastern Health Board*[479] the plaintiff entered into a contract of employment, in which six paragraphs were dedicated to the issue of the circumstances in which employment might be determined. These provided that the employee could be dismissed upon being struck off the medical register; reaching 70 years of age; and on permanent infirmity of mind or body. The High Court held that the provisions regulating dismissal were exhaustive and that the implication of a right of dismissal on notice was eliminated. Accordingly the plaintiff could not be dismissed on notice.[480]

B. Cases Where the Ground of Dismissal Offends Public Policy

170. In the United States it has been recognised that there may be exceptional cases – cases of extreme abuse where the law might draw a limit to the employer's usual right of dismissal on notice.[481] A similar principle – that the employer may not be allowed dismiss for objectionable reasons – applies in Irish law. In *Maha Lingham* v. *Health Service Executive*[482] the Supreme Court seemed to suggest that there might be cases where the grounds of dismissal were so racist or abusive that the employer forfeited his common law privilege of dismissal on notice; one case might be where the employer was dismissed on purely racial grounds:

> according to the ordinary law of employment a contract of employment may be terminated by an employer on the giving of reasonable notice of termination and that according to the traditional law at any rate, though perhaps *modified to some extent in light of modern developments ...* No doubt, if the plaintiff/appellant had been able to produce a strong and clear body of evidence that the defendant in the present case was motivated by a policy of racial discrimination, the matter would be entirely different.

---

479. *Ibid.*
480. On the other hand, the plaintiff in *Sheehy* v. *Ryan* [2008] 4 IR 258 was employed on a contract which was said to be 'permanent'. The Supreme Court rejected the plaintiff's argument that this meant that she could not be dismissed on notice. 'Permanent' simply meant that the contract was not transitory or impermanent. It was conditionally permanent: the condition was that the employer did not exercise his common law right of dismissal on notice. Unlike the *Grehan* case the contract had not restricted the employer's general entitlement to dismiss on reasonable notice.
481. *Peterman* v. *Teamsters Local* 396 174 Cal. App. 2d. 184; 344 P. 2d. 25 (1959) (where the defendant had fired the employee for not giving false testimony). The court held that the dismissal was in breach of public policy and that the conventional power of dismissal-at-will could not be exercised for such a reason. It is almost certain that an Irish court would apply the same principle to the exercise of the employer's power of dismissal upon reasonable notice. In *Nees* v. *Hocks* 536 P 2d 512 (1975) the plaintiff was discharged for sitting upon a jury. The court held that the power of dismissal at will was subordinate to public policy, and could not be exercised for illegitimate reasons.
482. [2006] 17 ELR 137.

VII. Remedies for Wrongful Dismissal

A. Quantifying Damages

171. The mode of calculating damages follows from the right of the employer to dismiss on notice. Since an employer may lawfully terminate the relationship on giving reasonable notice, it follows that the measure of damages is what the employee would have received if proper notice had been given. In assessing damages the court must 'consider what the position would have been if his old employment had run its full course'. In *Lavarack* v. *Woods of Colchester*[483] the plaintiff was dismissed in 1965; the contract was due to expire in 1967. The court held that the measure of damages is what the employee would have earned if the employer had employed him for the period that he was required to employ him, the 'run-off period'. This was two years:

First, the court has to consider what the position would have been if his old employment had run its full course. It must calculate the sums which he might reasonably have expected to receive in his old employment. Secondly, the court has to consider what the plaintiff has done since his dismissal. It is his duty to act reasonably in mitigation of damages. If he has acted reasonably and obtained new employment, the court must calculate the sums which he has received for his work in his new employment during the run-off period.

In *Dooley* v. *Great Southern Hotels*[484] an employee was wrongfully summarily dismissed without being given the six months' notice to which he was entitled. The High Court held that his notice period represented his entitlement for wrongful dismissal: 'he was not given the requisite six months' notice. This was undoubtedly a breach of contract but one which entitles him damages amounting to six months gross salary.'

B. No Damages for Distress and Loss of Esteem

172. An employee who suffers wrongful dismissal may also suffer psychological distress, loss of self-esteem or depression through the withdrawal of employment. The general common law doctrine is that damages may not be awarded for the distress, or injured feelings generated by a wrongful dismissal. The leading authority is *Addis* v. *Gramophone Co. Ltd*[485] where Lord Lorborne LC stated:

> If there be a dismissal without notice the employer must pay an indemnity; but that indemnity cannon include compensation either for the injured feelings of the servant, or for the loss he may sustain from the fact that his having been dismissed of itself makes it more difficult for him to obtain fresh employment.

---

483. [1967] 1 QB 278.
484. High Court, 27 July 2001. *Nerney* v. *Thomas Crosbie Holdings* [2013] IEHC 127.
485. [1909] AC 488.

The *Addis* principle continues to represent the law in Ireland and England. In *Johnson* v. *Unisys Ltd*[486] the House of Lords held that Lord Lorborne's statement in *Addis* continued to represent the legal position. The *Addis* principle was confirmed by the Irish High Court. It was stated in *Pickering* v. *Microsoft* that 'damages for the manner of dismissal are confined to those damages to which an employee would be entitled for the notice period and do not include damages for the manner of a dismissal'.[487]

The principal reason for the existence of the rule in the context of wrongful dismissal is a corollary of the elementary rule that the loss must be caused by some breach of contract. But in the case of wrongful dismissal there is no nexus between the loss and the breach of contract. The breach of contract is the not giving the required notice. But that is not what causes the psychological damage. The cause of the distress is the breach of an expectation of keeping one's job. But an employer has a common law entitlement to withdraw employment on giving notice. The loss flows from something that the defendant is *entitled* to do. Once cannot recover damages where another does something that he or she is entitled to do.

C. The Duty to Mitigate

173. A dismissed employee is obliged to mitigate his loss by seeking alternative employment.[488] An employee who is wrongfully dismissed is not entitled to sit in the sun, and allow damages to accumulate. Reasonable self-reliance is expected. An employee must diligently seek suitable alternative employment.[489] Where an employee fails to mitigate, the amount which the employee would have earned if he had mitigated, is deducted from the damages award.[490]

D. Deduction for Taxation

174. On working out to what the employee is entitled by way of loss of earnings the court must make a deduction for what the employee would have had to pay by way of income tax on those earnings. Otherwise the employee would be better off having been dismissed than staying in work. In *British Transport Commission* v. *Gourley*[491] Lord Goddard CJ, rejecting the suggestion that damages should be paid net of tax, said:

> I cannot see on what principle of justice the defendants should be called upon to pay the plaintiff more than he would have received than if he had been able

---

486. [1999] 1 All ER 834.
487. [2006] 17 ELR 65.
488. *Lavarack* v. *Woods* [1967] 1 QB 278.
489. *Bruce* v. *Calder* [1895] 2 QB 253.
490. *Lavarack* v. *Woods* [1967] 1 QB 278.
491. [1956] AC 185.

to carry on his duties … Damages which have to be paid for personal injuries are not punitive still less are they a reward. They are simply compensation.

The principle in *Gourley* was endorsed in Irish law in *Glover* v. *BLN.*[492]

One problem with this principle is that it risks double taxation. The plaintiff is also subject to taxation on the sum which he obtains by way of damages for wrongful dismissal. Section 123 of the Taxes Consolidation Act 1997 subjects to income tax '*any payment made* in consequence of, or otherwise in connection with, *the termination of* the holding of an office or *employment*'. This is subject to an exemption of €10,160 which is not taxable.[493] In order to avoid over-taxation (being subjected to income tax under the *Gourley* principle *and* income tax under section 123) the Supreme Court in *Glover* v. *BLN* held that the *Gourley* principle should only be applied to the exempt sum of €10,160.[494]

E. Specific Performance

175. The common law position is that specific performance of a contract of employment is never permissible: *De Francesco* v. *Barnum.*[495] This view is justified on the ground that it would be oppressive to compel an employer to re-employ a person with whom his relationship had broken down. This principle has been followed in Irish law.

While there is no instance where such an order has been made, it has been commonly said that the conventional rule against specific performance may not be absolute in Irish law. In *Glover* v. *BLN*[496] Walsh J expressed reservations about the pro-employer bias of the rule disallowing reinstatement. In *Phelan* v. *Bic (Ireland) Ltd*[497] the High Court suggested that, in cases where the manner of an employee's dismissal was particularly outrageous, a court might order specific performance.[498]

F. The Dismissal Injunction

176. A very commonly used anti-dismissal remedy in Irish law is the dismissal injunction: an order suspending the effect of the dismissal until the ground of dismissal has been found to be lawful at a full trial, or until the dismissal has been procedurally lawfully implemented.

---

492. [1973] IR 432.
493. S. 201 (1)(a) Tax Consolidation Act 1997.
494. These principles were applied in *Nerney* v. *Thomas Crobie Holdings* [2013] IEHC 127.
495. (1890) 45 Ch D 430.
496. [1973] IR 388.
497. [1997] 8 ELR 208.
498. *Carroll* v. *Bus Atha Cliath* [2005] 4 IR 184; *Ryan* v. *ESB* [2013] IEHC 126.

The injunction is often when the employer is alleged to have failed to comply with the procedure regulating dismissal.[499] The injunction prevents the employer from dismissing without properly observing the procedure, and forces the employer to convene a second hearing. This has the advantage that, should the employee at the renewed hearing make a good defence, his effective chance of having the dismissal reversed may be increased. For instance, the plaintiff in *Philip Burke* v. *Independent Colleges Limited*[500] had been a senior manager in the private third level college. He had been dismissed in breach of the requirement in his contract that the process be approved by the entire board. He was granted an injunction directing the employer to rescind dismissal until it had complied with the contractual process, and the dismissal considered by the entire board.

Where it is alleged that the dismissal has been taken for an illegal reason the injunction prevents the dismissal taking effect until the trial. This will keep the relationship alive and the plaintiff entitled to wages pending the trial of action.[501] If at the trial it is found that the dismissal is substantively unjust (the dismissal, for instance, is on a ground not permitted by the contract) the court may reinstate the plaintiff. The combination of the specific performance after trial and the interlocutory injunction before trial gives the unjustly dismissed employee in Ireland a far superior remedy than the original common law remedy: damages subject to the duty to mitigate. Where, on the other hand, an injunction has been obtained the employee suffers no loss of continuity of income.

Two conditions must be established in order to obtain such a mandatory injunction. The first is the existence of a: 'strong and clear case' that the employer has not acted in accordance with the contractual process. In *Lingham* v. *HSE*[502] it was said that an order requiring the employer of a dismissed employee to comply with his contractual obligations was a mandatory injunction. In the case of a mandatory rather than negative injunction the test is whether there is a strong case. it followed that in this case the plaintiff was required to show a strong case that the defendant had acted illegally in law and fact:

> In substance what the plaintiff/appellant is seeking is a mandatory interlocutory injunction and it is well established that the ordinary test of a fair case to be tried is not sufficient to meet the first leg of the test for the grant of an interlocutory injunction where the injunction sought is in effect mandatory. In such a case it is necessary for the applicant to show at least that he has a strong case.

The second condition is to show that the balance of convenience favours granting the injunction. This means that the cost to the employee of not being granted the order must outweigh the cost to the employer of granting the order. This will usually

---

499. *Sheerin* v. *AIB* High Court, *Irish Times*, 12 March 2005; *Devine* v. *EBS Irish Times*, High Court, 24 June 2005; *Costello* v. *Cadburys* High Court, *Irish Times*, 21 July 2006; *Bergin* v. *Galway Clinic* [2007] IEHC 386.
500. [2011] 22 ELR 169.
501. *Evans* v. *IRFB Services* [2005] 2 ILM 358; *Carroll* v. *Bus Atha Cliath* [2005] 4 IR 184; *Ryan* v. *ESB* [2013] IEHC 126.
502. [2006] 17 ELR 137.

favour the employee. (In *Burke's* case the plaintiff's interest in being able to persuade the Board to retain him (with the possibility that the board might re-consider the case) outweighed the burden on the employer involved in hearing the employee.)

Chapter 10. The Unfair Dismissals Acts 1977–2007

177. Concurrent with the wrongful dismissal remedy is the statutorily created remedy of unfair dismissal, constituted by the Unfair Dismissals Acts 1977–2007. The effect of these Acts is to massively reduce the employer's right to dismiss on notice. In place of the general right to dismiss on notice, there is substituted a limited entitlement to dismiss which may be exercised only on one of a restricted set of grounds: Section 6(4) of the Unfair Dismissals Acts 1977–2007.

These Acts largely supersede the common law protection against dismissal. The common law remedy continues to provide a role where the applicant is not eligible to claim the Unfair Dismissals Acts 1977–2007, or where the common law remedy is superior to that under the Unfair Dismissals Acts 1977–2007.

§1. CONDITIONS FOR ENTITLEMENT TO CLAIM UNFAIR DISMISSAL

178. For a claimant to be able to be eligible to use the Unfair Dismissals Acts 1977–2007 he or she must be in a position to show that he or she is an 'employee'; that the contract of employment is enforceable; that 'dismissal' which corresponds to the definition in section 1 of the legislation has occurred. In addition, it must be shown that the employee has accumulated the required 'one year's continuous service' with the employer as required by section 2(1)(a); and that he or she does not fall within any of the excluded categories of employee to whom the legislation does not apply.

I. 'Dismissal'

179. The definition of 'dismissal' for the purpose of the Unfair Dismissals Act 1977 (as amended) is structured to include three modes of termination of an employment relationship: (i) the direct termination by an employer of the contract of employment; (ii) constructive dismissal; and (iii) non-renewal of a fixed-term contract of employment.

A. Unambiguous Words of Dismissal

180. The first of the three forms of termination included in section 1 is defined as occurring in circumstances involving direct dismissal: 'the termination by his employer of the employee's contract of employment with the employer, whether prior notice of the termination was or was not given to the employee'.

Dismissal will be legally effective as soon as unambiguous words of dismissal are used. In *Willoughby* v. *CF Capital*[503] an employer and employee were in the course of negotiating the possibility of the employee's early retirement. The employer by

---

503. [2011] IRLR 198.

clerical error in correspondence described the employee as having been dismissed. The employee responded by taking proceedings for dismissal. The employer responded by saying that the statement was an error and that he ought to have been allowed the chance to correct the mistake. The argument was rejected. The threshold is crossed as soon as unambiguous words are used.

B. Refusal to Permit Employee Re-entry after an Ineffective Resignation

181. There will be a dismissal where the employer insists on implementing a resignation which is itself legally ineffective. A resignation may be regarded as ineffective if a reasonable analysis of the act indicates that the resignation was the result of a 'heat of the moment' loss of self-control and not really intended.[504] In *O'Callaghan* v. *Quinnsworth*[505] the claimant who had been aggressively criticised over her work performance said 'I am leaving', and walked out. Within a few hours her husband had contacted the branch manager inquiring about her position. Later the employer sent Mrs O'Callaghan her social insurance card and made it clear that it understood her as having resigned. The EAT held that it was disingenuous to treat her as having resigned. Her purported resignation was made in the heat of the moment, and was clearly not intended. The active force in the process was the employer.

C. Resignation Induced by Duress

182. An employer may be held to have dismissed an employee who, under duress, tenders a formal resignation. In *Flood* v. *Regency Fare Ltd*[506] the employee worked for a Dublin café, was alleged to have pilfered food products. It was put to the claimant that she could either resign, or that the police would be called. She was given a piece of paper, and wrote on it as instructed. The EAT held that the resignation was not voluntary, but had been induced by the employer, so that she had, technically, been dismissed.

D. Non-renewal of a Fixed-term Contract

183. A fourth form of dismissal is the non-renewal of a fixed-term contract. Section 1 of the Unfair Dismissals Act 1977 includes within the definition of dismissal the expiry of a fixed-term contract without that contract being renewed. If this had not been included in the definition of 'dismissal' an employer would have an easy means of evasion: letting go employees hired on fixed term contracts would be legally analysed as termination 'by operation of law' and not 'dismissal'. For this reason section 1 was drafted in order to make non-renewal a species of dismissal.

---

504. *Sovereign House Security* v. *Savage* [1989] IRLR 115.
505. EAT [1978] UD 68/1978.
506. EAT [1988] UD 1036/1988.

Section 1 only applies in the case of a 'fixed-term contract'. In practice, one of the most common fixed term contracts is the contract for a certain period with a provision for earlier determination on notice; for instance, a fixed term contract for three years which is also determinable by either side on three months' notice. This is a hybrid; both fixed term and determinable earlier. Is this a fixed term contract? Is the non-renewal of such a contract a 'dismissal' caught by section 1? If it is not, an employer would have a convenient technique for avoiding the Unfair Dismissals Acts 1977–2007: employing workers under hybrid clauses. Non-renewal of such contracts would not constitute the expiry of a 'fixed term contract' (section 1) and would therefore not constitute a dismissal. In *Dixon* v. *BBC*[507] the English Court of Appeal, overturning a previous decision[508] which had held that such a contract was not a fixed-term contract for the purpose of unfair dismissals legislation, ruled that a fixed-term contract with provision for determination on earlier notice must be regarded as a fixed-term contract. If a contract with provision for earlier determination on notice was not read as a fixed-term contract the result would be that the non-renewal of such a contract would not be regarded as a dismissal, and could be used by employers as a method for avoiding the legislation. In order to prevent this outcome the Court of Appeal held that – in order to prevent evasion of the legislation– a contract with provision for earlier termination was still a fixed-term contract.

The English interpretation of 'fixed term contract' has been followed by the Irish EAT in *O'Mahony* v. *TCD*.[509] Here, the claimant had entered into a contract with Trinity College Dublin for three years ending on 31 December 1994. The contract also included the phrase: 'the contract will be terminable by three months' notice from either side'. The EAT, relying on *BBC* v. *Dixon*,[510] rejected the argument that a fixed term contract with a proviso for earlier determination could not be a fixed-term contract.

However, an employer may avoid the provisional liability for non-renewal of a fixed-term contract created by section 1, by availing of the fixed-term waiver contract under section 2(2)(b). Section 2(2)(b) provides that the non-renewal of a fixed term contract may be immunized from scrutiny under the Unfair Dismissals Acts 1977–2007 where the parties enter into a fixed-term contract which is (a) in writing, (b) which is signed by the employer and employee, and (c) which provides that the Act will not apply to a dismissal consisting only of the expiry of the contract. There is no dismissal:

> where the employment was under a contract of employment for a fixed term … and the dismissal consisted only of the expiry of the term without its being renewed under the said contract or the cesser of the purpose and the contract is in writing, was signed by or on behalf of the employer and by the employee and provides that this Act shall not apply to a dismissal consisting only of the expiry or cesser aforesaid.

---

507. [1979] ICR 281.
508. *BBC* v. *Ioannou* [1975] ICR 267.
509. [1998] 9 ELR 16.
510. [1979] ICR 281.

However, section 2(2)(b) is strictly construed. The exemption will only apply when the conditions to its operation have been scrupulously adhered to. In *Sheehan* v. *Dublin Tribune*[511] the contract was signed by both parties, and provided '[i]t is fully understood that on termination of this contractual arrangement you shall have no claim on the company arising from the termination of contract'. The EAT held that the section 2(2)(b) formula – the Unfair Dismissals Act, 1977 shall not apply to a dismissal consisting of the expiry or cessation of the contract – was mandatory. Accordingly, the immunity did not operate.

An important limit on the use of fixed term waiver clauses was introduced by the Unfair Dismissals (Amendment) Act, 1993[512] (as amended in 2007).[513] This proviso to section 2(2)(b) applies (i) where a fixed-term contract having expired, the parties, within three months, enter into a subsequent fixed-term contract with a waiver clause; (ii) the second contract is not renewed; (iii) the purpose of the entry into the second contract was the avoidance of liability under the 1977 Act.

The section 2(2)(b) proviso was applied in *Cahill* v. *Teagasc*.[514] The claimant, who had previously worked under an indefinite contract, was asked to sign a fixed-term waiver contract to last between January 1993 and September 1993. He was then asked to enter into a second fixed-term waiver contract to last between September 1993 and September 1994. That second fixed-term contract was not renewed. The EAT held that the second fixed-term contract was entered into for the purpose of avoidance of liability. The change from indefinite to fixed term could only be rationalized on the basis that the employer had adopted legal advice that the use of fixed-term contracts provided a means of expanding the grounds for terminating an employment relationship. In *Brennan* v. *Board of Management of Rosses Community School*[515] the claimant worked from 4 October 2006 to 4 June 2007 and 27 August 2007 to June 2008. The second fixed-term contract was not renewed. The employee's argument, that the section 2(2)(b) proviso applied, was rejected. The use of the second fixed-term contract was 'not wholly or partly connected with the avoidance of liability under the Act' as provided for in section 2(2)(b). Here a Department of Education circular prevented full-time employment for economic reasons. This was why the School had entered into the fixed-term contracts.

E. Constructive Dismissal

184. Section 1 includes constructive dismissal within the definition of dismissal:

['Dismissal' includes] the termination by the employee of his contract of employment with his employer, whether prior notice of the termination was or

---

511. [1992] ELR 239.
512. S. 3(2)(b).
513. S. 25 of the Protection of Employees (Exceptional Collective Redundancies and Related Matters) Act 2007.
514. [1996] ELR 215.
515. EAT [2008] UD 618/2008.

was not given to the employer, in circumstances in which, because of the conduct of the employer, the employee was or would have been entitled, or it was or would have been reasonable for the employee, to terminate the contract of employment without giving prior notice of the termination to the employer.

The burden of showing that there was in fact constructive dismissal a is a high one, requiring, according to one formulation, proof that the employer's conduct falls outside the 'normal remit' of workplace culture.[516] An alternative test asks whether an employer conducts himself or his affairs 'so unreasonably that the employee cannot fairly be expected to tolerate it any longer and justifies the employee leaving'.[517]

The statutory definition of constructive dismissal requires that it must be 'reasonable' for the employee to resign. It is not 'reasonable' if there is an alternative means of redress. In a large number of determinations, employees have failed in constructive dismissal claims where they have not invoked internal grievance procedures. Employees' conduct in resigning without invoking such procedures makes it unreasonable for them to resign at that point. The general principle is that 'unless there are compelling reasons to the contrary agreed grievance procedures must be followed'.[518] In *Gilsenan* v. *County Meath VEC*[519] the EAT held that 'except in very limited circumstances [the employee] must exhaust all alternative remedies. The employee must give the employer an opportunity to deal with his concerns.'

II. One-year's Continuous Service

185. Section 2(1)(a) of the Unfair Dismissals Act 1977 provides that the Act shall not apply to: 'an employee (other than a person referred to in section 4 of this Act) who is dismissed, who, at the date of his dismissal, had less than one year's continuous service with the employer who dismissed him'.

There are two conditions here: 'continuity' and 'service'. The first is 'continuity'. Continuity of employment refers to an interval of time between the time that the employee was hired and the time that the employee was dismissed. The employee must have accumulated a continuous block of more than one year. The second concept is service: within a continuous block of at least one year the employee must also have accumulated 52 weeks of 'service' or work.

Section 2(4) provides that the concepts of continuity, and of service, are determined in accordance with the provisions of the First Schedule of the Minimum Notice and Terms of Employment Act 1973.

---

516. *Murphy* v. *Dalkia* EAT, 27 Apr. 2007.
517. *Hynes* v. *Westwood Golf Club*, EAT, 3 May 2006.
518. *Moore* v. *Dunnes Stores* EAT [2009] UD173/2009.
519. EAT [2010] UD 168/2010.

A. Continuity of Employment

186. Paragraph 1 of the First Schedule of the Minimum Notice and Terms of Employment Act 1973 regulates 'continuity'. This provides that 'the service of an employee in his employment shall be deemed to be continuous unless that service is terminated by— (*a*) the dismissal of the employee by his employer, or (*b*) the employee voluntarily leaving his employment'.

Since a 'dismissal' breaks continuity, an employer could avoid the 1977 Act simply by dismissing the employee when he or she approaches the one year qualifying point, and afterwards re-employing him or her. In order to prevent this paragraph 6 of the First Schedule provides that the dismissal of an employee followed by his *immediate re-employment* shall not break continuity: 'the continuous service of an employee shall not be broken by the dismissal of the employee followed by the immediate re-employment of the employee'. 'Immediately' is not construed literally.[520] In *Kenny* v. *Tegral*[521] the employee's contract of employment was terminated on 20 September 2003. He was re-employed on 15 October 2003. The EAT applying the principle that 'immediate' should not be construed literally, held that re-employment within three weeks and three days was 'immediate'. Accordingly, there was no break in continuity. In *Tomasiak* v. *W Cummmins Plasterers*[522] the employer had sent a text message saying that there was no more work. Three weeks later the employee was re-employed. The EAT held that there had been no break in continuity.

Paragraph 6 only maintains continuity where dismissal is followed by 'immediate' re-employment. Does that allow an employer to avoid the legislation by dismissing short of one year and then re-employing *non-immediately*? Section 2(5) of the Unfair Dismissal Act 1977 closes this loophole. Section 2(5) of the 1977 Act provides that the dismissal of an employee followed by the employee's re-employment within six months shall not break continuity where the purpose the dismissal was the avoidance of liability under the Act.

B. One Year's 'Service'

187. Paragraphs 8–13 of the Minimum Notice and Terms of Employment Act, 1973 constitute the principal source for determining the period of 'service' of an employee:

> 10. If an employee is absent from his employment for not more than twenty-six weeks between consecutive periods of employment because of—
>
> (a) a lay-off,
> (b) sickness or injury, or

---

520. *Martin Howard v. Breton* EAT [1984] UD 486/1984.
521. [2006] 17 ELR 309.
522. EAT [2009] UD720/2009.

(c) by agreement with his employer, such period shall count as a period of service.

11. If, in any week or part of a week, an employee is absent from his employment because he was taking part in a strike in relation to the trade or business in which he is employed, that week shall not count as a period of service.

Paragraph 10 recognizes periods of absence from work of less than 26 weeks which either are by agreement with the employer, or due to sickness, as periods of 'constructive' service. Thus, periods of study leave or bereavement leave granted by an employer are counted as 'service'.

'Lay off' is defined as occurring where 'an employee's employment ceases by reason of the employer being unable to provide the work for which the employee was employed to do, and it is reasonable in the circumstances for the 'employer to believe that the cessation of employment will not be permanent, and the employer gives notice to that effect to the employee prior to the cessation'.[523] In *Driscoll* v. *United Fish Industries Ltd*[524] the employee was a trawler employee. In the first season he worked from 3 January 2002 until 25 April 2002. In the second season he worked from 8 February 2003 until 14 April 2003. The Tribunal held that that the claimant was laid off on both 25 April 2002 and 14 April 2003: on both occasions work was suspended on the assumption that it would be resumed in the next fishing season. Accordingly he could include six months of that period in the 'computable weeks' calculation. By contrast there was no lay-off in *Doyle* v. *Morelli*.[525] The claimant had worked during her school holidays from June 2003 to October 2003. Under pressure from her parents she left in order to resume her schooling. She was re-employed in June 2004. She was then dismissed. The claimant argued that she had the required service since the period was one of lay-off. The Tribunal held that the period was not one in which 'the employer was unable to provide the work for which the employee was employed to do'. Here, the employee had withdrawn for non-economic reasons. Accordingly there was no 'lay-off' during which the employee was deemed to be at work.

§2. The Legal Conditions for a Lawful Dismissal Under the Unfair Dismissals Acts 1977–2007

I. The Standards Regulating Dismissal: the General Scheme

188. Section 6(1) of the Unfair Dismissals Act 1977 provides:

Subject to the provisions of this section, the dismissal of an employee shall be deemed, for the purposes of this Act, to be an unfair dismissal unless, having

---

523. By a complicated chain of cross-reference the 1977 Act requires that one year's service be calculated according to the rules in the Minimum Notice and Terms of Employment Act 1973; that Act provides that the definition of 'lay-off' is that which is constituted by s. 11 of the Redundancy Payments Act, 1967.
524. EAT [2005] UD310/2005.
525. EAT [2005] UD 523/2005.

regard to all the circumstances, there were substantial grounds justifying the dismissal.

Section 6(4) of the 1977 Act goes on to provide:

> Without prejudice to the generality of subsection (1) of this section, the dismissal of an employee shall be deemed, for the purposes of this Act, not to be an unfair dismissal, if it results wholly or mainly from one or more of the following:
>
> (a) the capability, competence or qualifications of the employee for performing work of the kind which he was employed by the employer to do,
> (b) the conduct of the employee,
> (c) the redundancy of the employee, and
> (d) the employee being unable to work or continue to work in the position which he held without contravention (by him or by his employer) of a duty or restriction imposed by or under any statute or instrument made under statute.

A further condition to the legality of a dismissal subject to the Acts is imposed by section 6(7):

> Without prejudice to the generality of subsection (1) of this section, in determining if a dismissal is 'an unfair dismissal, regard may be had, if the rights commissioner, the Tribunal or the Circuit Court, as the case may be, considers it appropriate to do so (a) to the reasonableness or otherwise of the conduct (whether by act or omission) of the employer in relation to the dismissal …

The combined effect of subsections (7), (4) and (1) is that a dismissal may only be justified (i) where the findings correspond to one of the circumstances specified at paragraphs (a) to (d); (ii) where there were 'substantial grounds' supporting the findings; and (iii) where the dismissal has been administered in a manner which is 'reasonable'.

II. 'Substantial Grounds Justifying the Dismissal'

189. Section 6(1) requires that there be *substantial evidential grounds* justifying the decision to dismiss.

An approach sometimes adopted by the EAT, when resolving evidential disputes, has been to adopt 'the range of reasonable responses' standard. According to this view, it is not for the Tribunal to decide whether *it* would have made the same finding on the evidence. Rather it is merely required to decide whether the conclusion is one which a reasonable employer *could have* reached. Where the evidence suggests that a reasonable employer could have so decided, the Tribunal is obliged to uphold the dismissal, and cannot overturn the decision merely because it might have reached a different conclusion on the evidence. In *Looney* v. *Looney*[526] the claimant had been accused of pilfering Mars bars from the grocer's shop for which he worked. He disputed the finding that he had stolen the goods. The EAT declined to resolve the dispute. Instead it said that it was only required to determine whether the finding was one which a reasonable employer might have made:

> It is not for the Tribunal to seek to establish the guilt or innocence of the claimant, nor is it for the Tribunal to indicate whether we in the employer's position, would have acted [as the employer] did in his investigation or concluded as he did. To do so would be to substitute our own mind and decision for that of the employer. Our responsibility is to consider against the facts what a reasonable employer in … [the employer's] position and circumstances at that time, would have done and decided at that time, and to set this up as [the] standard …

The 'range of reasonable responses' test is an import from English law. In *Burchell* v. *British Home Stores*[527] the employee had been dismissed on grounds of fraudulent abuse of a staff discount purchasing scheme. The EAT, rejecting the employee's argument that the evidence did not support the finding, held that it was sufficient that the finding was one which a reasonable employer might make:

> First of all, there must be established by the employer the fact of that belief; that the employer did believe it. Secondly, that the employer had in his mind reasonable grounds upon which to sustain that belief … It is not relevant, as we think, that the tribunal would themselves have shared that view …

However, the English standard of review must be read in the light of its legislative background. Section 57(3) of the Employment Protection (Consolidation) Act, 1978 (the English Act being applied in *Burchell*) provided that the:

> determination of the question whether the dismissal was fair or unfair shall depend on whether the employer can satisfy the Tribunal that in the circumstances (having regard to equity and the substantial merits of the case) he acted *reasonably* in treating it as a sufficient reason for dismissing the employee.

However, there is a difference between the employer's reasonableness standard in the English legislation, and the higher 'substantial grounds justifying the dismissal' standard in the (Irish) 1977 Act. The Irish standard appears more exacting. 'Substantial' is higher than 'reasonable'. Section 6(1) deems a dismissal to be unfair unless the Tribunal finds that there are *substantial* grounds or evidence justifying the dismissal. It is not enough, as it is in English law, that the employer was acting *reasonably*. 'Substantial' grounds arguably means something near 'strong' or 'significant'. 'Reasonable', on the other hand, can mean something as low as merely 'plausible'.

---

526. EAT [1984] UD 843/1984.
527. [1978] IRLR 379.

III. The Reasonableness Requirement; Section 6(7)(a) of the Unfair Dismissals Act 1977

190. A further requirement in section 6(7)(a) of the Unfair Dismissals Act 1977 is that the employer act 'reasonably'. This encompasses a number of sub-principles: (a) that the decision to initiate dismissal proceedings have been preceded by prior warnings, or notice, that such conduct might result in dismissal; (b) that, where dismissal follows a finding of fact about the conduct of the employee, that the employer have carried out an investigation of reasonable depth; (c) that the disciplinary procedure have been put into motion and completed without unnecessary delay; (d) that the enquiry have been conducted without pre-judgement or bias; (e) that fair procedures have been observed during the hearing; (f) that the findings of fact be supported by the evidence; (g) that the decision to dismiss be a proportionate one.

IV. Fair Warning of Standards

191. It is unreasonable (and thus contrary to section 6(7)) for an employer to dismiss an employee for falling short of a particular standard when that employee has not been put on notice that compliance with that standard is expected. This may be particularly relevant where social standards are undergoing a process of revision. In 1996 in *Allen* v. *Dunnes Stores*[528] the claimant, an elderly security guard had been dismissed after allegedly attempting to kiss one of his co-employees, and commenting on the perfume she was wearing. The determination should be read in its historical context. The case was decided in the mid-1990s when attitudes to harassment were in transition. The Employment Appeals Tribunal observed that the employee may have been genuinely unsure whether such conduct was legitimate or not. The Tribunal concluded that there was an obligation on the employer to put in place a programme to inform, educate, and instruct its employees on the issue of sexual harassment. In *Smith* v. *Brien*[529] the claimant was dismissed for smoking marijuana. The respondent did not have a clear policy outlawing the use of marijuana and the dismissal was held unfair.

V. Compliance with Fair Procedures

192. The employer must precede any dismissal decision with an enquiry must be conducted in compliance with fair procedures. In *Gunn* v. *NCAD*[530] the Supreme Court rejected the old common law view that natural justice or fair procedures was confined to the office holder[531] and did not extend to the ordinary employee. The Supreme Court held that such status differentiation and elitism was repugnant to

---

528. [1996] ELR 203.
529. EAT [2004] UD 210/2004.
530. [1990] 2 IR 168.
531. *Ridge* v. *Baldwin* [1964] AC 40.

republican Irish constitutional values: 'The application of the rules of fair procedures does not depend upon whether the person concerned is an office-holder as distinct from being an employee of some other kind'.

The High Court and the Supreme Court have generated a body of case law on the contents of constitutional fair procedures in the context of actions for wrongful dismissal. These require: (i) that there be notice of the charge and time for preparation; (ii) that the employee be allowed the assistance of legal representation;[532] (iii) that the employee have the constitutional right of access to incriminating witness statements[533] and (iv) the right of cross-examination of incriminating witnesses.[534]

These constitutional standards are incorporated into unfair dismissals adjudication through the section 6(7) 'reasonableness' condition: an employer cannot be said to act 'reasonably' under section 6(7) if he acts unconstitutionally. Therefore compliance with the constitutional standards is part of the assessment of reasonableness.

A. The Right of Notice and Access to Witness Statements

193. The rights to access to witness statements was infringed in *Redmond* v. *Ryanair.*[535] A complaint had been made against a flight attendant alleging that she had blocked off the first two rows of a Ryanair flight between Durham and Dublin. The employee was summoned to a meeting, but she was not informed of the charges. She was not given copies of the witness statements and the names of the witnesses were erased. The Tribunal held that fair procedures required a 'reasonable means of defence' and that 'reasonable' included 'being furnished with a copy of the evidence which reflected on her good name and the right to cross-examine his accusers'. The Tribunal stressed that it was a fundamental principle that the claimant be provided with an effective right of cross-examination of incriminating witnesses.

B. The Rule against Bias

194. The rule against bias must be observed. The dismissal process should be administered without the involvement of a person affected by bias or prejudice against the employee. In *Kelly* v. *Dundalk FC*[536] the dismissal decision was taken by the CEO of the club. The CEO and the employee, who had been employed as director of marketing, had been involved in a romantic relationship which had just terminated. The decision-maker was held to have a 'personal interest in the matter contrary to the *nemo judex* principle'.

---

532. *Maher* v. *Irish Permanent* [1998] 9 ELR 77.
533. *Cassidy* v. *Shannon Castle Banquets* [2000] ELR 248.
534. *Ibid.*
535. EAT, 17 October 2006.
536. EAT [2009] UD 39/2009.

VI. Consistency in Dealing with Similar Cases

195. The consistency principle requires consistency with previous disciplinary precedent. In *Post Office* v. *Fennell*[537] the employee was summarily dismissed for assaulting a co-employee in a works canteen. In previous similar cases, the employer had not used the ultimate sanction of dismissal. In overturning the dismissal the English High Court held an employer acted unreasonably where he dismissed an employee for conduct which he had treated more leniently in the past. In *Honeywell International Technologies Ltd* v. *The Rights Commissioner*[538] the employer administered a no-smoking policy. The claimant had been caught smoking and was dismissed. In previous incidents involving other employees a lesser sanction had been imposed. The dismissal was held illegal on grounds of inconsistency.

VII. Proportionality

196. One of the key principles regulating the reasonableness of dismissal is compliance with the principle of proportionality. The proportionality principle is a component of the general section 6(7)(a) principle of reasonableness. Proportionality is also a condition of the 'substantial grounds for dismissal' requirement in section 6(1). An employer does not have substantial grounds for dismissal if some other sanction would have sufficed.

In *McCurdy* v. *Adelphi*[539] the claimant, a cinema usher, disregarded the manager's instruction not to take time off to watch the Ireland v. Malta World Cup qualifying game on television, and was dismissed. The Tribunal held that the employer's response was disproportionate, and that a day's suspension without pay would have been a more appropriate response.

The most common ground of dismissal in the period 2009–2011 has been redundancy. The requirement of proportionality in the context of redundancy means that an employer lacks proportion if he dismisses on grounds of redundancy where lesser alternatives are available. This principle has its origins in the English case, *Williams* v. *Compair Maxim Ltd*[540] which laid down the requirement that the employer should 'see whether instead of dismissing an employee he could offer him alternative employment'. This principle has been adopted in Irish law. In *Caroline Dower* v. *Waterford News*[541] the EAT emphasized that the employer would act disproportionately if he failed to adopt alternative feasible alternatives such as reduced hours or wage reductions:

> The loss of one's employment has a significant financial and personal impact on an individual and in deciding on the appropriate changes to make in a workplace when faced with an economic downturn the employer must conduct itself

---

537. [1981] IRLR 221.
538. EAT [2007] UD1090/2005.
539. [1992] ELR 14.
540. [1982] IRLR 83.
541. EAT [2010] UD 151/2010.

in a reasonable fashion ... any reasonable employer would consult with all employees whose employment is potentially affected; would invite representations and would consider all reasonable alternatives ... Consideration [should be given to] ... options such as pay reduction hour reduction and voluntary redundancies.

However, the proportionality condition is sometimes mitigated by the doctrine of 'reasonable responses'.[542] In *Schaff* v. *Boots Retail (Ireland) Ltd*[543] the claimant was alleged to have embezzled some nail polish from her employer. The Tribunal, despite the relatively minor nature of the offence, again deferred to the employer, applying the 'range of reasonable responses' test:

the task of the Tribunal in determining any case before them is not to consider what sanction the Tribunal might impose but rather to determine whether the employers reaction and the sanction imposed lay within the range of responses which a reasonable employer might make.

The range of reasonable responses standard suggests that a decision to dismiss will be upheld if it is a response which a hypothetical reasonable employer might plausibly adopt. Again it is arguable that the test is not appropriate in the context of the Irish law. Section 6(1) of the 1977 Act requires that the employer have 'substantial grounds'. 'Substantial grounds' seems to suggest that it is not enough that the justification is merely 'reasonable' or just plausible. The EAT has expressed concerns about whether the range of reasonable responses standard was part of Irish law. In *Brennan* v. *Carlow IT*[544] the employee a security guard at a university had shut, and alarmed, the Library while a reader was still present. The employer defended the proportionality of the dismissal on the ground that it fell within the range of reasonable responses. The EAT doubted whether this doctrine was the proper approach in Ireland.

§3. Redress for Unfair Dismissal

197. Three remedies are constituted by the Unfair Dismissals Acts 1977–2007: the remedies of re-instatement, re-engagement, and compensation. In practice, compensation is the most common remedy, with re-engagement and re-instatement very much marginal remedies. In 2010 the Employment Appeals Tribunal awarded compensation (amounting to €3,485,898) in 217 cases. Reinstatement was ordered in six cases and re-engagement was ordered in three cases.[545]

---

542. In *Fleming* v. *Horseware* EAT [2001] UD60/2001 the EAT held: 'The Tribunal finds that the respondent company's suspicions and beliefs were well founded and their actions were reasonable in the circumstances. It is well established that the test to be applied is the test of reasonableness in the actions of the respondent company.'
543. EAT [2006] UD328/2005.
544. EAT [2011] UD 281/2011.
545. *Employment Appeals Tribunal Annual Report 2010.*

I. Reinstatement

198. The employee who has been unfairly dismissed will often want life to return to normal and to return to his employment. Section 7 of the Unfair Dismissals Act 1977 provides two remedies under which the employee may obtain the recovery of his pervious employment: reinstatement and re-engagement.

The reinstatement order is the most superior of the remedies. It treats the dismissal as void, so that the employee is regarded, for purposes of remuneration, benefits, pension, or seniority, as never having been dismissed. In other words, the employee is not just entitled to his job back. He is entitled to all that he would have earned if he had not been dismissed.

In practice, reinstatement is rarely ordered. It is usually confined to cases where the employer has been guilty of groundlessly dismissing the employee, and where the employee has been blameless. In most cases the employer will have acted genuinely, even if the process of dismissal has been illegally administered. Occasionally, however, an employer will have acted without any good reason at all. In such cases the Tribunal has sometimes been prepared to punish the employer by ordering the employee's reinstatement. In *Maher* v. *Greyhound Waste Disposal*[546] the employee was sacked in favour of a cheaper non-national. The dismissed employee had done nothing to merit dismissal. The Tribunal held that the appropriate remedy was reinstatement. In *Bagge* v. *Vodafone*[547] a whistle blower who had exposed fraud committed by Vodafone on its customers was dismissed. The employee had done nothing wrong and the employer had no good reason for dismissal. The Tribunal ordered reinstatement. These decisions seem to mean that the employer cannot inflict arbitrary dismissal and then buy his way out by paying compensation. The Tribunal may order reinstatement.

II. Re-engagement

199. Re-engagement, by contrast, does not necessarily treat the interval between dismissal and re-commencement of employment as a period when the dismissal was ineffective. Section 7(1) (b) defines re-engagement as the re-employment of the dismissed worker either in the position 'which he held immediately before his dismissal or in a different position which would be reasonably suitable for him on such terms and conditions as are reasonable'.

Re-engagement is the more flexible of the remedies. The key words are 'on such terms and conditions as are reasonable'. This phrase allows the Tribunal flexibility: the flexibility to mould a remedy which gives the employee his old job back while building in a period of suspension without pay. It achieves this by delaying the point of re-engagement. This delayed re-employment can be punitive. It restores the relationship, while at the same time permitting the Tribunal to register its disapproval of the employee's contributory misconduct. The interval is treated, in effect, as a

---

546. *Irish Times*, 3 February 2006.
547. *Irish Examiner,* 28 March 2012.

period of suspension without pay.[548] In *Lewis* v. *Dunne Stores*[549] the employee, a security guard was dismissed in November 2002. The dismissal was held to be unlawful. However the employee, who had been aggressive to customers. had been guilty of contributory misconduct. In order to accommodate this contributory misconduct, the Tribunal ordered that he be treated as re-engaged from July 2003. The intervening period was treated as a period of suspension without pay.[550]

III. Compensation; 'Financial Loss Attributable to the Dismissal'

200. The principal remedy ordered in cases where unfair dismissal is established is that of compensation. The jurisdiction is detailed in section 7(1)(c). Compensation is awarded for 'financial loss'. The amount of the compensation may not exceed an amount equivalent to two years' earnings:

> if the employee incurred any financial loss attributable to the dismissal, payment to him by the employer of such compensation in respect of the loss not exceeding in amount 104 weeks remuneration … as is just and equitable having regard to all the circumstances

The only category of loss which is compensated by the Act is 'financial loss'. By definition, non-financial loss – emotional loss, loss of self-esteem, humiliation, or depression – are not compensatable. Section 7(1) (c) of the Unfair Dismissals Acts prevents the employment Appeals Tribunal from awarding compensation for anything other than 'financial loss'. This was confirmed in *Quigley* v. *Complex Tooling.*[551]

Section 7(3) defines 'financial loss' as including 'any actual loss and any estimated prospective loss of income attributable to the dismissal'. Loss of income is divided into 'actual' loss of income, and 'estimated prospective' loss of income. 'Actual loss' of income compensates the employee for loss of income between the point of dismissal and the date of hearing: loss is calculated (i) by assessing the employee's earnings, if any, during this period, and (ii) deducting this from the earnings which the employee would have made if he had remained in employment.

'Prospective loss of income' is assessed by estimating (i) the period for which the original employment was likely to continue, and the income likely to have been generated between the date of the determination and the date on which that employment would have determined,[552] and (ii) deducting from that sum, the income (if any) that the employee is likely to earn in alternative work. In *Graham* v.

---

548. See e.g. *McDonald* v. *Des Gibney Ltd* EAT [1985] UD 329/1985; *Lynch* v. *Sunbeam* EAT [1977] UD 20/1977.
549. EAT [2003] UD 597/2003.
550. *Crawford* v. *Donegal Meat Processors* [2003] ELR 329: employee contributed to dismissal by uncertified sick leave; order that re-engagement deemed to have taken place three months prior to determination by the EAT.
551. [2005] IEHC 71.
552. See e.g. *McDermot* v. *Allied Irish Banks* EAT [1978] UD 166/1978; *Raou* v. *Civil Aviation Authority* [1994] IRLR 241.

Portroe Stevedores[553] the claimant was dismissed following an incident at a Christmas party. The claimant was earning €70, 000 per year. He was likely to be employed for a further eleven years until retirement. He had found employment as a taxi driver earning about €40,000 per year. The EAT calculated his future estimated loss as €330,000. Since this was in excess of the statutory maximum this was reduced to €140, 000 (two year's wages).

The assessment of these two contingencies is, as the legislation acknowledges, imprecise. In estimating the duration of future likely unemployment, the Tribunal may take into account: the period for which the employee is likely to remain unemployed by reason of illness;[554] the age of the employee as a factor which may make it more difficult to locate alternative work;[555] or the fact that the circumstances of the dismissal have stigmatized the employee.[556]

From the figure arrived at in calculating the employee's financial loss a series of deductions may then be imposed. The grounds of deduction are referred to in section paragraphs (b), (c) and (f) of section 7(2):

> (b) the extent (if any) to which the said financial loss was attributable to an action, omission or conduct by or on behalf of the employee, …
> (c) the measures (if any) adopted by the employee or, as the case may be, his failure to adopt measures, to mitigate the loss aforesaid, …
> (f) the extent to which the conduct of the employee (whether by act or omission) contributed to the dismissal.

Section 7(2)(b) permits contributory conduct to be built into the compensation order. In *Hickey* v. *Budget Travel*[557] the Tribunal found that the dismissal of the complainant (for bullying) had been procedurally unfair. On the other hand, the complainant was incontestably at fault. The Tribunal took this factor in reducing the quantum of compensation by the large percentage of 60 per cent.

Under section 7(2)(c) a deduction may be imposed to take into account a failure to mitigate.[558] In fixing the amount to be deducted in assessing the scale of deduction for failure to mitigate the usual process is (i) to identify the steps which should have been taken; (ii) to estimate the date by which such steps would have produced an alternative income; and (iii) to reduce compensation by reference to the alternative income which would have been generated.[559]

In *O'Sullivan* v. *Berkeley Court Hotel*[560] the claimant, a hotel porter, was found to have been unfairly dismissed; however, he had made no positive efforts to find alternative work, beyond asking friends if they had heard of work opportunities. The

---

553. EAT, 12 February 2008.
554. *Allen* v. *Independent Newspapers* [2002] ELR 84.
555. *Cavanagh* v. *Dunnes Stores* EAT [1994] UD 820/1994.
556. 436 *Byrne* v. *Board of Management, Scoil Mhichil Naofa* EAT [2002] UD 757/2002.
557. EAT [2003] UD 319 2003. *Sialys* v. *JC Savage Supermarket* EAT [2009] UD 50/2009: failure to take break when directed; preferring to take break when girlfriend free; no fair hearing; dismissal unfair; but compensation reduced to take account of the contributory misconduct of the employee.
558. *O'Sullivan* v. *Berkeley Court Hotel* EAT [2005] UD483/2005.
559. *Gardiner-Hill* v.. *Roland Berger Technics Ltd* [1982] IRLR 498
560. EAT [2007]UD483/2005.

claimant indicated that he intended to take out a taxi licence, but did not complete the application. Efforts to seek alternative employment were limited to asking a small number of individuals of his acquaintance if they were aware of any openings. The claimant did not apply for any actual vacancies himself.

The Tribunal held that the applicant had failed to mitigate his loss and reduced the amount he would have earned if he had made reasonable efforts to locate alternative work.

Chapter 11. The Redundancy Payments Acts 1967–2007 and the Protection of Employment Act 1977

201. Under the Redundancy Payments Acts 1967–2007 an employee who is dismissed by reason of redundancy, or who is kept on short term or is laid off is entitled to a redundancy payment.[561]

§1. THE REDUNDANCY PAYMENTS ACTS 1967–2007

I. Continuous Employment for 104 weeks

202. The employee must have been employed for a period of 104 weeks' continuous employment.[562] The requirement of continuous employment means that the employee must accumulate 104 reckonable weeks in an overall period of continuous service. Service is continuous unless it is terminated by dismissal or resignation. A week is reckonable either where the employee is at work; or absent due to illness, and where the period of absence does not exceed 26 weeks; or where the absence has been authorized by the employer.[563] However, none of the following absences, where they occur in the three-year period ending with the termination of employment, is allowable: (a) an absence in excess of 52 weeks by reason of an occupational accident or disease; (b) absence in excess of 26 continuous weeks by reason of any other illness; (c) absence by reason of lay-off by the employer;[564] (d) absence by reason of participation in a strike.[565]

II. The Definition of Redundancy

203. Redundancy is defined in section 7(2) of the Redundancy Payments Act 1967, as amended by the Redundancy Payments Act, 1971. Five grounds are recognized as constituting redundancy. The first is: (a) the fact that the employer has ceased, or intends to cease, to carry on the business for the purposes of which the employee was employed by him, or has ceased or intends to cease, to carry on that business in the place where the employee was so employed.

Part (a) refers to cases of business closure, or cases where the work location is proposed to be moved. In *Brady* v. *Donegan*[566] the employee worked on a construction site building apartments. Due to a fall in sales, the site was closed. It was held that the circumstances fell within section 7(2)(a). The phrase 'the place where the employee was employed' has been controversial. There have been two conflicting interpretations. According to one (the geographical test) of those interpretations the

---

561. S. 7 of the Redundancy Payments Act 1967.
562. Ss. 7(1)(a) and 7(5) of the Redundancy Payments Act 1967.
563. Schedule 3, para. 8, as amended by the Redundancy Payments Act 2003.
564. *Ibid.*
565. Schedule 3, para. 10, as amended by the Redundancy Payments Act 2003.
566. EAT [1980] UD 280/1980.

employee is employed at the place where he actually works, whether or not this coincides with the place where he is contractually required to work. According to the second (the contractual test), the employee is employed at the place where he might be required to work under the contract of employment.[567] However, while the issue has not been tested in Irish law, the geographical test is preferred in English law.[568]

The second ground is: (b) the fact that the requirements of that business for employees to carry out work of a particular kind in the place where he was so employed have ceased or diminished or are expected to cease or diminish.

In *Farren* v. *Lee*[569] the employee was a shop assistant in a department store. New retail practices were introduced which resulted in shop assistants being required to give less personal assistance to customers, and to work mainly at cash registers. The EAT held that there was a qualitative change in the character of the work required to be done, and that section 7(2)(b) applied. In *Limerick Health Authority* v. *Ryan*[570] Kenny J. observed that 'the kind of work, not the type of employee, is the decisive factor under para (b) of sub-section 2'. 'Work of a particular kind' is characterized both by the essential conditions under which the work is carried out, as well as by the job function itself. The claimant in *Kelliher* v. *St. James Hospital Board*[571] had been employed as a part-time nurse. The employer requested her to cease working under a part-time contract. Although there was no diminution in the need for employees to do work of the type which she previously undertook, there was a reduction in the need for employees to undertake work under 'similar [contractual] conditions'. 'Expected to cease or diminish' means *imminently* 'expected to cease or diminish'. In *Keenan* v. *The Gresham Hotel*[572] the employee, a hotel catering worker, was dismissed by her employer in light of a gloomy business prognosis. She was then re-employed, and it was only some ten months later that the need to contract finally arose. The Tribunal said:

> We think that this diminution must be expected to occur at or within a very short time after the time of the alleged redundancy, as otherwise an employer who merely expects that this requirement for employees to do work of a particular kind may diminish at some distant time in the future could greatly reduce the redundancy entitlement of such employees.

The third ground is: (c) the fact that his employer has decided to carry on the business with fewer or no employees, whether by requiring the work for which the employee had been employed (or had been doing before his dismissal) to be done by other employees or otherwise.

Part (c) is distinguished from (b) in that the cause of the reduction of employees need not be a reduction in the need of the business for employees to carry on work of a particular kind. The business may still require the original number of

---

567. *Sutcliffe* v. *Hawker Siddeley Aviation Ltd* [1973] ICR 560.
568. *High Table* v. *Horst* [1997] IRLR 513.
569. EAT [1979] UD 496/1979.
570. [1969] IR 194.
571. EAT [1977] UD 59/1977.
572. EAT [1988] UD 478/1988.

employees, but may for cost cutting reasons be forced to shed employees. In *Nolan* v. *Griffin Furniture*[573] the employer, in light of falling sales, dismissed the office secretary, and took over secretarial functions himself. Although there was no reduction in the need for work of that type to be carried out, the circumstances fell within Part (c).

The fourth and fifth grounds are: (d) the fact that his employer has decided that the work for which the employee had been employed (or had been doing before his dismissal) should henceforward be done in a different manner for which the employee is not sufficiently qualified or trained; (e) the fact that his employer has decided that the work for which the employee had been employed (or had been doing before his dismissal) should henceforward be done by a person who is also capable of doing other work for which the employee is not sufficiently qualified or trained.

Parts (d) and (e) were inserted in the Redundancy Payments Act 1971 in response to the decision of the High Court in *Limerick Health Authority* v. *Anna Ryan*.[574] There the High Court, working under the original 1967 definition of redundancy, which included only Parts (a) and (b), held that there was no redundancy when the defendant decided to replace its midwifery service with a community nurse service, employing nurses competent to act both as midwives and community nurses. There was, the High Court held, no closure of the business for the purpose for which the plaintiff had been employed; nor had the employer ceased to require employees to undertake work of the type which the employee undertook.

An employee is also entitled to a redundancy payment where he has been kept on lay-off, or on short-time for the minimum period.[575] Lay-off occurs where an employee is suspended from work on economic grounds; where the employer reasonably believes that the lay-off is temporary and the employer gives notice to that effect.[576] Short time occurs where an employee's normal hours are reduced, or where his remuneration is less than one-half and where it is reasonable for the employer to believe that the diminution in work is not permanent and notice to this effect is given to the employee.[577] An employee who has been laid off, or placed on short time, is entitled to claim redundancy payment where: (i) he has been laid off, or placed on short time, for four or more consecutive weeks or (ii) within a period of thirteen weeks the employee has been on lay-off or short time for a period of six or more weeks. Here there is no requirement that the period be consecutive.[578] However, the right to a redundancy payment on the ground of lay-off or of being put on short time does not apply where the employer responds with a counter-notice.[579] Such a counter-notice is served where the employer reasonably believes that there will follow a period of not less than 13 weeks during which the employee will not be laid off or kept on short time.

573. EAT [1980] M 7888/1980.
574. [1969] IR 194.
575. S. (7)(1) of the Redundancy Payments Act 1967.
576. S. 11(1).
577. S. 11(2).
578. S. 12 (2).
579. S. 13.

204. The amount of the redundancy payment is the calculated as follows: the product of two weeks' normal weekly remuneration multiplied by the number of years of continuous employment with the employer; plus a sum equivalent to the employee's normal weekly remuneration.[580]

§2. COLLECTIVE REDUNDANCIES

205. Council Directive 98/59 of July 20 1998 on the approximation of the Laws of the Member States Relating to Collective Redundancies is implemented in Irish law by the Protection of Employment Act 1977 as supplemented by the Protection of Employment Order 1996[581] and by the European Communities (Protection of Employment) Regulations, 2000[582] and the Protection of Employment (Exceptional Collective Redundancies) Act 2007.

I. The Conditions Activating the Consultation Duty

206. The duty of consultation is activated by the existence of a 'collective redundancy'. The term collective redundancy is made up of a combination of (i) the existence of a redundancy related dismissal affecting more than the prescribed number of employees; (ii) the fact that these workers are employed at the same establishment; (iii) the fact that the redundancies occur in any period of 30 days. Section 6(1) as amended provides:

> For the purpose of this Act, 'collective redundancies' means dismissals effected by an employer for one or more reasons not related to the individual concerned where in any period of 30 consecutive days the number of such dismissals is
>
> (a) at least 5 in an establishment normally employing more than 20 and less than 50 employees,
> (b) at least 10 in an establishment normally employing at least 50 but less than 100 employees,
> (c) at least ten per cent of the number of employees in an establishment normally employing at least 100 but less than 300 employees, and
> (d) at least 30 in an establishment normally employing 300 or more employees.
>
> (2) For the purpose of calculating the number of redundancies where the number of dismissals is at least 10 in an establishment normally employing more than 20 and less than 100 employees, terminations of a contract of employment which occur to the individual workers concerned shall be assimilated to redundancies provided there are at least 5 redundancies.

---

580. Schedule 3 of the Redundancy Payments Act 1967 as amended by s. 11 of the Redundancy Payments Act 2003.
581. SI No. 370 of 1996.
582. SI No. 488 of 2000.

(3) In this section 'establishment' means an employer or a company or a subsidiary company or a company within a group of companies which can independently effect redundancies.

A redundancy based dismissal may exceed the prescribed 10 per cent in one unit of the overall business, while falling beneath the threshold by reference to the overall organization. In the *Rockfon*[583] case, the business Rockwol A/S had a workforce of over 300 distributed among a number of subsidiary companies. As a matter of corporate organization all dismissal decisions had to be sanctioned by a centralized personnel department. One of the subsidiary companies, Rockfon, dismissed on grounds of redundancy 24 employees out of its workforce of 162. Rockwol A/S argued that the meaning of 'establishment' consisted of a corporate group as a whole, and relied upon the Danish law implementing the directive which provided that a subsidiary would only be regarded as an 'establishment' where it had 'a management which can independently effect large scale dismissals'. This was not so here, and, it was argued, the directive did not apply. The European Court of Justice held that the term 'establishment' referred to every local employment unit. It was not necessary that the unit have an independent power of ordering redundancies:

> The term 'establishment' appearing in article 1(1)(a) of Directive (75/129/EEC) must be understood as meaning, depending on the circumstances, the unit to which the workers made redundant are assigned to carry out their duties. It is not essential, in order for there to be an 'establishment', for the unit in question to be endowed with a management which can independently effect collective redundancies.

In the light of *Rockfon*, the definition of 'establishment' in the section 6(3) of the 1977 Act as a subsidiary which can 'independently effect redundancies' appears to infringe European law.

II. The Timing of the Consultation

207. Section 9 of the 1977 Act provides that 'where an employer proposes to create collective redundancies he shall … initiate consultations'. The duty is triggered by the employer 'proposing' to hold a consultation. In *Tangney* v. *Dell Products*[584] the High Court rejected the proposition that the trigger point arose when the employer was planning to make a decision which 'foreseeably or inevitably, will lead to collective redundancies'. Instead it held that the employer's obligation to begin consultations concerning collective redundancies arises 'when a strategic or

---

583. *Rockfon A/S* v. *Specialarbejderforbunet i Danmark* [1996] IRLR 168.
584. [2014] ELR 61.

commercial decision is taken which compels the employer to contemplate or to plan collective redundancies'.[585]

III. Consultation with Whom?

208. Under the Protection of Employment Act 1977, as originally drafted, consultation was required to be carried out only with officials of a trade union or staff association. But, where there was no recognized trade union, there was no obligation to consult. Following the initiation by the European Commission of enforcement proceedings against Ireland on the ground that the limited definition of employee representative amounted to a failure to effectively implement the directive, the European Communities (Protection of Employment) Regulations 2000[586] was enacted. Under the 2000 Regulations the definition of employee representative in section 2 of the 1977 Act was expanded to provide that in the absence of a trade union, consultations must be carried out with 'a person or persons chosen (under an arrangement put in place by the employer) by such employees from amongst their number to represent them in negotiations with the employer'.

---

585. The High Court applied *Akavan* v. *Fujitsu Siemens* Computers C-44/08 [2009] ECR I-8163 and *United States of America* v. *Nolan* [2012] IRLR 1020 (ECJ).
586. SI No. 488 of 2000.

Chapter 12. Protection Derived from the Transfer of Undertakings Directive 2003

§1. TRANSFER PROTECTION

209. Directive 2001/123 on the protection of employee rights on a transfer of undertaking is implemented in Irish law by the European Communities (Protection of Employees on Transfer of Undertakings) Regulations, 2003.[587]

The rights in the Transfer of Undertakings Directive are triggered by the acquisition of an 'economic entity', for which it is intended to retain 'continuity of identity'. The acquisition must correspond to the form of a 'transfer' recognized by the directive.

Article 1 of Directive 2001/123 provides:

(a) This Directive shall apply to any transfer of an undertaking, business, or part of an undertaking or business to another employer as a result of a legal transfer or merger.
(b) Subject to subparagraph (a) and the following provisions of this Article, there is a transfer within the meaning of this Directive where there is a transfer of an economic entity which retains its identity, meaning an organized grouping of resources which has the objective of pursuing an economic activity, whether or not that activity is central or ancillary.

Article 3 of the implementing Irish Regulations, the European Communities (Protection of Employees on Transfer of Undertakings) Regulations, 2003[588] provides:

> These Regulations shall apply to any transfer of an undertaking, business, or part of an undertaking or business from one employer to another employer as a result of a legal transfer (including the assignment or forfeiture of a lease) or merger:
>
> 'transfer' means the transfer of an economic entity which retains its identity;
>
> 'economic entity' means an organised grouping of resources which has the objective of pursuing an economic activity whether or not that activity is for profit or whether it is central or ancillary to another economic or administrative entity.

§2. THE SCOPE OF APPLICATION OF THE TRANSFER REGULATIONS

I. 'Economic Entity'

A. The Background to the Suzen *Case*

210. The directive only applies where there has been the acquisition of an 'economic entity'. The definition of economic entity –'an organized group of resources

---

587. SI 131 of 2003.
588. *Ibid.*

which has the objective of pursuing an economic activity' – incorporates the stricter test, propounded by the Court of Justice in *Süzen* v. *Zenhacker*,[589] for identifying the circumstances in which an acquisition activates the Directive.

An 'economic entity' may be viewed along a spectrum. At one end of the band an incoming undertaking may acquire all of the assets (physical, personnel, and economic). At the other end of the spectrum, an incoming business may merely *succeed to the right to carry on the business carried on by a previous business* without acquiring the plant, premises and workforce associated with that economic asset. Does the acquisition of the right to carry on a business constitute the acquisition of an 'economic entity'?

In *Christel Schmidt* v. *Spar*[590] the European Court of Justice ruled that the directive would apply where the incoming party merely acquired the right to carry on a business without obtaining any of the enabling assets – workforce or materials – of that undertaking. Christel Schmidt was employed by the Savings and Lending Bank as a cleaner. In February 1992 Christel Schmidt was dismissed because the bank decided to contract out cleaning to Spiegelbank, the firm responsible for cleaning other branches. Christel was not re-employed by the other cleaning company.

The European Court of Justice held that there was, none the less, a transfer of an 'economic entity'. The court emphasized that the purpose of the directive was to protect workers. This objective was best accomplished by giving the directive a wide interpretation. It was sufficient that all that Spiegelbank had acquired was one intangible asset: the right to carry out a business. The *Schmidt* case suggested that the Transfer of Undertakings Directive was activated simply where the new party acquired a 'right to carry out business'. Thus, the acquisition of a franchise in succession to another party might be sufficient. By 1994, a business could find itself encumbered by the directive in two situations: (i) in the case of a full tangible asset transfer, where a business and its central tangible operational assets, were acquired; (ii) in the case of an intangible asset transfer, where an undertaking simply succeeded to the entitlement to carry on a business.

Within just three years of *Schmidt* the Court of Justice committed a *volte face*. In *Süzen* v. *Zehnacker*[591] The plaintiff had been employed as a cleaner at a private school/church. As in *Schmidt*, the defendant was awarded the cleaning contract. By contrast with *Schmidt*, the European Court of Justice refused to find that this constituted a full transfer. A mere acquisition of a right to carry on a business was not the acquisition of an 'economic entity'. The European Court of Justice formulated a new test: 'the term entity refers to an organized grouping of persons and assets facilitating the exercise of an economic entity which pursues a particular objective'.

The stress had now shifted to the acquisition of tangible assets. The ECJ specifically held that it was not sufficient that there is a transfer of the right to carry on a business. The emphasis was on conveyances involving the acquisition of those assets which enable the entity to carry out its business: its employees, and its physical assets. The European Court stated:

---

589. *Ayse Süzen* v. *Zehnacker Gebäudereinigung GmbH Krankenhausservice* [1997] IRLR 255.
590. [1994] IRLR 302.
591. [1997] IRLR 255.

Article 1(1) of the Directive is to be interpreted as meaning that the Directive does not apply to a situation in which the person who had entrusted the cleaning of his premises to a first undertaking terminates his contract with the latter and, for the performance of a similar work, enters into a new contract with a second undertaking, *if there is no concomitant transfer from one undertaking to another undertaking of significant tangible assets or the taking over by the new employer of the new workforce, in terms of their numbers and skills, assigned by his predecessor to the performance of the contract.*

B. The Human Capital Intensive/Asset-reliant Distinction

211. The directive is activated only by acquisition of the central *operating* assets, rather than the entitlement to engage in business. The central question post-*Süzen* is to identify the principal or most significant assets in the operation of the business. This depends on a process of characterisation. Where the business is *human capital intensive* the employees constitute the 'economic entity'. Therefore the acquisition of the employees will constitute the acquisition of an economic entity. Where (as is more usually the case) the business is *asset-reliant* the assets constitute the 'economic entity'. Therefore, acquisition of the assets will constitute acquisition of that 'economic entity'.

The principle that in labour-based activities the workforce constitutes the asset by which the business is enabled to operate, with the result that re-employment of the workforce attracts the Directive, was re-iterated in *Hernandez Vidal.*[592] Here the plaintiff was employed by the cleaning company Contratas y Limpiezas as a cleaning worker. She was allocated to Hernandez Vidal, a company engaged in the manufacture of sweets. In 1994 the contract was terminated by Vidal, the company itself wishing to carry out the activity. None of the employees were transferred. Nor were any significant tangible assets transferred. The European Court of Justice stated that, in certain human-capital intensive businesses, the workforce could constitute the heart and soul of the economic entity. 'In labour intensive industries, a group of workers engaged in a joint activity may constitute an economic activity.'

An Irish instance of the labour intensive principle is *Dignan* v. *Sheehan Security Corporation Ltd.*[593] The claimant was employed by a security firm; 13 of the undertaking's 14 employees were re-employed by a second firm (but no assets, plant, or buildings were transferred). The EAT held that the undertaking was a labour intensive one. Private security does not require a considerable tangible asset base.

Oy Liikenne AB[594] involved the acquisition by the defendants of the right to operate seven local bus routes. The former drivers were re-employed, though on less favourable terms and conditions. No vehicles or other assets connected with the bus routes was acquired. The employees, who believed that the acquisition of an undertaking had occurred which entitled them to the benefit of the conditions previously

---

592. [1998] ECR 1-8179.
593. [2005] 16 ELR 222.
594. *Oy Liikenne Ab* v. *Pekka Liskojärvi and Pentti Juntunen* [2001] IRLR 171.

enjoyed, sought an order that there had been the transfer of an undertaking. The European Court of Justice proposed an approach based on the central enabling assets of the business. Where (as in the case at hand, bus transport) a business is asset-reliant those assets must be acquired if the directive is to operate:

> In a sector such as scheduled public transport by bus, where the tangible assets contribute significantly to the performance of the activity, the absence of a transfer to a *significant extent* from the old to the new contractor of such assets, which are necessary for the proper functioning of the entity, must lead to the conclusion that the entity does not retain its identity.

Accordingly, in the case of a labour intensive business, acquisition of the workforce will attract the directive. In the case of an asset-reliant business, there will have to be acquisition to a 'significant extent' of the tangible assets which facilitate the carrying out of the work.

The *Oy* case was applied by the Irish EAT in *Farrell* v. *United Cargo Services*.[595] The respondent had carried out transport services. The company was acquired by a former employee. The successor re-employed 10 of the 12 drivers used by the old employee. It did not acquire the trucks belonging to the old business, but bought six new trucks. The claimant was not re-employed and was dismissed by the old employer. The Tribunal held that since there was no acquisition of the old fleet there was no transfer of undertaking:

> The Tribunal is satisfied that the circumstances in the instant case are similar to those pertaining in [the *Oy* case]. The business of the second named respondent is similar to bus transport in that it requires substantial plant and equipment and cannot similarly be regarded as an activity based essentially on manpower ... there was no transfer of tangible assets between the respondents and the plant and equipment now being used by the second named respondent was brought new. The Tribunal is satisfied that the circumstances in this instant case are such that the reasoning of the European Court in the *Liikenne* case applies.[596]

II. The Nature of a 'Transfer' for the Purpose of the 2003 Regulations

212. The paradigm of a 'transfer' is the acquisition by one business of the ownership of another business. But, the legal definition of 'transfer' now encompasses situations far broader than that simple paradigm. If the notion of transfer had not expanded in this way, the directive would be capable of easy evasion, with conveyancing devices being contrived in order to evade application of the directive.

---

595. EAT [2004] UD 96/ 2004.
596. In *Sheils* v. *Integrate Ireland and the VEC* [2010] 21 ELR 41 the franchise to carry out English language classes was awarded to Dublin City Vocational Colleges (Dublin VEC). Dublin VEC did not acquire the premises or equipment of the previous franchisee; nor did it re-employ the staff. The Directive, it was held, did not apply.

A. *Acquisitions Where There Has Been an Acquisition of the Entity by Indirect Means*

213. The transfer may be direct or may be indirect or complex. In *Daddy's Dance Hall*[597] A leased a restaurant to B. A then terminated the lease with B with effect from a specified date and agreed that C should take the lease from that date. The directive was held to apply despite the fact that C did not acquire the undertaking *directly* from the transferor, B, and that there was no commercial contact between B and C. The European Court of Justice held that the only condition to the directive was that the old employer had been superseded by a newer one. It did not matter *how* this had happened; it was irrelevant that the transfer process of transfer was indirect or complex. If the rule was otherwise the directive could be simply evaded by indirect conveyances.

B. *Transfers in the Context of Judicially Monitored Insolvency Proceedings*

214. Article 5.1 of Directive 2001/23/EC provides:

> Unless Member States provide otherwise, Articles 3 and 4 shall not apply to any transfer of an undertaking, business or part of an undertaking or business where the transferor is the subject of bankruptcy proceedings or any analogous insolvency proceedings instituted with a view to the liquidation of the assets of the transferor and are under the supervision of a competent public authority.

This exclusion probably had its origins in the observation of the European Court of Justice in *Abels* v. *Administrative Board*[598] that the application of the directive in insolvency cases could be socially counterproductive. Liquidators may sell a business in two ways: (i) they may sell the assets alone (asset-stripping), or (ii) they may sell the business as a going concern. The second is the socially optimum outcome: it involves the maintenance of employment. The argument in *Abels* was that, if the directive applies to an insolvency sale, liquidators may be dissuaded from selling the business as a going concern (since purchasers may be reluctant to take on the old workforce).

Ireland has, with one exception, 'opted in'. Regulation 6 of the Protection of Employees Regulations, 2003 provides: 'Regulations 3 and 4 of these Regulations shall not apply to any transfer of an undertaking, business or part of an undertaking or business where the transferor is the subject of bankruptcy proceedings or insolvency proceedings.'

Insolvency proceedings are defined narrowly: 'proceedings where the transferor may be wound up under section 213(e) of the Companies Act of 1963'. In other words, the regulations apply to insolvency transfers except 'proceedings where the

---

597. [1988] ECR 739.
598. *Abels* v. *The Administrative Board of the Bedrijfsvereniging voor de Metaalindustrie en de Electrotechnische Industrie* [1985] ECR 469.

transferor may be wound up under section 213(e) of the Companies Act of 1963'.[599]

The exception to the application of the directive is quite restricted. It does not apply to all cases where a business is insolvent. It does not apply to the disposal of an undertaking by a creditor's receiver. Neither does it apply to a disposal following a creditors' voluntary-winding up under section 256 of the Companies Act 1963 (which occurs where a company is unable to pay its debts and where the company recognises that it is defunct and agrees to wind itself up). In *Re PSK Construction*[600] a company was wound up by voluntary creditors' meeting. The contracts and employees were acquired by another construction company, PLK Plant and Equipment Hire Limited. PSK owed unpaid wages to its employees which, if the Regulations applied, would pass to PLK. PLK attempted to argue that the directive did not apply because the transfer had occurred in analogous insolvency proceedings. However, the Tribunal held that the exemption only applied to proceedings under section 213(e). Here, however, 'PSK was not wound up compulsorily i.e. by court order. It was wound up by a creditors' voluntary winding-up some three to four weeks after the workforce moved from PSK to PLK.' Accordingly the Regulations applied.

In addition, Regulation 6(3) includes a specific anti-avoidance provision under which the Regulations apply where the sole reason for the institution of bankruptcy or insolvency proceedings is the evasion of the employer's transfer obligations: ' '(3) Notwithstanding paragraph (1), if the sole or main reason for the institution of bankruptcy or insolvency proceedings in respect of a transferor is the evasion of an employer's legal obligations under these Regulations, the Regulations shall apply to a transfer effected by that transferor.'

C. The Transfer Must Involve a Change in the Identity of the Employer

215. The transfer must be a transaction which results in the new party becoming the new employer. Article 2(1)(b) of the 2001 Directive defined 'transferee' as: 'any natural or legal person who, by reason of a transfer within the meaning of Article 1(1), *becomes the employer in respect of the undertaking, business or part of the business'.*

Thus, the process of transfer must result in the emergence of another employer.

This means that the directive will not apply where the acquisition is structured so that the formal identity of the employer remains the same even though the effective power has shifted to a new party. The workers in *Brookes* v. *Borough Care Services*[601] were employed by Borough Care Services Ltd (BCS). BCS was taken over by a company called CLS. In order to avoid the directive the acquiring party (CLS) chose to retain the name BCS. Effective control changed: BCS directors were removed. CLS directors became the board members. The personnel changed. But

---

599. S. 213 (f) provides that a company may be wound up by the High Court if 'the company is unable to pay its debts'.
600. EAT [2007].
601. [1998] IRLR 636.

CLS did not extinguish the old company. The employees remained the employees of the old company BCS. There was no change in the identity of the original employer, BCS. The English Court of Appeal held that, since there had been no change in the identity of the employer, the directive did not apply. This was a means of evasion which the Community could have blocked, but had chosen not to do so:

> The Regulations and the Directive refer quite specifically to the change of employer and to a transferor and transferee being any natural or legal person ... The Directive could have addressed, but did not, circumstance in which the shareholding membership of the legal person changed though its separate legal identity remained untouched.

§3. THE RIGHTS GUARANTEED BY THE DIRECTIVE

I. The Protection against Dismissal

216. Article 4 of the 2001 directive prohibits the dismissal of an employee which is related to the transfer of an undertaking.

A. The Economic, Technical or Organizational Defence to Dismissal

217. The transfer of an undertaking, business or part of a business shall not itself constitute grounds for the dismissal by the transferor or the transferee. However, a transfer-related dismissal may still be defended if it is on grounds of an economic, technical or organizational reason entailing the necessity of a change in the workforce: 'This provision shall not stand in the way of dismissals that may take place for economic, technical or organizational reasons entailing a change in the workforce.'

There may be an 'economic' or 'organizational' reason where the business would not be viable if the employees were retained. In *Purcell* v. *Bewleys*[602] the claimants were dismissed in the same month that the defendant's bakery was transferred to another enterprise. The Circuit Court held that the dismissal was for an 'economic, technical or organizational reason'. The bakery was losing £20,000 a month. It was essential that it contract its workforce. 'Economic, technical or organizational reasons entailing a change in the workforce' may arise where there is a change to the way in which the work is carried out. In *Porter* v. *Queen's Medical Centre*[603] a transferee acquired the business of supplying paediatric care in Nottingham. It was considered essential that the service be provided not by general paediatricians, but by experts in neonatology, neurology and in community health care. The current paediatricians were generalists. Their dismissal was held not to infringe the directive.

---

602. [1990] ELR 68.
603. [1993] IRLR 486.

B. Remedies against a Transfer-connected Dismissal

218. The ordinary remedy for dismissal contrary to Article 4/Regulation 5 is by means of a claim under the European Communities (Protection of Employees on the Transfer of Undertakings) Regulations.[604] The EAT may make an award of damages or re-instatement. While the remedy of reinstatement is usually very difficult to obtain in cases of actions for unfair dismissal, it is much more likely to be ordered in cases of dismissal contrary to the Transfer Directive. The general European law principle is that remedies for the breach of rights deriving from European law should be genuinely effective and dissuasive.[605] In *Wendelboe* v. *LJ Music Aps*[606] Advocate General Slynn stated:

> whether the remedy for the dismissal consists in a court order declaring that dismissal to be a nullity or the award of damages or some other effective remedy is for the Member State to determine. In any event, the Member States are obliged to provide a remedy which is effective and not merely symbolic.

This view has been adopted by the Irish EAT as a justification for awarding *reinstatement* (rather than just compensation) where an employee has been dismissed in breach of his or her 2001/23 Directive rights. In *MacDonnell* v. *Compass Catering*[607] the employee had been dismissed for a transfer-connected reason. The EAT – which is normally so reluctant to order re instatement – held that the remedy of reinstatement was the appropriate redress.

II. The Continuity of Existing Rights and Obligations

219. Article 3 of Directive 2001/123 provides:

> The transferor's rights and obligations arising from a contract of employment, or from an employment relationship existing on the date of a transfer within the meaning of Article 1 (1) shall, by reason of such transfer, be transferred to the transferee.

The right of an employee to have his existing terms and conditions maintained is the source of a companion principle: that a transferred employee cannot voluntarily waive his existing rights. In *Daddy's Dance Hall*[608] the European Court of Justice held, however, that an employer could not vary a pre-existing contract even by agreement. The reasoning was paternalistic. If employees could vary their contract there was a danger that they might be pressurized into variations. The prohibition on consensual variation only applies where the variation is made for reasons connected with the transfer. It does not prevent changes for reasons 'other than the

---

604. SI No. 131 of 2003.
605. *Von Colson* v. *Land Nordrhein* [1984] ECR 1891.
606. [1985] ECR 457.
607. EAT [2009] UD 1137/09.
608. [1988] IRLR 315.

transfer'. The European Court of Justice made this qualification clear in *Daddy's Dance Hall*:

> Insofar as national law allows the employment relationship to be altered in a manner unfavourable to employees in s*ituations other than the transfer of an undertaking* ... such an alteration is not precluded merely because the undertaking has been transferred in the meantime and the agreement has therefore been made with the new employer.

In *Smith* v. *Trustees of Brooklands College*[609] a school was acquired by a transferee. The transferee noticed that the employees were being mistakenly overpaid. They were being paid as if they were working for 35 hours; in fact, they were only working for 25 hours. The employees agreed that their wages had to be reduced. The court applied the principle that all that was prohibited was a transfer connected variation. A transfer-connected alteration would be one in which the sole reason was an employer's wish to 'harmonize terms and conditions' between the old and new groups of workers. However, here the change was not motivated by a wish to harmonize. It was connected with a wish to correct an over-payment.

This same principle non-transfer-connected principle was applied in Ireland in *An Employee* v. *A Restaurant*.[610] The transferee had taken over the business in July 2008. Within weeks the global economic crisis had erupted. The transferee negotiated a wage reduction with the staff to which they consented. Subsequently one staff member argued that the change was not binding and contravened the *Daddy's Dance Hall* principle. The EAT held that the change was not transfer-connected. It was not inspired by a desire to harmonize. Accordingly, the change was binding.

---

609. UK EAT, 5 September 2011.
610. EAT [2010], 2 June 2010.

Chapter 13. Protection against Discrimination on Grounds of Sex in Employment

§1. Equal Pay under the Employment Equality Acts 1998–2011

220. Part III of the Employment Equality Acts 1998–2011 proscribes discrimination on grounds of sex in employment. The prohibition is divided into discrimination in relation to remuneration; and discrimination in relation to matters other than remuneration.

The right to equal pay in Irish law derives ultimately from Article 157 of the Treaty on the Functioning of the European Union: 'Every member State shall ensure that the principle of equal pay for male and female workers for equal work or work of equal value is applied'. In *Defrenne* v. *Sabena*[611] the European Court of Justice classified the right in Article 157 as a personal right which was directly enforceable between private parties. The effect of the *Sabena* ruling is that an individual has a default constitutional right to equal pay deriving from European law. The status of Article 157 as a personal right has practical utility. As a superior right, Article 157 may be invoked in default of domestic law in cases where domestic law is insufficient. The domestic source of the right to equal pay is section 19(1) of the Employment Equality Acts 1998–2011:

> It shall be a term of the contract under which A is employed that, subject to this Act, A shall at any time be entitled to the same rate of remuneration for the work which A is employed to do as B who, at that or any other relevant time, is employed to do like work by the same or an associated employer.

I. The Conditions for an Equal Pay Claim

A. The Comparator Must Do 'Like Work'

221. The concept of 'like work' is defined in section 7(1) of the Employment Equality Acts 1998–2011:

(a) both perform the same work under the same or similar conditions, or each is interchangeable with the other in relation to the work;
(b) the work performed by one is of a similar nature to that performed by the other and any differences between the work performed or the conditions under which it is performed by each either are of small importance in relation to the work as a whole or occur with such irregularity as not to be significant to the work as a whole; or
(c) the work performed by one is equal in value to the work performed by the other, having regard to such matters as skill, physical or mental requirements, responsibility and working conditions.

---

611. [1976] ECR 455.

Category (a) refers to cases where the work is identical. Category (b) refers to cases where the work though identical is of similar nature, and where differences in work function or of qualification are of small overall importance. In *O'Leary* v. *Minister for Transport*[612] a group of women communications assistants claimed that they were entitled to have their pay set at the same rate as that paid to radio operators. It was accepted that the work was 'similar in nature'. The question then arose whether any differences were of 'small importance in relation to the work as a whole'. The Supreme Court held that the higher qualifications and greater responsibilities of radio operators were not of small importance in relation to work as a whole.

Category (c) arises where work, though not of the same character is equal in value 'having regard to such matters as skill, physical or mental requirements, responsibility and working conditions'. Here the Tribunal subjects the claimant's job and the comparator's job to a job evaluation study, scoring the demands which the job makes by reference to the five factors of 'skill, physical or mental requirements, responsibility and working conditions'. The complainant will succeed where the demands made of the comparator in respect of each of the five criteria, or a majority of those criteria, are as great as those made of the comparator. An example of the application of the process is *161 Named Employees* v. *TCD*[613] where a group of female catering assistants claimed that they were entitled to the same rate of pay as paid to male grounds maintenance staff. The Equality Officer carried out a work inspection, and found that the demands made on the claimant in terms of skill, physical effort and working conditions were the same as those made on the comparator, and that in terms of mental effort and responsibility the demands made on the claimant were higher. In *Six Named Employees* v. *Dublin Institute of Technology*[614] the complainants were male porters employed by the Dublin Institute of Technology. The comparator was a female housekeeper. The Equality Tribunal found that the demands made on the comparators in terms of physical requirements and working conditions were equivalent to the demands made on the female comparator. However, in relation to skills, mental requirements and responsibility the demands made on the female comparator were greater; since the value of the work done by the complainant was less than that of the comparator, the complaint was dismissed. In *Diageo* v. *O'Sullivan*[615] an assessment carried out by reference to the standards of working conditions, responsibility, skill, and mental effort showed that a female cleaner was doing work of equal value to a male yardman. In *Kenny* v. *Minister for Justice*[616] the CJEU was sceptical of the claim that clerical workers who had served in the *Garda Siochana*, and clerical workers who had not, undertook work of equal value. The former members had superior qualifications and did work (such as liaising with Interpol) which was not done by the clerical workers from a non-Garda background.

---

612. Supreme Court, 3 February 1998.
613. Equality Tribunal [2000] DEC-2-2000/04.
614. Equality Tribunal [2003] DEC E2003/020.
615. [2007] 18 ELR 150.
616. [2013] IRLR 463.

Following the decision of the European Court of Justice in *Murphy* v. *Bord Telecom Eireann*[617] the right to equal pay applies where the claimant does work of greater value than that carried out by the comparator. Section 7(3) of the 1998–2011 code provides:

> In any case where (a) the remuneration received by one person ('the primary worker') is less than the remuneration received by another ('the comparator'), and (b) the work performed by the primary worker is greater in value than the work performed by the comparator, having regard to the matters mentioned in subsection (1)(c), then, for the purposes of subsection (1)(c), the work performed by the primary worker shall be regarded as equal in value to the work performed by the comparator.

B. The Comparator Must Be Employed by the Same or an 'Associated' Employer

222. When is a claimant permitted to extend the search for a comparator to an associated employer? Section 2 of the 1998–2011 Acts provide that 'two employers shall be taken to be associated if one is a body corporate of which the other (whether directly or indirectly) has control or if both are bodies corporate of which a third person (whether directly or indirectly) has control'.

Undertakings are 'associated' either if one is a body corporate which has control over the other, or if both are bodies corporate under the control of the same third party.[618] The requirement of common control was found not to be satisfied in *Brides* v. *Minister for Agriculture*.[619] Here employees of Teagasc, an independent agency involved in agricultural training, claimed as their comparators for the purpose of an equal pay claim employees of the Department of Agriculture. The High Court dismissed the argument that the two institutions were associated: Teagasc was an entirely independent body, and was not within the sphere of control of the Department of Agriculture. Nor did any third party exercise control over both organizations.

In *Lawrence* v. *Regent Office Care*[620] the European Court repeated that the right to equal pay was not confined to workers within the same employment; it also arose between workers doing like work within the 'same establishment or service'. In *Lawrence* the European Court of Justice elaborated upon the meaning of 'same establishment or service', holding that it meant a 'single source':

---

617. [1988] ECR 673.
618. The restriction to employment within corporate groups is not necessarily consistent with European law. The statutory definition would not permit comparison within associated undertakings which were not 'corporations', but had some other legal form, such as trusts or unincorporated associations (even where the bodies are under the control of a third party). However, under European law the test is employment within the 'same establishment or service'. That is probably a wider concept than associated 'corporations'.
619. [1999] 4 IR 250.
620. [2003] ICR 1092.

It is not evident from the wording of Article [157] that the comparison must be confined to one and the same employer. The test is the 'same establishment or service' (see, inter alia, *Defrenne (No 2)*. This will occur where the regulation of the terms and conditions of employment actually applied is traceable to one source, whether it be the legislature, the parties to a collective works agreement, or the management of a corporate group.

Two examples of terms and conditions amongst different employments, but deriving from a 'single source' were instanced: (a) where several undertakings or establishments are covered by a collective agreement; (b) where terms and conditions of employment are laid down centrally for more than one organization or business within a holding company or conglomerate. The extent of the equal pay right under European law is wider than the right under section 22 of the Irish Employment Equality Acts 1998 (as amended). However, category (a) – several different undertakings covered by the same collective agreement – is not covered by section 22. That right must be claimed by invoking the right under Article 157.

C. The Comparator and the Complainant Must Have Been Employed 'at That or Any Other Relevant Time'

223. Under section 19(1) the complainant and the comparator must have either been employed contemporaneously, or 'at any other relevant time'. 'Relevant time' is defined in section 19(2)(b) as 'any time during the 3 years which precede, or the three years which follow the particular time'.

D. 'Employed'

224. The right in section 19(1) is confined to persons who are 'employed'. However, this does not mean that the right to equal pay is restricted to persons who are employed *under a contract of employment*. Section 19(2) provides that the word 'employed' includes certain types of contracts for services: 'employed includes, in addition to employment under a contract of employment, employment under a contract personally to execute any work or labour'. In 2004 the range of persons entitled to avail of the legislation was extended further to include partners. Section 13A(1) of the 1998 Act provide that 'references to an employee includes references to a partner'.

II. Defences to Alleged Direct Discrimination in Pay: 'Grounds Other than Gender'

225. Where a prima facie case of direct discrimination is established, the burden shifts to the employer to show that the lesser pay was justified by grounds other than gender. Section 19(5) of the Employment Equality Act 1998 provides that 'subject

to subsection 4, nothing in this Part shall prevent an employer from paying, on grounds other than gender different rates of remuneration to different employees'.

In attempting to prove that the differential was motivated by a ground other than sex, the High Court has held that it is irrelevant (in a case where the claim is made by a woman) that there are women in the higher paid comparator group.[621] The fact that there are women in the privileged group does not necessarily mean that the difference in pay was on alternative legitimate grounds.[622]

III. Indirect Discrimination in Pay

226. Where the employer identifies a ground other than sex for the discrimination, and an employee cannot, as a result, prove direct discrimination it is still open to the employee to raise a case of indirect discrimination. Indirect discrimination is defined in section 19(4) as occurring

> where an apparently neutral provision puts persons of a particular gender (being As or Bs) at a particular disadvantage in respect of remuneration compared with other employees of their employee'. The provisionally indirectly discriminatory provision may be justified where 'the provision is objectively justified by a legitimate aim and the means of achieving the aim are appropriate and necessary.

IV. The Components of Indirect Discrimination Affecting Pay

A. 'At a Particular Disadvantage'

227. A claim of indirect discrimination involves a statistical analysis in which all of those who are potentially affected are identified. From that group the percentage of men who are disadvantaged by the measure is compared with the percentage of women who are disadvantaged by the measure. In *Kenny* v. *Minister for Justice*[623] the Court of Justice of the European Union re-emphasized the requirement that the statistical evidence must be reliable. Statistics 'must cover enough individuals, [must not] illustrate purely fortuitous or short-term phenomena and ... in general ... appear to be significant'.[624] Statistics may lack reliability where the pool is small or where the differential is undermined by wide statistical variations over earlier years.[625]

---

621. *C & D Food Group* v. *Cunnion* [1996]1 IR 147.
622. However, the Labour Court has not always followed this analysis, refusing in some cases to find discrimination in cases where there were members of the opposite sex in the claimant group, or members of the same sex in the comparator group: *Irish Times Ltd* v. *SIPTU* [1999] 10 ELR 35.
623. Case C-427/11, 28 February 2013.
624. *Ibid.*, para. 44.
625. *Nationalist and Leinster Times* v. *Ashmore* [2013] 24 ELR 216

B. The Enderby *principle*

228. Although indirect discrimination usually requires the existence of an 'apparently neutral provision' this component is not always insisted upon. In *Enderby* v. *Frenchay Health Authority*[626] the European Court of Justice held that a prima facie case of indirect discrimination could arise where there are two occupational groups doing comparable work, with one group made up of one sex, and the other of the other sex, and being higher paid. The breakthrough made in this case was that the ECJ did not require, as a component of indirect discrimination that the applicant identify some 'condition' or 'apparently neutral provision' which filtered women into the disadvantaged group. It is sufficient that the underpaid group is composed of one sex and the better paid is composed of the other sex.[627] This principle is commonly applied in Irish equal pay claims. The *Enderby* principle was applied in *Department of Justice* v. *Civil & Public Services Union.*[628] Here clerical functions in the *Garda Siochana* were performed by two groups: (i) members of *An Garda Siochana* and (ii) clerical officers. Both groups performed work of equal value. The first group was overwhelmingly male; the second was overwhelmingly female. The Labour Court held that:

> the practice results in clerical work of equal value within the force being remunerated at a higher rate when it is performed by members of a group made up predominantly of men than when it is performed by a group made up almost exclusively of women. This, on the authority of the judgment of the European Court of Justice in *Enderby v. Frenchay Health Authority* Case C-127/92 [1993] E.C.R. 5535 discloses indirect discrimination.[629]

C. Defences to Alleged Indirect Discrimination in Pay

1. Wages Adjusted Pro Rata to Hours Worked

229. In *Lewen* v. *Denda*[630] the European Court of Justice held that an arrangement under which a bonus was enhanced or reduced according to the number of hours worked pursued the legitimate aim of rewarding employees according to the contribution measured in time provided by each employee. The *Lewen* principle

---

626. [1993] IRLR 591.
627. The *Enderby* principle has been held not to apply where the advantaged group is predominantly made up of one sex and the comparator group is gender neutral: *Health Service Executive* v. *238 Named Complainants* [2013] ELR 206.
628. Labour Court [2007] EDA 0713.
629. The principle was applied in *28 Civil Servants* v. *Courts Service,* Equality Tribunal [2007] DEC E2007-007. Here court messengers were 90 per cent male. These were underpaid by comparison with staff officers (90 per cent female). *Enderby* was applied: the burden shifted to the employer to justify the distinction. By contrast in *HSE* v. *Sheridan,* Labour Court [2008] EDA 0820 workers in the two groups were not doing work of equal value; therefore *the case did not* fall within the *criteria* in *Enderby.*
630. [1999] ECR 1-7243.

was applied in *Brady* v. *ESOP Trustees*[631] where it was alleged that the employee share ownership plan instituted by a bank was indirectly discriminatory against women. The scheme provided for a share allocation in lieu of a pay increase; the amount of the share allocation paid to employees would depend on the number of hours worked over the last twelve months. The Equality Tribunal held that the scheme was justified by the principle that salary may be reduced according to the amount of work done.

2. Compassionate Grounds: Socially Progressive Policies

230. The comparators in *UCC* v. *Aherne*[632] were female telephone operators who had been excused, in accordance with a policy which reduced the workload on employees with family responsibilities, from doing accounts works which other full time staff were expected to undertake. These workers, although doing slightly less work than the other persons in the same grade, continued to be better paid. However the Supreme Court held that the pay advantage was justified by the employer's progressive family policies which entailed advantages without loss of pay to some employees: 'Inequality of pay may be justified on compassionate grounds, as where persons originally in a higher wage category are, for health reasons, assigned to a lower work function, but, on compassionate grounds, are allowed to retain their original salary.'[633]

3. Possession of Superior Qualifications

231. In *25 Named Employees* v. *Irish Aviation Authority*[634] a group of air traffic control officers claimed parity with a comparator group composed of radio officers. The radio officers were required to hold third level degrees in electronics – a condition which it was alleged indirectly discriminated against women. The Equality Tribunal invoked *Handels-og*[635] in which it was held the possession of training may constitute an objective justification where it 'is of importance for the performance of the specific tasks which are entrusted to the employee'.

4. Industrial Relations

232. In *Kenny* v. *Minister for Justice*[636] the Minister for Justice, as part of an agreement with the representative association of the *Garda Siochana*, agreed that, in exchange for employing more civilians in the *Gardai*, a pool of clerical positions could be filled by members of the *Gardai*. It was also agreed that those *Gardai*

---

631. Labour Court [2005] EDA 053.
632. [2005] 16 297.
633. *Campbell* v. *Minister for Transport* [1996] ELR 106.
634. [2010] 21 ELR 211.
635. [1990] ECR 1-3979
636. C-427/11, 28 February 2013.

would enjoy the same rates of pay that they previously enjoyed. This group was predominantly male. The clerical workers who had not previously been serving members were less well paid. This group was overwhelmingly female. The CJEU held that prima facie indirectly differential could be justified by industrial relations considerations:

> the interests of good industrial relations may be taken into consideration by he national court as one factor among others in its assessment of whether differences between the pay of two groups of workers are due to objective *factors* unrelated to any discrimination on grounds of sex and are compatible with the principle of proportionality.

§2. SEX DISCRIMINATION AND THE EMPLOYMENT EQUALITY ACTS 1998–2011

233. Distinct from the rules against discrimination in matters of pay is a separate system of rules prohibiting discrimination in matters other than pay.

Under Article 1 of the Equal Treatment Directive (Directive 2006/54/EC) direct discrimination is defined as arising 'where one person is treated less favourably than another is, has been or would be treated in a comparable situation'. The definition in section 6 of the Employment Equality Act 1998–2011 corresponds to the standard European definition:

> (1) For the purposes of this Act and without prejudice to its provisions relating to discrimination occurring in particular circumstances discrimination shall be taken to occur where—
> (*a*) a person is treated less favourably than another person is, has been or would be treated in a comparable situation on any of the grounds specified in subsection (2) (in this Act referred to as the 'discriminatory grounds') which—
>
> (i) exists,
> (ii) existed but no longer exists,
> (iii) may exist in the future, or
> (iv) is imputed to the person concerned,
>
> (2A) Without prejudice to the generality of subsections (1) and (2), discrimination on the gender ground shall be taken to occur where, on a ground related to her pregnancy or maternity leave, a woman employee is treated, contrary to any statutory requirement, less favourably than another employee is, has been or would be treated.

I. Establishing Direct Discrimination on Grounds of Sex under the Employment Equality Acts 1998–2011

234. Conceptually, four conditions must be established in order to establish direct discrimination on grounds of sex under the Employment Equality Acts

1998–2011. These are (i) the imposition of some less favourable treatment than is imposed on another person; (ii) the fact that a comparator would not have been so treated; (iii) the fact that the treatment was on grounds of sex; (iv) the inappropriateness of any of the limited defences to direct discrimination on grounds of sex.

A. *Less Favourable Treatment*

235. A controversial application of the 'less favourable treatment' principle can be found in the case law on employment interview cases.[637] Direct discrimination in relation to access to employment has been held to occur where during an employment interview a candidate of one sex has been asked to dispel objections which would not, in all likelihood, be raised in the case of persons of the other sex. In *Chaney* v. *UCD*[638] an applicant for a post in a university was asked how she proposed to look after her children. The question would not, it was assumed, have been asked of a male applicant and was held discriminatory. On the other hand, questions which are asked of both male and female applicants about children will not constitute direct discrimination. Thus, in *Smith* v. *MGI*[639] there was held to be no discrimination where both male and female applicants were asked about childcare arrangements.

Different treatment is not necessarily less favourable treatment. An application of such an 'equivalence of treatment' analysis may be found in the approach to the issue of dress codes. In *Burdett* v. *West Birmingham Health Authority*[640] the claimant was a nurse who objected to the requirement to wear a special starched linen nurse's cap. Male nurses had to wear a white tunic with epaulettes, but no cap. The applicant refused to wear the cap, and was disciplined. The EAT (UK) upheld a finding by the industrial tribunal that the applicant had not been discriminated against, since the requirement to wear a uniform applied equally to male and female employees. The position in Ireland was, originally, different. The traditional approach under the Irish case law was that there was less favourable treatment when *details* in a dress code required of one sex were are not imposed upon members of the other sex.[641] This was revised in favour of a more intermediary approach. In *O'Byrne* v. *Dunnes*[642] the Labour Court rejected the argument (the position which had been adopted earlier) that a dress code must be identical item by item. Instead the approach was to ask whether 'it applies a common standard of neatness, conventionality and hygiene to both men and women and does not unreasonably bear more

---

637. See L. Flynn, 'Discriminatory Questions at Job Interviews' (1993) ILT 221.
638. Equality Tribunal [1983] EE15/1983.
639. Equality Tribunal [1998] EE 04/1998.
640. [1994] IRLR 7.
641. See *Pantry Franchise* v. *A Worker Labour Court* [1993]EEO97 (prohibition on male employees wearing long hair directly discriminatory); *45 Female Employees* v. *Tesco* Labour Court [2000] EE06-2006 (requirement that female employees wear skirts and not trousers held directly discriminatory on grounds of sex); *Keane* v. *CERT* Equality Officer [2000] EE 2000-08 (requirement that female hotel workers wear dress and apron directly discriminatory).
642. [2004] 15 ELR 96.

heavily on one gender than it does on the other'. A dress code would be discriminatory if it more significantly restricted the right of men rather than women to determine their appearance. In this case the Labour Court found that, judged as a whole, the employer's code made a greater number of restrictions on the freedom of appearance of its male employees that it did of its women employees.

B. 'On Grounds of Sex'

236. The differential treatment must be 'on grounds of sex'. The Labour Court routinely adopts the argument that, since Article 2 of (Directive 2006/54/EC) prohibits any discrimination 'whatsoever', it is unnecessary to show that the 'discriminatory ground relied upon was the only, or the dominant, reason for the impugned treatment'. Any case in which the gender of the victim plays a motivational part will be 'on grounds of sex' unless the employer can show that the 'ground was anything other than a trivial influence'.[643]

C. Discrimination on Grounds of Pregnancy Is Usually Sex Discrimination

237. While it is ordinarily a condition of direct sex discrimination that it be on 'grounds of gender', certain forms of discrimination are recognized as constituting sex discrimination where the link with gender is more indirect. The classic example of this is pregnancy discrimination. Strict application of the comparator rule would mean that less favourable treatment on grounds of pregnancy would usually not constitute discrimination on grounds of sex. In *Turley* v. *Alders Department Stores*[644] the applicant was dismissed because she was pregnant. Two arguments were made by the court in rejection of her sex discrimination claim: (i) that it was logically impossible to identify the male comparator of a pregnant woman: 'In order to see if she has been treated less favourably than a man the sense of the section, is that you must compare like with like, and here you cannot. When she is pregnant a woman is no longer just a woman. She is a woman, as the authorized version puts it, with child, and there is no masculine equivalent.'[645] (ii) The alternative, less extreme, argument was that there might, in certain limited circumstances, be a comparator: a sick male, who sought leave of absence for a period equivalent to the period requested by the pregnant woman. Since it was likely that a male who was absent for such an extended period would be also dismissed there was no discrimination.

However, English and Irish law was transformed by the judgment of the European Court of Justice in *Dekker* v. *Stichting Wormings*.[646] The European Court of Justice held that under the Equal Treatment Directive (Article 2 of which provided

---

643. *Ely Property* v. *Boyle* Labour Court [2009] EDA0902.
644. [1980] IRLR 4.
645. *Ibid.* p. 5
646. [1991] ECR 1-3941.

that 'the principle of equal treatment shall mean that there shall be no discrimination whatsoever on grounds of sex, either directly or indirectly') discrimination on grounds of pregnancy was discrimination on grounds of sex:[647]

Whether a refusal to employ is direct discrimination on grounds of sex depends on whether the most important reason for the refusal is a reason which applies without distinction to employees of both sexes, or whether it applies exclusively to one sex. As employment can only be refused because of pregnancy to women, such a refusal is direct discrimination on grounds of sex.

In *Gillespie* v. *Northern Health and Social Services Board*[648] the European Court of Justice was asked to rule whether it was direct discrimination for an employer to pay an employee absent on maternity leave less than her normal wages. A logical application of the *Dekker* principle would suggest that since a disadvantage on grounds is sex discrimination should follow that not to pay a pregnant employee is sex discrimination. However, the European Court of Justice reverted to the comparator requirement. The European Court held that it was necessary to show that a male in a comparable situation would not have been so treated. However, a pregnant woman on maternity leave was not comparable with a working male employee. It was not, in this case, enough that the cause of the disadvantage was her pregnancy:

> It is well settled that discrimination involves the application of different rules to comparable situations or the application of the same rule to different situations ... The present case is concerned with women taking maternity leave provided for by national legislation. They are in a special position which requires them to be afforded special protection, but *which is not comparable either with that of a man or with that of a woman actually at work.*

Furthermore, the European Court of Justice has distinguished the period from the start of pregnancy to the conclusion of maternity leave from the period after maternity leave. During the first period no disadvantage may be imposed on grounds of absence or inability to work. This is because the disadvantage is related to pregnancy and pregnancy discrimination is sex discrimination. *Herrero* v. *Instituto Madrileno de la Salud*[649] concerned a rule under which the period spent on maternity leave was not counted towards seniority. Although the same rule was applied in the case of an absent sick male, the European Court of Justice held that the rule infringed the rule against the discrimination on grounds of sex:

> the court has held that a female worker is protected in her employment relationship against any unfavourable treatment on the ground that she is, or has been, on maternity leave and that a woman who is treated unfavourably because of absence on maternity leave suffers discrimination on the ground of her pregnancy and of that leave.

---

647. This principle was incorporated into Irish law by s. 6(2) of the Employment Equality Acts 1998–2011.
648. [1996] ECR 1-475.
649. [2006] ECR I-01513.

However, after the end of maternity leave, pregnancy-related illness or absence may be assessed in the same way as absence by a male member of staff. If a male is liable to be dismissed there is no discrimination. In *Hertz*[650] an employee who took 100 days post-natal leave was held not to have been discriminated against on grounds of sex where a sick male would have been treated in the same way after a similar absence. The *Hertz* principle was endorsed in *Brown* v. *Rentokil*.[651] Here the European Court of Justice held that illness which occurred during the period from the beginning of pregnancy to the end of maternity leave was based on pregnancy, and, therefore, sex-based. On the other hand, the absence after maternity leave, even if, in medical terms, pregnancy-related is not legally regarded as sex-related. If the absence persists for such a length of time that a male would, if absent for an equivalent period, be dismissed, than dismissal is not regarded as sex-based.

In line with established European law, Irish law deems discrimination on grounds of pregnancy to be discrimination on grounds of sex: section 6(2A) of the Employment Equality Acts 1998–2011 provides:[652] 'discrimination on the gender ground shall be taken to occur where on a ground related to her pregnancy or maternity leave, a woman is treated, contrary to any statutory requirement, less favourably than another employee is has been or would be treated'.

The Labour Court has applied the requirement laid down by the European Court in *Paquay* v. *Société d'architectes Hoet + Minne SPRL*[653] that the redress for dismissal on grounds of pregnancy 'must have a genuine dissuasive effect with regard to the employer and must be commensurate with the injury suffered'.[654]

D. Sexual Harassment as Sex Discrimination

238. In order to remove doubts as to whether sexual harassment is treatment on grounds of sex (as opposed to some other ground)[655] section 23 of the Employment Equality Acts 1998–2011 deems sexual harassment to constitute 'discrimination by A's employer, on the gender ground, in relation to A's conditions of employment'. Sexual harassment is defined in section 14A(7) of the Employment Equality Acts 1998–2011 as:

> any form of unwanted verbal, non-verbal or physical conduct of a sexual nature, being conduct which in either case has the purpose or effect of violating a person's dignity and creating an intimidating, hostile, degrading, humiliating or offensive environment for the person. ... such unwanted conduct may

---

650. [1990] ECR 1-3979.
651. [1998] ECR 1-4185.
652. *Justitia* v. *McGarvey*, Equality Tribunal [2009] DEC-E2008-041 (pregnant employee selected for redundancy dismissal; employer failing to rebut presumption that the dismissal was not on ground of pregnancy). *Corcoran Auctioneering* v. *Martin* Labour Court [2011] EDA 1133 (employer permanently transferring job to another employee while claimant on maternity leave).
653. [2007] ECR 1-8511.
654. *Trailer Care Holdings* v. *Healy*, Labour Court [2012] EDA128.
655. J. Dine and B. Watt, 'Sexual Harassment: Moving Away from Discrimination' (1995) 58 MLR 343.

consist of acts, requests, spoken words, gestures or the production, display or circulation of written words, pictures or other material.

The employer is regarded as having been guilty of discrimination either where he is responsible, or where the conduct is committed by 'a client, customer or other business contact of the employer' and 'the circumstances of the harassment are such that A's employer ought reasonably to have taken steps to prevent it'.[656] Section 14(2) creates a due diligence defence: 'it shall be a defence for the employer to prove that the employer took such steps as are reasonably practicable ... to prevent the person from harassing or sexually harassing the victim or any class of persons which includes the victim'.

Section 14 (2) has been held to mean that the employer should be:

consciousof the possibility of sexual harassment occurring and have in place reasonable measures to prevent its occurrence as well as policies and procedures to deal with such harassment where it is found to have taken place. This requires the employer to show, at a minimum, that a clear anti-harassment or dignity at work policy was in place before the harassment occurred and that the policy was effectively communicated to all employees. Moreover, management personnel should be trained to deal with incidents of harassment and to recognise its manifestations.[657]

An employer who takes action which is 'in all the circumstances as much as the employer could reasonably have been expected to do' may be exonerated.[658]

E. Proof of Direct Discrimination

239. Section 85A of the Employment Equality Acts 1998–2011 provides that:

where in any proceedings facts are established by or on behalf of a complainant from which it may be presumed that there has been discrimination in relation to him or her, it is for the respondent to prove the contrary.

The employee does not carry the burden of proving on the balance of probability that he or she was discriminated against on grounds of sex. It is sufficient if he or she raises facts of 'sufficient significance to raise an inference of discrimination'.[659] The Labour Court has held that it is sufficient to shift the burden of proof that the inference 'is within the *range of inferences* which can reasonably be drawn from

---

656. S. 14(A).
657. *A Worker* v. *A Hotel* [2010] 21 ELR 72.
658. *Boy's Secondary School* v. *Two Female Teachers* Labour Court [2002] DEE021. *A Female Teacher* v. *Board of Management of a Secondary School* [2013] 24 ELR 16. S. 56 of the Employment Equality Act 1998 enables the Minister to issue codes of practice which have the objective of the promoting the 'elimination of discrimination in employment'. The Employment Equality Act 19998 (Code of Practice) (Harassment) Order 2012 (SI 208/2012) enacted under section 56 provides guidance on the drafting of effective anti-sexual harassment policies.
659. *Mitchell* v. *Southern Health Board* [2001] 12 ELR 201.

these facts'.[660] On the other hand, in order to shift the burden of proof, the claimant must present some credible evidence: 'mere allegations unsupported by any corroborative evidence are insufficient to establish a prima facie case and so transfer the burden of proof'.[661]

F. The 'Genuine and Determining Occupational Requirement' Defence

240. Article 14(2) of Directive 2006/54/EC introduces a defence to sex-related bars to access to employment where by reason of the 'nature of the occupational activities' or 'the context in which they are carried out' the sex of the worker 'constitutes a genuine and determining occupational requirement' so long as the objective is legitimate and the requirement is proportionate.

Corresponding to this, section 25(1) of the Employment Equality Acts 1998–2011 provides:

> A difference of treatment which is based on a characteristic related to the gender ground in respect of access to employment in a particular post shall not constitute discrimination under this Part or Part II where, by reason of the particular occupational activities concerned or of the context in which they are carried out—
>
> (a) the characteristic constitutes a genuine and determining occupational requirement for the post, and
> (b) the objective is legitimate and the requirement proportionate.

The objective is, without rigidly defining the exceptions in advance, to provide for cases where it is essential to the effective performance of the job in question that the applicant should belong to one sex. In *M* v. *A Language School*[662] the Equality Tribunal held that it was not an objective justification that the position of manager of a language school be restricted to a female. The respondent had attempted to justify the restriction on the ground that 'the position involved visiting host families to check the standard of the homes, dealing extensively with the "lady of the house", and coping with homesick or emotional Italian students.' The Tribunal held that the circumstances did not constitute sex as a determining, or indispensable, requirement for the position.

The Employment Equality Acts 1998–2011 exempt sex-exclusive assignments in the *Garda Síochána* or in the prison service, taken in order to 'guard violent individuals or to quell riots or violent disturbances, or in order to disarm violent individuals or disperse crowds or … in the interests of privacy or decency'. The legislation also permits the application of differential height requirements for male and female recruits. Section 27(1)(b) provides that the Act does not prevent:

---

660. *A Worker* v. *A Hotel* 22 [2011] ELR 72
661. *Melbury Developments* v. *Arturs Valpetters* [2010] 21 ELR 64; *IBM* v. *Svoboda* Labour Court [2011] EDA 1116; *Ilesview Ltd* v. *Dabkowska* Labour Court [2012] EDA 1212.
662. [2005] 16 ELR 35.

the application of one criterion as to height for men and another for women, if the criteria chosen are such that the proportion of women in the State likely to meet the criterion for women is approximately the same as the proportion of men in the State likely to meet the criterion for men.

There is no express exclusion exempting the defence forces. However, discriminatory measures may be justified here by reference to 'the genuine and determining occupational requirement' defence laid down in section 25(1).

G. Measures of Affirmative Action

241. Article 3 of the 2006 Council Directive, and Article 157(4) of the Treaty on the Functioning of the European Union provide the basis for a restricted power of direct, or 'positive' , discrimination which operates in the interest of the members of sex which is underrepresented in a particular employment. Article 157(4) of the TFEU provides:

> With a view to ensuring full equality in practice between men and women in working life, the principle of equal treatment shall not prevent any Member State from maintaining or adopting measures providing for specific advantages in order to make it easier for the under-represented sex to pursue a vocational activity or to prevent or compensate for disadvantages in professional careers.

Article 3 of the Equal Treatment Directive incorporates the sense of Article 141: 'Member States may maintain or adopt measures within the meaning of Article 141(4) of the Treaty with a view to ensuring full equality in practice between men and women.'

Section 24 of the Employment Equality Act 1998 (as amended by section 15 of the Equality Act, 2004) implements this form of legitimate discrimination in Irish law:[663]

> (1) This Act is without prejudice to any measures—
> maintained or adopted with a view to ensuring full equality in practice between men and women in their employments, and
> providing for specific advantages so as—
>
> (i) to make it easier for an under-represented sex to pursue a vocational activity, or
> (ii) to prevent or compensate for disadvantages in professional careers.

---

663. The wording in s. 24 may, in fact, go further than is envisaged by European measures. The only measures allowed by Article 141 and by the Equal Treatment Directive are measures which make it easier for the under-represented sex to pursue a vocational activity, or to prevent or compensate for disadvantages in professional careers'. S. 24, on the other hand, permits measures 'adopted with a view to ensuring full equality in practice between men and women in their employments'.

II. Indirect Discrimination on Grounds of Sex

A. The Definition of Sex Discrimination on Grounds of Sex

242. Section 22(a)[664] of the Employment Equality Act 1998–2011 is the source of the domestic statutory prohibition of sex-based indirect discrimination. Section 22 defines indirect discrimination as operating where:

> an apparently neutral provision puts persons of a particular gender (being As or Bs) at a particular disadvantage in respect of any matter other than remuneration compared with other employees of their employer.
> (*b*) Where paragraph (*a*) applies, the employer shall be treated for the purposes of this Act as discriminating against each of the persons referred to (including A or B), unless the provision is objectively justified by a legitimate aim and the means of achieving that aim are appropriate and necessary.
> (1A) In any proceedings statistics are admissible for the purpose of determining whether subsection (1) applies in relation to A or B.

Article 1(b) of the Equal Treatment Directive 2006/54/EC defines indirect discrimination as arising:

> where an apparently neutral provision, criterion or practice would put persons of one sex at a particular disadvantage compared with persons of the other sex, unless that provision, criterion or practice is objectively justified by a legitimate aim, and the means of achieving that aim are appropriate and necessary.

It has been noted that the Irish definition (which covers a neutral provision but does not cover practices or criteria) does not comport fully with the definition of that concept set out in 2006/54/EC.[665]

B. The Legitimate Aim Defence to Indirect Discrimination

243. Section 22 recognizes a defence where there is a legitimate aim and the means of achieving that aim are appropriate and necessary. The following section is a sample of Irish case law applying this defence.

1. Seniority Requirements

244. In *Conlon* v. *University of Limerick*[666] the disappointed applicant for the Professorship of Law in the University of Limerick challenged as indirectly discriminatory the requirement that applicants have 'several years experience at a

---

664. By s. 13 of the Equality Act, 2004.
665. *Department of Justice, Equality and Law Reform* v. *CPSU* [2008] 19 ELR 140.
666. [1999] ELR 155.

senior academic level', claiming that this was a condition with which fewer female applicants could comply. The legitimacy of the condition was upheld by the High Court: even if the job could be performed by persons less qualified, it was important to the standing of the university that its most senior posts be filled by persons who were distinguished at senior academic level.

2. Measures Disadvantaging Job-sharing Workers

245. It has sometimes been argued that a refusal to allow part-time work constitutes indirect discrimination on the grounds of sex. Even if this so, an employer may justify refusal where it is 'objectively justified by a legitimate aim, and the means of achieving that aim are appropriate and necessary'. In *Burke* v. *University College Galway*[667] it was accepted that in principle refusal to offer part time work might be indirectly discriminatory. However, here the employee (a university library information officer) was found (by both the equality tribunal and the Labour Court) to hold a position for which full time work was indispensable.

Assuming that an employer does permit job-sharing, defending less favourable treatment of those job-sharers may entail difficulties. In *Hill and Stapleton* v. *Revenue Commissioners*[668] the European Court of Justice held that an Irish civil service rule which provided that when job sharers converted from job-sharing to full-time work their accrued service for the purpose of fixing their salary increment would be calculated as half a year's service for each year of job sharing employment did (i) put women workers at a particular disadvantage; and (ii) was not justified. The European Court of Justice distinguished part time workers and job sharing workers.

> The specific feature which distinguished job-sharing from full term employment is that in the case of job-sharers the work and responsibilities are shared between two employees. Full term commitment and co-ordination of responsibilities related to the job being shared can be required of the job sharer.

Accordingly the Irish government's argument that the pay scheme constituted a legitimate incentive to civil servants to choose a method of work which was of greater value to the employer was rejected by the Court of Justice.

---

667. DEC E2000/06/AEE/01/13.
668. [1998] ECR 1-3739.

Chapter 14. The Law on Discrimination on Grounds of Age, Disability and Race

§1. DISCRIMINATION ON GROUNDS OF DISABILITY

I. The Definition of Disability

246. Discrimination on grounds of disability in employment is outlawed by the Employment Equality Acts 1998–2011. The definition of disability (which is borrowed from the Australian Disability Discrimination Act 1992) is made up of five alternative conditions. The first five of these conditions are:

(a) the total or partial absence of a person's bodily or mental functions, including the absence of a part of a person's body;

(b) the presence in the body of organisms causing, or likely to cause, chronic disease or illness.

It has been held that (b) does not capture conditions which are not caused by organisms. In *A Civil Servant* v. *The Office of the Civil Service and Local Appointments Commissioners*[669] the Equality Tribunal held that asthma did not fall within section 2(b) since asthma is caused by the narrowing of the smaller bronchi and bronchioles; it is not caused by an organism.

(c) The malfunction, malformation or disfigurement of a part of a person's body. Category (c) is the definition with the widest application. In *A Civil Servant (represented by the CPSU)* v. *The Office of the Civil Service and Local Appointments Commissioners* [670] the Equality Tribunal held that irritable bowel syndrome and asthma did fall within the definition in 2(c). In *A Computer Component Company* v. *A Worker*[671] the Labour Court held that epilepsy fell within the definition in 2(c). A back injury caused by a road accident has been held to be a 'malfunction';[672]

(d) a condition or malfunction which results in a person learning differently from a person without the condition or malfunction; or

(e) a condition, illness or disease which affects a person's thought processes, perception of reality, emotion or judgement or which results in disturbed behaviour.

Section 2(e) embraces a whole range of psychiatric conditions. In *The Civil Service Commissioners* v. *A Complainant*[673] the Labour Court assumed that the definition included persons suffering from paranoid schizophrenia. In *A Health and Fitness Club* v. *A Worker*[674] anorexia was held to be disability covered by section 2(e): (presumably on the ground that it is a 'condition' which affects 'thought processes and

---

669. Equality Tribunal [2004] DEC-E2004-029.
670. *Ibid.*
671. Equality Tribunal [2001] EED 013.
672. *An Grianan Hotel* v. *Langford*, Labour Court [2012] ADE/12/2.
673. Labour Court [2002] EDA 024
674. Labour Court [2003] EED 037.

perception of reality). In *A Complainant* v. *Café Kylemore*[675] it was held that alcoholism was a 'disease' which caused 'disturbed behaviour' and therefore, fell within section 2(e). Transsexualism has been held to be a disability.[676] In *O* v. *A Named Company*[677] the Equality Tribunal held (overruling the employer's objections that the symptoms did not fall within the definition of 'disability') that an employee who suffered from anxiety and depression caused by work-related stress suffered from a disability. The High Court has doubted whether obesity was a disability within any of the five definitions.[678]

II. The Concept of Direct Discrimination on Grounds of Disability

247.   Direct discrimination is defined in section 6 (2) (g) of the Employment Equality Act 1998:

> For the purposes of this Act, discrimination shall be taken to occur where, on the ground that [one is a person with a disability and the other either is not or is a person with a different disability] one person is treated less favourably than another is, has been or would be treated.

Article 2 of Directive 2000/78/EC, establishing a framework for equal treatment, provides that the principle of equal treatment means that there shall be no direct or indirect discrimination 'whatsoever' on any of the protected grounds. This is routinely interpreted as meaning that it is sufficient that disability be a significant, or more than trivial, influence. It is not necessary that the employee's disability be the sole influencing factor.[679] In *Alzheimer Society* v. *A Worker*[680] the claimant had not been returned to her post as nursing officer of a day care centre following a period of illness. The Labour Court held that it was enough that the disability was one of the grounds for the decision. It was not necessary to prove that it was the sole ground.[681]

The comparator may be actual or hypothetical. The Labour Court has said that in constructing a hypothetical comparator '[it] should establish the factual criterion for the impugned decision and consider if that criterion would have similarly been applied in the case of a person without the protected characteristic'.[682] The comparator may also suffer from a disability and the claimant suffer from a 'different' disability. This is necessitated by the very broad definition of disability. If this provision was not included, it would be open to an employer to use some disability

---

675. DEC-S2002-024, followed by the Labour Court in *A Government Department* v. *An Employee* Labour Court [2006] EDA 062.
676. *Hannon* v. *First Direct Logistics* [2011] 22 ELR 215.
677. DEC-E2003/052.
678. *Eagle Star Assurance Co* v. *Director of the Equality Tribunal* [2009] 20 ELR 295.
679. *An Grianan Hotel* v. *Langford* Labour Court [2012] ADE/12/2.
680. Labour Court [2007] EDA 075.
681. Similarly: *A Worker* v. *A Hotel* [2008] 19 ELR 73; *A Company* v. *A Worker* (ADE 09/21, 21 May 2010).
682. *A Worker* v. *Two Respondents* Labour Court [2011] ADE 11/16.

affecting the advantaged comparator's to disprove the allegation that the treatment was on grounds of disability. In *The Civil Service Commissioners* v. *A Complainant*[683] the complainant, who suffered from schizophrenia, had applied for a position as clerical officer in a competition which was restricted to persons with a disability. The claim fell within the legislation since it involved a claim that he was discriminated against relative to persons who suffered from a 'different' disability.

The definition of discrimination in section 6(1) of the Employment Equality Acts 1998–2011 corresponds to the European 'associative discrimination' principle (established in *Coleman* v. *Attridge Law*).[684] Section 6(1) extends discrimination to cases where a person who is associated with another person and is 'by virtue of that association treated less favourably' and where similar treatment of that other person would constitute discrimination.[685]

III. The Concept of Indirect Discrimination on Grounds of Disability

248. Section 31 of the Employment Equality Acts 1998–2011 defines indirect discrimination on grounds of disability as occurring where:

(a) an apparently neutral provision puts persons of a particular gender (being As or Bs) at a particular disadvantage in respect of any matter other than remuneration compared with other employees of their employer.

(b) Where paragraph (*a*) applies, the employer shall be treated for the purposes of this Act as discriminating against each of the persons referred to (including A or B), unless the provision is objectively justified by a legitimate aim and the means of achieving that aim are appropriate and necessary.

In practice all job descriptions are likely, in some way, to be indirectly discriminatory. The key element will be whether the measure may be justified as an 'appropriate' and 'necessary' means of pursuing a 'legitimate aim'. The complainant in *Gorry* v. *Civil Service Commissioners*[686] challenged as indirectly discriminatory a requirement that applicants for the position of executive officer in the Civil Service have passed the Leaving Certificate English examination. Gorry, who suffered from dyslexia, had not passed the examination. The Equality Tribunal accepted that the Leaving Certificate requirement put persons who suffered from this disability at a particular disadvantage. The Tribunal went on to find that the requirement that Executive Officers should hold the Leaving Certificate did pursue a 'legitimate aim' and was both 'appropriate' and 'necessary'.

---

683. Labour Court [2002] EDA 024.
684. [2008] IRLR 722.
685. The *Coleman* principle was applied in *A Worker* v. *Two Respondents* Labour Court [2011] ADE/11/16.
686. Labour Court [2006] EDA 0164.

185

IV. The 'Reasonable Accommodation' Requirement

249. Section 16 is the source of the 'reasonable accommodation' requirement required by Article 5 of Directive 2000/78/EC. Section 16 begins by providing that an employer may refuse to recruit, or may dismiss, a disabled person if the person is not fully competent to undertake the duties attached to the job.

> Nothing in this Act shall be construed as requiring any person to recruit or promote an individual to a position, to retain an individual in a position, or to provide training or experience to an individual in relation to a position, if the individual- will not undertake (or, as the case may be, continue to undertake) the duties attached to that position or will not accept (or as the case may be continue to accept) the conditions under which those duties are, or may be required to be, performed, or is not (or, as the case may be, is no longer) fully competent and available to undertake, and fully capable of undertaking, the duties attached to that position, having regard to the conditions under which those duties are, or may be required to be performed.

However, the employer may only prove lack of competence where he also establishes that no measure of 'reasonable accommodation' by him could make the employee competent. Section 16(3)(a) incorporates the 'reasonable accommodation' condition:

> For the purposes of this Act a person who has a disability is fully competent to undertake, and fully capable of undertaking, any duties if the person would be so fully competent and capable on reasonable accommodation (in this subsection referred to as 'appropriate measures') being provided by the person's employer.

'Duties' are interpreted as meaning the 'central duties' attached to the position. The complainant in *A Computer Component Co.* v. *A Worker*[687] was a factory worker who suffered from epilepsy. The respondent, concerned that her work involved operating heavy equipment, dismissed her. The ground of dismissal was that her continued employment exposed others and herself to physical danger. The Labour Court[688] held that the dismissal was discriminatory on grounds of disability. First, it interpreted the phrase 'the duties attached to the position' as meaning the *central* duties attached to the position. Therefore, while the respondent did have some heavy machinery, not all production workers were required to use it, and the respondent could have arranged his affairs so as to have some other operative carry out the work. Accordingly, she was able to carry out the duties attached to the position.'

Secondly, the Labour Court has held that the words 'on the basis of an objective and thorough investigation' should be inserted and read before the phrase 'not fully

---

687. Labour Court [2001] EED O13.
688. S. 77(2) provides that a claim alleging discriminatory dismissal must be initiated before the Labour Court and should not be brought before the Director.

competent'. In *A Worker* v. *A Health and Fitness Club*[689] the Labour Court held that employer should consult the employee about his or her needs:

> Before coming to the view [that an employee is other than 'fully competent and available to undertake the duties attached to a position'] the employer would normally be required to make adequate enquiries so as to establish fully the factual position in relation to the employee's capacity. The nature and extent of the enquiries which an employer should make will depend on the circumstances of each case. At a minimum, however, an employer should ensure that he or she is in full possession of all the material facts concerning the employee's condition and that the employee is given fair notice that the question of his or her dismissal for incapacity is being considered. The employee must also be allowed an opportunity to influence the employer's decision.[690]

In the absence of such a dialogue the employer will not be able to objectively establish that the employee is incompetent; nor will the employer be able to properly undertake its duty to put in place 'appropriate measures'.[691]

'Appropriate measures' may include the supply of facilities or training to enable a disabled employee to be fully competent to undertake the duties of the position. The complainant in *An Employee* v. *A Local Authority*[692] suffered from a learning difficulty. He had been employed by the local authority in a junior clerical position, whose duties involved routine clerical functions such as photocopying and writing letters of acknowledgement. The employee was found to be excessively slow and unreliable in carrying out these functions, and was dismissed. It was held that although not fully capable of carrying out his work, the employer did not consider the option of a job coach to assist the worker. The Equality Tribunal held that the costs involved in retaining a job coach would not exceed a 'nominal' cost to this employer. 'Appropriate measures' may include the provision of a different work regime, such as permitting the worker to work at different hours, or part time, or remotely.[693] In *An Employer* v. *A Worker*[694] the Labour Court said that 'appropriate measures' may involve

---

689. Labour Court [2003] EED037; principles applied in *Rattigan* v. *Connacht Gold Co-op* [2008] 19 ELR 348 and *Mr O* v. *An Industrial Management Waste Co* [2014] ELR 106.
690. The complainant in *McCrory Scaffolding* v. *A Worker* Labour Court [2005] EED055 was a scaffolding worker who had suffered epileptic fits while working. He was summarily dismissed on the grounds that his epilepsy made him dangerous and incompetent. The Labour Court held that the employer, in failing to carry out a medical examination, in conjunction with the employee had not carried out the assessment required by s. 16(1): *Rattigan* v. *Connacht Gold Co-op* [2008] 19 ELR 348.
691. *Mid Staffordshire General Hospitals NHS Trust* v. *Cambridge* [2003] IRLR 566.
692. Equality Tribunal [2002] DEC-E/2002/4. 'Appropriate measures' may include tolerance of a period of absence or interrupted work. In *O* v. *A Named Company,* Equality Officer [2003] DEC-E2003-052 it was held that an employer was required to allow an employee, who was undergoing psychiatric treatment following a nervous breakdown, the opportunity to return to work on a phased basis for a number of weeks. The principle was also applied in *A Worker* v. *A Telecommunications Company* [2011] 22 ELR 41.
693. *A Worker* v. *A Telecommunications Company* [2011] 22 ELR 41.
694. Labour Court [2004] EDA 0413.

affording the person with a disability more favourable treatment than would be accorded to an employee without a disability. Thus it may be necessary to consider such matters as adjusting the person's attendance hours or to allow them to work partially from home. The duty to provide special treatment may also involve relieving a disabled employee of the requirement to undertake certain tasks which others doing similar work are expected to perform.

However, the measure must be one which will restore the employee so that he is 'fully competent and capable' of undertaking the original position. It is not enough that the measure will enable the employee merely to work in some reduced capacity. In *Department of Justice* v. *Kavanagh*[695] the Labour Court emphasized that the measure must be one which restored the employee to full competence: the purpose of section 16 is to render the disabled person 'fully capable to undertake the full range of duties associated with their posts'.

Section 13(3) limits the economic costs of 'reasonable accommodation': 'a refusal to provide for special treatment shall not be deemed reasonable unless such provision would give rise to a cost, other than a nominal cost, to the employer'. As originally drafted, the Employment Equality Bill had been framed so as to deny the right to discriminate where 'with the assistance of special assistance or facilities the employee would be fully capable of carrying out the work'. However, in *The Employment Equality Bill 1996 Reference*[696] the Supreme Court struck down the provision as an unjust interference with the property rights of employers. The court held that it was unjust that employers should bear the full economic cost of installing remedial measures. The effect of the measure, it was held, was to impose on one social constituency, employers, the burden of remedying a general social problem. Section 13(3), as revised in light of the Supreme Court decision, now provides that 'a refusal to provide for special treatment shall not be deemed reasonable unless such provision would give rise to a cost, other than a nominal cost, to the employer'. Accordingly, where the cost of making an adaption would not give rise to anything more than a nominal cost, the employer is obliged to make the change. In *Kehoe* v. *Convertec*[697] an employee with cerebral palsy was held to have been discriminated against on grounds of disability where he was dismissed because his productivity was less than a target rate set by the employer. The employer could, by making a reasonable accommodation (lowering the productivity demand, and reducing pro rata the claimant's wage), have continued the claimant in employment.

V. Measures to Enable a Person Who Has a Disability 'to Have Access to Employment'

250. Section 16(3)(b) (inserted by the Employment Equality Act 2004) now imposes a series of positive obligations on the employer to make it feasible for a person to apply for the position in the first place:

---

695. [2012] 23 ELR 34.
696. [1997] 3 IR 321.
697. Equality Officer [2001] DEC E2001-34.

(*b*) The employer shall take appropriate measures, where needed in a particular case, to enable a person who has a disability—

(i) to have access to employment,
(ii) to participate or advance in employment, or
(iii)to undergo training, unless the measures would impose a disproportionate burden on the employer.

(*c*) In determining whether the measures would impose such a burden account shall be taken, in particular, of—

(i) the financial and other costs entailed,
(ii) the scale and financial resources of the employer's business, and
(iii)the possibility of obtaining public funding or other assistance.

In *Harrington* v. *East Coast Area Health Board*[698] the respondent was held to have infringed section 16(3)(b) by holding an interview in a room which was not wheelchair accessible. The claimant, who was a wheelchair user, and had been unable to participate in the interview, was awarded €1,270 for distress suffered. In *O'Sullivan* v. *Department of Justice*[699] the Equality Tribunal held that an employer was required to defer the time at which an interview was to be held with a prospective employee, who suffered from a disability and would not be able to attend at the time originally scheduled because he was undergoing disability-related surgery.[700]

Discrimination on grounds of disability may be direct or indirect.[701] The Act outlaws discrimination in relation to access to employment: *see Harrington* v. *Eastern Health Board*[702] where physical inaccessibility of premises to a physically disabled person attending an interview was held to constitute direct discrimination on grounds of disability.

VI. The Occupational Qualification, Significantly Increased Costs and Emergency Services Defences

251. Section 37(2) provides a derogation from the equality principle in a case where it is an occupational qualification for the post that the employee have a particular characteristic, which the disabled person does not possess. A further

---

698. Labour Court [2002] DEC E2002-001.
699. DEC-E2004-076.
700. In *O'Sullivan* v. *Siemens Business Service Ltd* Equality Tribunal [2006] DEC-E2006-058
    the employee had sought a position as IT support officer. There was a preliminary examination for candidates which the applicant was unable to sit. The applicant applied for permission to sit an electronic version of the test. This was refused. The Tribunal held that the employer had failed to take appropriate measures to ensure accessibility as required by s. 16(3)(b).
701. Ss. 6, 8 and 31 of the Employment Equality Act 1998–2011.
702. DEC E/2002/001.

qualification arises in a case where there is clear actuarial evidence that significantly increased costs would result if discrimination was not permitted.[703]

The prohibition on disability discrimination does not apply to employment in the defence forces.[704]

VII. Remedies for Disability Discrimination

252. The Equality Tribunal and the Labour Court are given a flexible spectrum of remedies where discrimination is proven. These range from compensation; to an order for equal treatment; to an order for for reinstatement or re-engagement.[705] The maximum sum that may be awarded by the Equality Tribunal where the 'complainant was in receipt of remuneration at the date of the reference of the case' should not exceed 104 times the amount of weekly remuneration, or €40,000, whichever is the greater sum.[706] Where the employee is not in receipt of remuneration at the time of discrimination the maximum is €13,000.[707] The powers of the Labour Court are more extensive: to order compensation for the effects of discrimination which occurred not earlier than six years before the discrimination.[708] There is no maximum damages limit. The Labour Court has stressed that where compensation is ordered that the Labour Court is bound to apply the principle in *Von Colson and Kamann* v. *Land Nordrhein Westfalen*[709] and to ensure that any sanction is 'effective and has a deterrent effect and ... amount to more than purely nominal compensation'.[710] There is no limit on the sum may be awarded by the Circuit Court where the complainant elects to use his right to litigate in that court.[711]

§2. Discrimination on Grounds of Age

253. Directive 2000/78 outlaws discrimination on grounds of age in employment. Section 8 of the Employment Equality Acts 1998–2011 provide that in relation to (a) access to employment, (b) conditions of employment, (c) training or experience for or in relation to employment, (d) promotion or re-grading, or (e) classification of posts, an employer shall not discriminate on ground of age against an employee or prospective employee.

---

703. S. 34(3) of the Employment Equality Act 1998.
704. S. 37(5) of the Employment Equality Act 1998.
705. Ss. 81 and 82 of the Employment Equality Act 1998.
706. S. 82(3) as amended by the Civil Law Miscellaneous Provisions Act 2011, s. 25(1).
707. The European Committee of Social Rights has held that the maximum of €40,000 infringes one of the incidents of the rule against discrimination; the principle that compensation must be proportionate and sufficiently dissuasive. European Committee of Social Rights. Conclusions. 2012. Ireland. 7 http://www.coe.int/t/dghl/monitoring/socialcharter/conclusions/conclusionsindex_en.asp accessed 15 June 2014.
708. S. 82(2) of the Employment Equality Act 1998.
709. [1984] ECR 1891.
710. *Bus Eireann* v. *Wynne*, Labour Court [2012] EDA 1216.
711. S. 82 (3) ('and no enactment relating to the jurisdiction of the Circuit Court shall be taken to limit the amount of compensation or remuneration which may be ordered by the Circuit Court').

I. The Scope of the Rule against Discrimination on Grounds of Age

254. The protection against age discrimination applies to a wide range of workers and is not just confined to persons working under a contact of employment. (i) The phrase 'contract of employment' is extended, beyond its normal common law meaning, to include certain forms of self-employment (arrangements under which an individual agrees with another person personally to execute any work or service for that person).[712] (ii) The protection of self-employed persons was extended by the Equality Act 2004[713] which included persons working personally for an undertaking. (iii) Partners are also protected. Section 13A(1), again an improvement effected by the Equality Act 2004, provides that the 'reference to an employee include references to such a partner'.

Section 37(6), as originally drafted, had provided that the protection against age discrimination did not apply to employment: (a) in the defence forces; (b) in the *Garda Síochána*, or (c) in the prison service. This was revised in 2004. There is no longer any general exemption from discrimination within the *Garda Síochána* or within the prison service. Instead the Minister may introduce maximum age limits for recruitment but only where such age limits are operationally necessary. Section 37(4) operates where: 'the Minister is of opinion that the age profile of members of the Garda Síochana, prison service or any emergency service is such that its operational capacity is or is likely to be adversely affected'.

On the other hand, the general exemption of the defence forces from the age discrimination rule has been maintained.[714] The Supreme Court in *The Employment Equality Bill 1996 Reference*[715] remarked disapprovingly on the unqualified nature of the defence forces exception. It was not clear, the Court remarked, why such a restriction on the right of non-discrimination should be necessary in the case of non-combatant members of the defence forces.

II. Proof of Discrimination on Grounds of Age

255. The claimant is not required to positively directly prove that the actual cause of non-appointment was the respondent's discrimination on grounds of age. It cannot be expected that the respondent will admit age discrimination: 'It is well settled that those who discriminate rarely do so overtly and will not leave evidence of the discrimination within the complainant's power of procurement'.[716] Accordingly, the claimant is entitled to prove discrimination by circumstantial evidence. The task of proof by circumstantial evidence is assisted by section 85A of the Employment Equality Acts 1998–2011; section 85A, implementing Article 10 of the Directive 2000/78,[717] provides that where:

---

712. S. 2 Employment Equality Act 1998–2011.
713. S. 3 Employment Equality Act, 2004.
714. S. 37(5).
715. [1997] 2 IR 321, at p. 368
716. *Cork City Council* v. *McCarthy* Labour Court [2008] EDA 0821.
717. Article 10 provides: 'Member States shall take such measures as are necessary, in accordance with their national judicial systems, to ensure that, when persons who consider themselves wronged

facts are established by or on behalf of a complainant from which it may be presumed that there has been discrimination in relation to him or her, it is for the respondent to prove the contrary.

This has been interpreted as meaning that the facts be of 'sufficient significance' to require that the court probe further. In *Rescon* v. *Scanlon*[718] it was said that burden of proof shifts when

> the complainant [proves] on the balance of probabilities the primary facts upon which he seeks to rely in raising a presumption of unlawful discrimination. Secondly, those facts, if proved, must appear to the court to be of sufficient significance to raise the presumption contended for.

Where the complainant raises evidence of 'sufficient significance' the burden of proof shifts to the employer. In *Donnellan* v. *An Garda Commissioner*[719] the High Court said:

> if a claimant can establish a *prima facie* case that age was a material causal factor in the decision, then the burden of proof shifts to the respondent to show that age was not such a factor, or else that it was justified. The fact that one candidate is preferred over another of a different age will clearly not be enough to shift the burden.

III. Evidence of 'Sufficient Significance' to Shift the Burden of Proof to the Employer

A. Where Older Candidate Is Better Qualified

256. The fact that the elder unsuccessful claimant is better qualified than the younger successful claimant may raise a prima facie case.

The burden will then transfer to the employer to show some non-age related ground for non-appointment. In *Mr A* v. *Government Department*[720] the applicant had been rated as an 'excellent official'. He was, despite his first rate appraisal, refused promotion. The employee's favourable appraisal in comparison with the younger appointee was held to shift the burden of proof. The employer did not give evidence in rebuttal. Therefore, the Tribunal was bound to find that the complainant had shifted the burden of proof:

> it is difficult to reconcile the review of the complainant in January 2005 which described him as an 'excellent official' (see 2.12 above) with this

---

because the principle of equal treatment has not been applied to them establish, before a court or other competent authority, facts from which it may be presumed that there has been direct or indirect discrimination, it shall be for the respondent to prove that there has been no breach of the principle of equal treatment.'
718. Equality Tribunal [2008] DEC-E2007-037.
719. [2008] IEHC 467.
720. 21 August 2006.

overwhelmingly negative assessment, without possibility of improvement, in April 2005. As the Principal Officer did not give evidence, I was unable to question him regarding his conclusions.

In *Meehan* v. *Leitrim CC*[721] the claimant had applied for a position of fireman with the respondent. He was, by reference to the criteria, more highly qualified than the successful applicant. Yet the employer had graded him equally with the less experienced younger competitors. The Tribunal held that the burden shifted to the employer to explain this disparity. The employer was unable to do this. The Tribunal noted that 'there is no evidence as to how the Interview Board reached their decision to award identical marks to both candidates for experience and knowledge, given the complainant's significantly greater experience as detailed above'.

B. Reliable Statistical Evidence Showing Preference for Younger Candidates

257. Where employment selection or promotion is part of a large competition a pattern of preference for younger candidates may raise an inference of discrimination. In *O'Mahony* v. *Revenue Commissioners*[722] the claimants had unsuccessfully applied for the position of higher executive officer in the customs' service of the Revenue Commissioners. The statistics as to successful applicants showed a pattern of discrimination in favour of younger candidates. In six of the ten locations, nobody over 50 years of age was placed on the panel despite the fact that in each case there were such applicants, and all of these employees had previously been rated highly in earlier internal assessments. The Labour Court held that the burden shifted to the respondent. In order to rebut the presumption of discrimination it was necessary to 'offer a creditable explanation for the marks actually awarded to the complainants'. The interview notes did not show grounds which justified non-appointment.

In *Rath* v. *UCD*[723] an analysis of results from a university promotions' round demonstrated that (i) 66 per cent of applicants aged under 60 were successful; only 40 per cent of candidates over 60 were successful. This disparity was counted as of sufficient significance to transfer the burden of proof. On the other hand, a statistically founded allegation of discriminatory historical practice will not succeed unless the evidence is statistically significant. The statistical pool must be sufficiently wide. In *McCormick* v. *Dublin Port*[724] the complainant presented figures which showed that there had been eleven candidates for a competition in 1992, of which one alone was aged over 50, and in 1998 twelve candidates for a competition, of whom two were aged over 50, and that in neither case had the older applicant been appointed. The Tribunal held that the 'figures involved in both competitions were too small to draw meaningful statistical conclusions … two competitions with respectively one and two candidates over the age of fifty, from a

---

721. Equality Tribunal [2006] DEC-E2006-014.
722. Labour Court [2003] EDA 033.
723. Labour Court [2011] EDA119.
724. DEC E2002-046.

pool of twenty three candidates do not that demonstrate that older candidates were deliberately not promoted by the respondent.'

C. Age-related Questions at Interview

258. Prima facie evidence that age is an operating consideration may be deduced from age-related questions asked at interview, or from the fact that the applicant is asked to furnish his age. Age-related questions will not be definitive proof of discrimination. Instead, the burden will shift to the employer to prove that the questions were not a factor in the challenged decision.[725] In *Cunningham* v. *BMS Promotions*[726] the employee was asked to provide his age in the application form. When the applicant refused, the respondent pursued the matter with him. This concern with age was held to shift the burden on to the employer, which the employer failed to rebut. In *O'Conghaile* v. *Scoil Mhuire*[727] the question 'can you offer the Selection Committee a brief outline as to why you feel, at this stage in your career, that you are the most suitable candidate for the position of Principal?' was held to betray a suspect attention to age.

D. Indirectly Discriminatory Appointment Criteria

259. Employment appointment criteria are also subject to review on the grounds of indirect discrimination on grounds of age. Section 31 defines the elements of indirect discrimination on grounds of age:

> where an apparently neutral provision puts persons of a particular [age] at a particular disadvantage … compared with other employees of their employer … the employer shall be treated for the purposes of this Act as discriminating … unless the provision is objectively justified by a legitimate aim and the means of achieving that aim are appropriate and necessary.

Thus, requirements such as physical fitness, or the possession of certain forms of qualification, may, in practice, be capable of being complied with by a considerably higher proportion of employees of one age group than employees of another, older age group. That alone will not make the measure indirectly discriminatory. In all cases, the key question will be whether the measure is justified by a legitimate aim, and that the measure is necessary to achieve this aim. In *O'Connor* v. *Lidl Ireland*[728] the complainant had responded to an advertisement which read: 'the ideal candidate should be a graduate, ideally with not more than two to three years' experience in

---

725. *McEniff* v. *Jurska* Labour Court [2011] EDA1122 (advertisement inviting applications to join a 'young' team; respondent showing that non-selection was due to a non-age related reasons; Labour Court held that while reference to age was 'inappropriate' age played no role in the ultimate selection process).
726. [2008] 19 ELR 165.
727. [2008] 19 ELR 107.
728. Equality Officer [2005] DEC-E2005-12.

a commercial environment'. The complainant had five years' post-qualification experience. He was not called to interview. The Equality Officer found that the requirement of not more than three years' post-qualification experience was one with operated to the disadvantage of older applicants as opposed to ones in their twenties and thirties. The employer was unable to show any objective justification for the measure. Accordingly, it was held to have indirectly discriminated.[729]

IV. Discriminatory Advertising

260. It was discriminatory age advertising which provoked the first age discrimination case in Irish law. Section 10 of the Employment Equality Act, 1998 provides that a person shall not publish or cause to be published or displayed an advertisement which relates to employment and which (a) indicates an intention to discriminate, or (b) might reasonably be understood as indicating such an intention. In *Equality Authority v. Ryanair*[730] *a*n advertisement stated that the applicant should be a 'young and dynamic professional.' It was held that Ryanair had published an advertisement which indicated an intention to discriminate on grounds of age. Rynair's defence – that the reference to young meant young as a matter of temperamental disposition, rather than young as a matter of age – was rejected.

V. Defences to Age Discrimination

A. Genuine and Determining Occupational Requirement

261. The rule against discrimination in relation to access to employment is subject to a number of qualifications. Firstly, there is an occupational qualification defence. Section 37(2) provides:

> For the purposes of this Part a difference of treatment which is based on a characteristic related to any of the discriminatory grounds (except the gender ground) shall not constitute discrimination where, by reason of the particular occupational activities concerned or of the context in which they are carried and—
>
> (a) the characteristic constitutes a genuine and determining occupational requirement, and
> (b) the objective is legitimate and the requirement proportionate.

The CJEU in *Prigge* v. *Deutsche Lufthansa*[731] held that essential physical capabilities for piloting aircraft which diminish with age could fall within the 'genuine and

---

729. A similar finding of indirect discrimination on grounds of age was made about a requirement of two to three years' post qualification experience in *Noonan* v. *Accountancy Connections* DEC 2004/42.
730. Equality Tribunal [2000] DEC -2000-14.
731. [2011] ECR-1-8003.

determining characteristic related to age formula'. In *Wolf* v. *Stadt Frankfurt*[732] the CJEU held that a high level of physical fitness required of a fire fighter constituted a genuine and determining occupational requirement related which justified an upper age limit for recruitment of 30. However, in *Donnellan* v. *An Garda Commissioner*[733] the High Court rejected the assertion that a compulsory retirement age of 60 for an assistant commissioner of An Garda Commissioner corresponded to an occupational qualification. The court said that Article 4 'only applies where the characteristic of age itself, goes towards an applicant's ability to perform a particular job'. The High Court went on to instance occupations such as acting, or modelling clothes aimed at a particular age group. The court approved the conditions articulated in Canada in *Law* v. *Canada (Minister of Employment and Immigration)*[734] and the Australian case of *Qantas* v. *Christie*:[735]

> are the characteristics that are cited to justify the act of discrimination legitimate and justifiable grounds for distinguishing between two people, b) is age an effective and reliable proxy for the relevant characteristics or a necessary differentiating tool for determining whether an individual possesses those characteristics?

In that case the High Court held that a rule which required that an assistant commissioner of *An Garda* Commissioner should not be aged more than 60 did not correspond to a genuine occupational qualification.

The age of the Assistant Commissioner formed no part of the '*occupational requirement*', of that position (as it could be of a job like child modelling). There was nothing inherent about the age used in the Regulations which would mean that a person of a certain age was required for the job. There was no essential characteristic for the position the possession for which age was a 'necessary differentiating tool.

B. '*Legitimate Aim*' Defence

262. Article 6(1) of Directive 2000/78 provides that:

> Notwithstanding Article 2(2), Member States may provide that differences of treatment on grounds of age shall not constitute discrimination, if, within the context of national law, they are objectively and reasonably justified by a legitimate aim, including legitimate employment policy, labour market and vocational training objectives, and if the means of achieving that aim are appropriate and necessary.

---

732. Case C-229/08.
733. [2008] IEHC 467.
734. [1999] 1 SCR 143.
735. (1998) 152 ALR 1295.

In *Donnellan* v. *An Garda Commissioner*[736] the High Court upheld a provision in the *Garda Síochána* (Retirement) Regulations 1996[737] under which an Assistant Commissioner was required to retire at the age of 60. The measure was justified on two grounds: (i) reducing the age profile of assistant commissioners would create a wider competitive pool of candidates from which the position of Commissioner might be chosen; and (ii) a turnover of vacancies in the office ensured motivation and dynamism through increased prospect of promotion. The High Court then applied the necessary' proportionality requirement (as elaborated in *Félix Palacios de la Villa* v. *Cortefiel Servicios SA*).[738] The measure was not excessively oppressive since under Regulation 6(b) the appointment could, on an application for an extension, be extended until the age of 65: 'Regulation 6(b) of the 1951 regulation serves to temper the severity of what would otherwise be an absolute retirement age; thereby rendering it, in my opinion, proportionate. It cannot therefore be entirely equated with a blanket policy type position.'

C. The Compulsory Retirement Age Defence

263. Section 34(4) of the Employment Equality Acts 1998-2011 validates non-selective compulsory retirement ages:

> … it shall not constitute discrimination on the age ground to fix different ages for the retirement (whether voluntarily or compulsorily) of employees or any class or description of employees.

Section 34(4) of the Employment Equality Acts 1998–2011 exempts dismissal consequential upon a retirement age which applies to 'employees or any class or description of employees'. It only operates where the provision is non-selective. It would not justify random or selective compulsory retirement ages. In *Leahy* v. *Limerick City Council*[739] where the complainant, a fire fighter, was dismissed at the age of 55 in accordance with the Council's policy of compulsory retiring fire fighters. The claimant pointed out that fire *officers* were not subject to this requirement, and that therefore the employer had not fixed different retirement ages for all employees of the same 'class or description'. However, the equality officer held that fire officers formed a distinct 'class or description' of employees. They were required to hold a third-level degree, and usually took control of a fire-fighting operation. The employer had fixed a distinct age for retirement of a class of employees and the measure was not capable of being complained of under the 1998 Act.

The legality of section 34(4) is now under pressure for infringing European Law. During the Select Committee debates on the Equality Bill 2004 an attempt was

---

736. [2008] IEHC 467.
737. SI 16/1996.
738. [2007] ECR 1-8531.
739. E/2003/38.

made to introduce an amendment which would have abolished the mandatory retirement age. The Minister, Willie O'Dea TD, opposed the amendment saying:[740]

> Compulsory retirement ages are a factor of many types of employment in both the public and private sectors. They have been agreed over time and, in many cases, following collective bargaining processes. The removal of existing … arrangements in the private sector with respect to compulsory retirement age is a matter for discussion with the social partners.

It is not clear whether any 'legitimate aim' can be uncovered from this explanation. The observations of the Third Chamber in *R(Age Concern)* v. *Secretary of State for Business*[741] that legitimate aims are social policy objectives and are 'distinguishable from purely individual reasons particular to the employer's situation such as cost reduction or improving competiveness'.[742] In *Donellan* v. *An Garda Commissioner*[743] the High Court, while not expressing any view on the legality of section 34, rehearsed the European law on the topic. Relying on *de la Villa*,[744] it was pointed out that in order to comply with Article 2(2) a compulsory retirement age must serve a legitimate purpose, and be an appropriate and proportionate means of accomplishing that objective:

> national measures relating to compulsory retirement ages are not excluded from consideration under Directive 2000/78/EC. Any discrimination with regards to age must, as put by that directive, serve a legitimate aim or purpose, and the means taken to achieve that purpose must be appropriate and should go no further than is necessary, i.e. they should be proportionate.[745]

Irish employment tribunals now reconcile section 34 with European law by reading the phrase to 'fix different ages' as meaning 'to fix' in accordance with the Article 6(1) of Directive 2000/78 'objective justification' test.[746] Therefore, a compulsory retirement age in an undertaking may be justified where it realizes, in a proportionate manner, a legitimate employment objective (such as promoting good personnel management).[747]

---

740. *Oireachtas* Debates. Select Committee on Justice, 22 June 2004, col. 1097.
741. [2009] ECR 1-1569, para 46.
742. *Ibid.*, para 46.
743. [2008] IEHC 467 25 July 2008.
744. [2007] ECR I-08531 (16 October 2007). This judgment was elaborated upon in *Fuchs* v. *Land Hessen* [2011] IRLR 1043, [2011] 3 CMLR 47, [2011] EUECJ C-159/10.
745. In *McCarthy* v. *HSE* [2010] IEHC 75 the High Court touched on the legality of section 19 of the Health Act 1970 which lays down a compulsory retirement age of 65. Finding nothing wrong with the requirement, the High Court said that '*de la Villa* adequately affirms that a law providing for a retirement age of 65 could not be seen as discriminatory or unreasonable in its effect. Indeed such provision is almost universal throughout the European Union'.
746. *Doyle* v. *ESB International* [2013] ELR 34.
747. *Ibid.*

D. Occupational Benefits Schemes and Age

264. Section 34(3) of the Employment Equality Act 1998 exempts from age discrimination provisions which take into account the period between the employee leaving employment and his or her compulsory retirement age – provisions which, for instance, allow an employer to pay a reduced sum to an employee who is about to reach compulsory retirement age. The Irish Labour Court has held that the aim of preventing workers close to retirement from receiving a windfall was a legitimate aim within Article 6 of Directive 2000/78.[748]

§3. DISCRIMINATION ON GROUNDS OF RACE

265. Section 6(2)(h) of the Employment Equality Acts 2008–2011 prohibits discrimination on grounds of race, colour, nationality or ethnic or national origins.

In practice, complaints of discrimination on grounds of race have rarely succeeded. They most commonly fail on the ground that the ground that the applicant has failed to raise a *prima facie* case.[749] Section 85A of the Employment Equality Acts 1998–2011 provide that

> where in any proceedings facts are established by or on behalf of a complainant from which it may be presumed that there has been discrimination in relation to him or her it is for the respondent to prove the contrary.

The phrase 'facts from which it may be presumed that there has been discrimination' has been interpreted as requiring 'facts from which discrimination [on grounds of race] may be inferred',[750] or facts on credible evidence of sufficient significance' to generate an inference of discrimination.[751] There have been a number of instances in which complainants have managed to shift the burden of proof to the employer. In *Munck* v. *National University of Ireland Maynooth*[752] emphasis placed by a university interview board, appointing a Professor of Sociology, to the applicant's knowledge of the 'Irish scene' was held to generate an inference of discrimination on racial grounds. The fact that a non-national employee, accused of theft, was not afforded the same disciplinary processes as would have been afforded to an indigenous employee shifted the burden of proof to the employer to *disprove* racial discrimination.[753] A non-national who was dismissed for an offence for which a person of another race in the same employment would have received a lesser sanction shifted the burden of proof of non-discrimination to the employer.[754]

---

748. *Hospira* v. *Rogan* [2013] ELR 263.
749. *Gedrimas* v. *Mulleadys* [2010] 21 ELR 133; *Valpeters* v. *Melbury Developments* [2010] 21 ELR 64; *Bozs* v. *Damoli Construction* [2011] 22 ELR 34.
750. *Campbell Catering* v. *Rasaq* [2004] 15 ELR 310.
751. *Gedrimas* v. *Mulleadys* [2010] 21 ELR 133.
752. [2005] 16 ELR 342.
753. *Campbell Catering* v. *Rasaq* [2004] 15 ELR 310.
754. *Ntoko* v. *Citibank* [2004] 15 ELR 116.

Chapter 15. Non-competition Covenants

266. Covenants against post-employment competition by former employees are regulated in Ireland by two sources of law: (i) the common law, and (ii) by the Competition Acts, 1991–1996.

§1. Post-Employment Non-compete or Non-disclosure Clauses

I. The Principles Required to Justify a Non-competition Clause

267. Since a non-competition clause interferes with an employee's freedom to work a non-competition clause – which by its nature restricts the type of work which the employee may be able to undertake – are only justified in limited circumstances.[755] The burden rests on the employer to show that this justification is in place.

Two principles condition the justification of such a clause: (i) the principle of a protectible interest, and (ii) the principle of least restrictive means.

The principle of the protectible interest means that the employer must be able to identify some important business interest. He must be in a position to show that that interest would be damaged if the employee engaged in competition. The protectible interests recognized at common law include the employer's customer base; the employer's confidential information; and the employer's interest in retaining key staff.

The principle of least restrictive means requires that, having established the existence of a legitimate protectible interest, the covenant should be drafted so as to impose only the most minimum restrictions upon competition. A covenant which exceeds that minimum will be regarded as null and void, and unenforceable.

II. The Protection of the Ex-employer's Customer Base

268. Where the protectible interest sought to be preserved by a restrictive covenant is the employer's customer base it must be demonstrated that the particular employee has such an intense customer hold, that were the employee to relocate, the customer would transfer his business to that former employee. It follows that not all employees are legally capable of being restrained by a covenant. In *Dosser* v. *Monaghan*[756] a restrictive covenant which prevented a musician who worked with an orchestra was held void. The employer's customers had no relationship with the individual musician such that if he was to move they would transfer their business to the new employer. Factors like exceptional skill, or the fact that customers entrust personal confidence to the particular employee, may generate 'customer hold'. Therefore, a highly skilled hairdresser 'agreeable and attractive to customers', or a

---

755. *Murgitroyd* v. *Purdy* [2005] 3 IR 12, 21.
756. [1932] NI 302.

solicitor to whom clients would entrust delicate information, have been held susceptible to restrictive covenants.[757]

The least restrictive means principle requires that, even if an employer establishes customer hold, the covenant must not exceed what is absolutely necessary to preserve the employer's interests. Restrictive covenants may take two forms: the non-compete clause and the non-solicit clause. The non-compete clause forbids the ex-employee from competing within the geographical market in which the ex-employer operates. The narrower non-solicit clause merely prevents the employee soliciting those customers with whom he or she has some customer connection. It is now accepted that only a non-solicit and not a non-compete clause may be used. The use of a non-compete clause would deny the ex-employee access to customers with whom he may have no customer connection, and would exceed what is strictly necessary to protect the employer's interests.[758]

Assuming that a non-solicit clause is the appropriate technique, two important drafting principles, both of them applications of the principle of least restrictive means, apply. The first is the principle that the contract must be drafted so as to prohibit dealing only with those customers with whom the employee has actually dealt. It is only these customers that the ex-employee is in a position to cause real harm. Second, the contract must be designed so as to prohibit soliciting or dealing only in the line of work originally carried out by the employee, and in which capacity he developed the customer hold.

John Orr Ltd v. *John Orr*[759] provides an example of a covenant which had the effect of barring the employee from a sector different from that in which he had 'customer hold'. The defendant employee worked for a company which manufactured general fabrics. Its parent company (Vescom) traded in wall coverings. The restrictive covenant provided that the employee should not:

> have any interest in any other firm or company, nor be employed by, or act as representative or agent for any other company, which manufactures or trades or markets similar or competing goods to those manufactured or traded by the company of by Vescom.

Under the strict terms of the covenant the ex-employee was prevented from working in a company which also traded in products different from those manufactured by his ex-employer. An employer does not have a protectible interest in a market in which he does not operate, and cannot prevent an employee working in a business which also pursues some other line of business.[760]

The prohibition on competition must not exceed what is necessary to protect the employer's customer base. A restrictive covenant must define the territorial limits of this customer base. In *Mulligan* v. *Corr*[761] a restrictive covenant which prevented the solicitor from practising within 20 miles of the town of Ballaghadareen was held

---

757. *Oates* v. *Romano* [1950] ILTR 161; *Mulligan* v. *Corr* [1925] 1 IR 179.
758. *Office Angels* v. *Rainer Thomas* [1991] IRLR 214.
759. [1987] ILRM 703.
760. *Business Seating* v. *Broad* [1989] ICR 713.
761. [1925] 1 IR 169.

to be geographically over broad. The practice was only carried on in the town of Ballina. The Supreme Court held that 'a restriction imposed to protect a business which was not in fact being worked and might never be set up was quite unreasonable'. In *John Orr Ltd* v. *John Orr*[762] the restrictive covenant prevented the ex-employee from being employed anywhere in any business carrying on any business equivalent to that done by the ex-employer. The ban was worldwide. Yet the company only traded in Europe and North America. The ban was held unenforceable.

The non-solicit clause must specify the period of time for which the contract is to endure. The cardinal principle is that the non-solicit clause must not exceed the period of time which is necessary for the employer to establish a relationship with the former customer base.[763]

III. The Protection of Confidential Information by Restrictive Covenant

269. The employer's interest in the non-disclosure of confidential information (as opposed to the protection of customer base) may be protected. According to one view a non-compete clause (forbidding the employee from working for a competitor who works in the same sector as the former employer) is acceptable. Although a narrower clause – one simply prohibiting the employee from using the information – may be more consistent with the minimal impairment principle, the English courts have accepted the legality of a non-compete clause in this context. The reasons for this are that identification of the information which is not to be disclosed may be difficult to detail, and that a non-disclosure clause, although narrower than a non-compete clause, may be difficult to enforce.[764]

Irish authority has taken a more critical view of a clause preventing a former employee engaging in a competing business when he is not actually using confidential information. A clause which forbids an ex-employee merely working for a competitor to whom the information may be useful is too broad; it should be narrowed to a prohibition on use of the confidential information.[765]

IV. Restrictive Covenants to Protect the Employer's Workforce

270. A restrictive covenant may prohibit an employee from inducing co-employees to leave the former employer.[766] However, an employer only has a protectible interest in key employees whose resignation would cause significant damage the ex-employer's business. In addition, the covenant may only prohibit the employer from approaching those employees with whom the ex-employee has had a special connection, or familiarity.[767]

---

762. [1987] ILRM 702.
763. *Middleton* v. *Brown* [1878] 47 LJ Ch. 411.
764. *Littlewoods Organization* v. *Harris* [1977] I WLR 1472.
765. *Net Affinity Limited* v. *Conaghan* [2011] IEHC 160; *Murgitroyd* v. *Purdy* [2005] 3 IR 12; *European Paint Importers* v. *O'Callaghan* [2005] IEHC 280; *Hernandez* v. *Vodafone ltd* [2013] 24 ELR 194.
766. *TSC Europe* v. *Massey* [1999] IRLR 22.
767. *Ibid.*

§2. The Competition Acts 1991–1996 and Restrictive Covenants

271. Section 4(1) of the Competition Act 1991 provides:

> subject to the provisions of the section, all agreements between undertakings, decisions by associations of undertakings and concerted practices which have as their objective or effect the prevention, restriction or distortion of competition or trade are prohibited and void.

An undertaking is defined in section 3 of the Act as 'a person, being an individual, a body corporate or an unincorporated body of persons engaged for gain in the production, supply or distribution of goods'. The view of the Competition Authority (the statutory authority which administers the Competition Acts) is that while an employee is usually not an undertaking, an employee may become an undertaking where he decides to commence trading on his own behalf.[768] At the moment that an employee commences in business on his own account he becomes an undertaking.

Employees are normally acting on behalf of an undertaking and therefore do not constitute an undertaking themselves. However, from the moment an employee pursues his own economic interests, and where they are different from his employer's interests, he might become an undertaking within the sense of Article 85.

There will, at that point, be an agreement between two undertakings and section 4 may apply. Restrictive covenants which 'prevent, restrict or distort' competition will then be subject to the sanctions provided under the competition code. (The question of whether this interpretation of section 3 – that it regulates restrictive covenants- is correct has not yet been settled by the High Court).

Assuming that the interpretation is correct, an ex-employee may, if the interpretation is correct, be able to resist injunctive proceedings for breach of a covenant on the basis that the agreement is contrary to Section 4 of the Competition Act, 1991 and unenforceable.

---

768. Competition Authority, Decision No. 20 Apex Fire Protection Ltd/Mr. Noel Murtagh.

Chapter 16. Employees and Intellectual Property

§1. Patents and Employees

272. The Irish law of patents is regulated by the Patents Act of 1992. Section 9 of the 1992 Act governs the definition of patentability: an invention is patentable if it is susceptible of industrial application, is new, and involves an inventive step. The Act excludes from the definition of patentability the following categories: (i) a discovery, a scientific theory, or a mathematical method; (ii) an aesthetic creation; (iii) a scheme, rule or method for performing a mental act, playing a game or doing business, or a programme for a computer; (iv) the presentation of information. (v) It also excludes a method for the treatment of the human or animal body by surgery or therapy.

Section 16 deals with the ownership of a patent: 'The right to a patent shall belong to an inventor, or his successor in title, but if the inventor is an employee the right to a patent shall be determined in accordance with the law of the state in which the employee is wholly or normally employed.'

The relevant 'law of the State' is the common law. The common law position is that, in the absence of an express provision to the contrary, there is an implied term that an employee is a trustee of his employee in relation to an invention made in the course of that person's duty as an employee. In *Patchett* v. *Sterling Engineering*[769] Lord Reid stated: 'it is, in my judgment, inherent in the legal relationship of master and servant that any product of the work which the servant is paid to do belongs to the master'.

However, the duty of accountability is restricted to cases (i) where the invention is made in the course of normal duties; (ii) where the invention is made in the course of carrying out duties specifically assigned to the employee; (iii) where the employee occupies a special office, such as that of director, under which he is expected to further the interests of the employer. Furthermore, the duty to account may be rebutted by a provision in the contract of employment displacing the ordinary common law rule of employee accountability for inventions.

§2. Copyright and Employees

273. The law of copyright is regulated in Ireland by the Copyright and Related Rights Act 2000. Copyright is defined as subsisting in (a) original literary, dramatic, musical or artistic works, (b) sound recordings, films, broadcasts, or cable programmes, (c) typographical arrangements of published editions. The issue of the ownership of copyright in the case of employment is dealt with by section 23:

> The author of a work shall be the first owner of the copyright unless (a) the work is made by an employee in the course of employment in which case the

---

769. (1955) 12 RPC 50.

employer is the first owner of any copyright, subject to any agreement to the contrary.

In *Stevenson Jordan Harrison* v. *McDonald*[770] the test applied for determining whether work was produced 'in the course of the author's employment' was whether the copyright originated in work which the employee might have been ordered to do. If it did, the work belonged to the employer. On the other hand, intellectual property generated during work which is done in the course of employment but was not strictly work of a type which the employee undertook to do, would not necessarily belong to the employer. Here a person originally employed as an engineer wrote academic lectures. Although the work was done with the sanction of the company, it did not constitute one of the functions specified in the contract of employment. Accordingly, copyright belonged to the employee.

Section 10(2) provides a separate rule in the case of journalistic employees. Where a literary, dramatic or artistic work is made by an author in the course of his employment by a newspaper or magazine, the author may use the work for any purpose other than for the purpose of retailing the piece to another newspaper.

---

770. [1952] TLR 101.

Part II. Collective Labour Relations

Chapter 1. The Historical Development of Trade Union Legitimacy: Trade Unions and the Constitution

§1. THE HISTORY OF TRADE UNIONISM IN IRELAND

I. Trade Unions and the Law in the Eighteenth and Nineteenth Centuries

274. In the early modern period trade unions were suppressed by a combination of statute law and common law. An Irish Act of 1729[771] incriminated persons who subscribed to, or who were knowingly concerned in, the constitution of a trade union. This was followed by an Act of 1743.[772] This Act declared all meetings of trade union organizations to be as unlawful assemblies. The premises in which such meetings were held were deemed a common nuisance. A series of these anti-union Acts were local in their focus: the City of Cork Regulation Act, 1771[773] was specific-ally directed against union organization in the city of Cork. Another Act of the same year[774] was directed against the activities of Dublin tailors and ship-wrights in their attempts to secure wage increases.

The common law also regarded trade unions as illegal. The legal objection was that trade union discipline interfered with the liberty of its members to work for whom, and on what conditions, they pleased; in other words, that trade unions oper-ated in restraint of trade. It was considered that agreements in restraint of trade, such as the rules of a trade union were not merely unlawful, but amounted to a criminal conspiracy at common law.[775] As organizations in restraint of trade (an interference with the free operation of the market), they were unlawful bodies to whose agree-ments the courts would afford no protection. Their funds were denied the benefit of the criminal law. The embezzlement of union funds was not regarded as crimi-nal.[776] More importantly, the coercive strategies pursued by trade unions were regarded as criminal conspiracies. The union-organized strike was regarded as a

---

771. An Act to Prevent Unlawful Combinations of Workmen; 3 Geo. III, Chapter XIV.
772. 17 Geo. II, Chapter 8.
773. 12 and 13 Geo. III, Chapter 18.
774. 11 and 12 Geo. III, Chapter 33.
775. *R.* v. *Bykerdike* (1832) 1 Mood and R. 179.
776. *Hornby* v. *Close* (1867) LR 2 QB 153.

criminal conspiracy[777] on the theory that it was a criminal conspiracy to agree to compel others to change the way in which they conducted their business affairs.

In 1824 a Parliamentary Select Committee (the Select Committee on the State of the Law in the United Kingdom respecting the Combination of Workmen to Raise Wages[778] recommended liberalization of the rules restricting trade unions, and a repeal of the Combination Acts. These recommendations were implemented by the Combination Repeal Act 1824, which repealed all earlier Combination Acts. The Trade Union Act of 1871 continued the process of legitimization: the funds of trade unions were declared lawful property.

However, criminal liability for strike activities remained. Strikes continued, notwithstanding the Act of 1871, to be regarded as criminal conspiracies: *R* v. *Bunn*.[779] In 1875, however, *R* v. *Bunn*[780] was reversed. Acts done in contemplation or furtherance of a trade dispute were not to be regarded as criminal unless the act, if done by a single person, would be regarded as unlawful.[781]

Distinct from the issue of criminal liability, was the civil responsibility of trade unions and individual union officials. While criminal liability was eliminated, civil responsibility remained. Officers, or organisers, engaged in trade disputes were potentially liable for the commission of a series of civil torts: inducing breach of contract (in the case of organisers of strikes); nuisance (in the case of picketers). In *Taff Vale* v *Amalgamated Society of Railway Servants*[782] the House of Lords declared that the principle of the vicarious responsibility of a corporation for the acts of its employees or agents applied to trade unions. Unions were held to be quasi-corporations. 'The *Taff Vale* decision was a smashing blow to trade union activity.'[783] The principle of vicarious responsibility threatened the very viability of trade unions, since unions now faced the prospect of being made answerable for the potentially enormous economic loss caused by strike activity. This threatened union funds, and union viability.

However, in 1906 the Liberal government enacted the Trade Disputes Act 1906. The *Taff Vale* decision was reversed, the 1906 Act declaring that no action could be taken against a trade union on the basis of its vicarious liability for the acts of its agents or servants.[784] The Act went on to immunize individuals from particular forms of civil liability. The Act provided that picketing which was carried out peacefully would not constitute the tort of nuisance. The Act also immunized union officials from the tort of inducing a breach of contract.

---

777. *R.* v. *Druitt* (1867) 10 Cox 592.
778. HC 1824 VI, 51.
779. (1872) 12 Cox 316.
780. *Ibid.*
781. S. 3 Trade Disputes Act 1906.
782. [1901] AC 426.
783. W. Citrine, *Trade Union Law* (London, 1967), 16.
784. S. 4 Trade Disputes Act 1906.

II. Twentieth-century Developments: the Trade Union Acts 1941 to 1990

275. In the twentieth century, trade unions became subject to a new form of state regulation: the requirement to obtain a negotiation licence. Section 6 of the Trade Union Act 1941 provides that 'it shall not be lawful for any body of persons, not being an excepted body, to carry on negotiations for the fixing wages unless such a body is the holder of a negotiation licence'.

At least two main disabilities may be incurred through not holding a negotiation licence. (i) Contravention of the requirement is a criminal offence, for which the members of the executive committee, and other officers, are guilty of a criminal offence, and subject to a fine of £1,000 and a fine of £200 for each day on which negotiations are carried out without a negotiation licence. (ii) A series of civil immunities are denied to a union which does not hold a licence: section II of the Industrial Relations Act 1990 (which removes civil liability from persons engaged in picketing), section 13 of the 1990 Act (which abolishes the vicarious responsibility of trade unions for the wrongs committed by its officials, or members, in the course of a trade dispute) and section 19 (which abolishes the entitlement to entitlement to obtain an injunction against strike organizers where a secret ballot has been held).

The requirement to hold a negotiation licence, in order to carry out negotiations for the fixing of wages or other conditions on employment, does not apply in the following six cases: (a) in the case of a body or (employer) carrying on negotiations for the fixing of wages or conditions of employment of its own (but no other employees); (b) in the case of a civil service staff association recognized by the Minister for Finance; (c) in the case of an organization of teachers recognized by the Minister for Education; (d) in the case of a joint labour committee; (f) in a case where the Minister for Jobs, Enterprise, and innovation has exercised his general power to exempt a body from the application of the negotiation licence requirement. An organization which is the subject of such a regulation is excused the need to obtain a negotiation licence. All of these exceptions are found in section 6(3) of the Trade Union Act 1941.

§2. FREEDOM OF ASSOCIATION IN IRISH LAW

I. Statutory Restrictions on the Right of Freedom of Association

276. Article 40(6)(1)(iii) of the Constitution, having provided for the right of citizens to form associations and unions, goes on to provide that 'laws may be enacted for the regulation and control in the public interest of the exercise of the foregoing right'.

The main statutory regulation of the right to form trade unions is the licensing requirement established by the Trade Union Act 1941. The 1941 Act, as described above, makes it a criminal offence for a trade union to carry on negotiations for the fixing of wages or other conditions of employment without the possession of a negotiation licence. The conditions which must be met in order to obtain a negotiation licence are relatively onerous: an applicant trade union must deposit in the High Court between €25,394.76 and €76,184.28, depending on the size of the trade union and must have a minimum of 1,000 members both at the time of, and eighteen months before, the application.

Two categories of worker are forbidden from joining ordinary trade unions and are instead limited to joining approved representative associations. The Garda Síochána Act 1924 forbids members from joining a trade union which has as its objects the influencing of pay or terms or conditions of service.[785] The 1924 Act also makes it a criminal offence for a person to cause disaffection among members of the *Garda Siochána*, or to induce, or attempt to induce any member of the *Garda Siochána* to withhold his services.[786] In *Aughey* v. *Ireland*[787] it was held that since the Act did not prevent the joining of a union which had objects other than those prohibited by section 4, the prohibition on union membership was not unreasonable or disproportionate.

The Defence Act 1954 incriminates a person who procures any person subject to military law to desert, or absent himself without leave.[788] The Defence (Amendment) Act 1990 enables the Minister for Defence to make regulations governing the formation of representative associations for members of the Defence Forces. Representative associations established under the 1990 Act may represent members of the defence forces in matters affecting remuneration, and other such matters as the Minister may designate, but excluding matters relating to any operation and the raising, maintenance, command, constitution and discipline of the defence forces.[789] A recognized representative association must be independent of and may not, without the consent of the Minister for Defence, associate with any trade union or other body.

II. No Right to Join a Trade Union in Irish Constitutional Law

277. No worker has a legal right to join the trade union of his choice. The leading Irish authority is *Tierney* v. *Amalgamated Society of Woodworkers*.[790] In *Tierney*'s case the High Court rejected the argument that a right to join a trade union is a corollary of the constitutional right to earn one's livelihood, and stressed the primacy of the union's autonomy. The general proposition that here is no right to join a trade union is, however, subject to a number of exceptions: (i) first, the decision whether to accept or reject a candidate for membership attracts fair procedures, and must be determined in accordance with natural justice;[791] (ii) where a trade union holds a monopoly in regulating access to particular trade, the court is entitled to grant relief where this monopoly on access to livelihood is abused;[792] (iv) the Employment Equality Acts 1998 and 2011 prohibit discrimination by *inter alia* 'an organization of workers or employers' against applicants for membership on

---

785. S. 4 Garda Síochána Act 1924.
786. S. 14 Garda Síochána Act 1924.
787. [1989] ILRM 87.
788. S. 255 Defence Act 1955.
789. S. 2(1).
790. [1959] IR 254.
791. *Ibid.*
792. *Murphy* v. *Stewart* [1973] IR 97.

grounds of gender, marital status, family status, religious belief, disability, race or membership of the travelling community;[793](v) European Economic Community Regulation No. 1612/68 provides that a worker who is a national of a Member State employed in the territory of another Member State shall enjoy equality of treatment as regards membership or trade unions and the exercise of rights attaching thereto.

III. The Issue of the Right to Recognition of a Trade Union

278. The Association of General Practitioners Ltd v. *Minister for Health*[794] is one of a series of cases which establish the proposition that an employer is not obliged to recognize, or to treat with, a particular union. There, the High Court held that there is no obligation imposed by ordinary law, or by the Constitution, on an employer to consult with or to negotiate with my organization representing his employees, when terms or conditions of employment are being reviewed or settled. In *Abbott and Whelan* v. *ITGWU and Southern Health Board*[795] the plaintiffs failed in their attempt to compel their employer to negotiate with the union (ITGWU) which they had joined. The High Court (McWilliam J) said:

> the suggestion in the pleadings that there is a constitutional right to be represented by a union in the conduct of negotiations with employers has not been pursued and, in my opinion, could not be sustained. There is no duty placed on any employer to negotiate with any particular citizen or body or citizens.

IV. Statutory Consultation/Recognition Duties

279. While there is no constitutional duty on an employer to deal with trade unions, legislation has imposed a series of miscellaneous duties of consultation and recognition. The content of these duties varies from (rarely) obligations requiring certain employers to involve trade unions in all arrangements relating to terms and conditions, to more restricted duties applying to limited categories of employers in respect of restricted matters only.

The most expanded duty of recognition and consultation applies in the case of the railway industry. The Railways Acts 1924–1933 require that all terms and conditions, as a condition to their legal validity, be negotiated between trade unions representative of the employees and the employer (section 55 Railways Act 1924; section 10, Railways Act 1933). The phrase 'union representative of the employees' means unions *lawfully* entitled to negotiate on behalf of the employees: it is therefore confined to unions which hold a negotiation licence under the Trade Union Act 1941.[796] Wages and other conditions of work agreed under the Railways Act 1924, between a union representative of employees and the company are binding on all

---

793. S. 13.
794. [1995] 1 IR 382.
795. [1982] JISLL 56.
796. *Iarnrod Éireann* v. *Holbrooke* [2001] 1 IR 237.

employees covered by the agreement, whether or not they are members of the union.[797]

Another technique is to impose a statutory obligation on the undertaking to put in place machinery between recognized staff associations and trade unions for the purpose of negotiations concerned with pay and conditions of service.[798]

A third variety of statutory duty requires that trade unions be consulted in the drawing up of internal rules. Section 26 of the Universities Act 1997, requires that the governing authority of universities establish procedures for the resolution of disputes following consultation with trade unions and staff associations representing employees of the university. Similarly, section 25(6) of the Universities Act 1997, makes it a condition to the suspension or dismissal of an employee that the university have first complied with a procedure enacted following consultation with a recognized trade union or staff association. The Education Act 1998 (section 28(1)) requires that recognized trade unions and staff associations be consulted in the drawing up of school grievance procedures. Section 22 of the Institutes of Technologies Act 2006 requires that trade unions be involved in the procedures for resolution of disputes.

The most common form of consultation clause is that found in legislation providing for the reorganization of public statutory bodies. This clause provides that the terms and conditions of employment previously enjoyed by employees shall not be interfered with except in accordance with a collective agreement negotiated with any recognized trade union or staff association. Instances of this clause include the Postal and Telecommunications Act 1983; the Forestry Act 1988 (section 43); the Dublin Transport Authority Act 1983 (section 15); the Labour Services Act 1987 (section 7); Health and Safety Act 1989 (section 20); the Roads Act 1983 (section 31); the Environmental Protection Agency Act 1992 (section 31); Radiological Protection Act 1991 (section 12); the Harbours Act 1996 (section 39); Meteorology Act 1996 (section 8); the National Standards Authority of Ireland Act 1996 (section 38); Irish Medicines Board Act 1995 (section 11); Courts Services Act 1998 (section 25); Turf Development Act 1998 (section 51); the National Cultural Institutions Act 1997 (section 30); *An Bord Bia* Act 1994: the Milk (Regulation of Supply) Act 1994 (section 12); the Horse and Greyhound Racing Act 2001 (section 27); the Health and Safety Act 2005 (section 54(3)); the Social Welfare (Miscellaneous Provisions) Act 2008 (section 36); the Student Support Act 2011 (section 11); the Child Care (Amendment) Act 2011; the Nurses and Midwives Act 2011 (section 100); Charities Act 2009 (section 25); the Broadcasting Act 2009 (section 15); the Health (Miscellaneous Provisions) Act 2004 (section 34).

A very important category applies generally (and not just to specified categories of employment) and requires that employers consult with their employees' trade union or representatives about particular terms or conditions, or prior to critical events affecting the business. The Organization of Working Time Act 1997 requires an employer to consult with his employees' trade union in determining the timing of employees' annual leave (section 21(I)(6) of the Organization of Working Time

---

797. *Transport Salaried Staff Association* v. *CIE* [1965] IR 180.
798. S. 16, Post and Telecommunications Act, 1983; Forestry Act, 1996.

Act 1997). The regulations implementing 2001/23/EC on the protection of employees in the transfer of undertakings – the European Communities (Protection of Employees on Transfer of Undertakings) Regulations 2003[799] – imposes a similar requirement in the event of a transfer of undertaking. The transferor and transferee must inform the employees' representatives – where reasonably practicable more than 30 days and in any event in good time before the employees of are affected: of (i) the date of the transfer; (ii) the reasons for the transfer; (iii) the legal economic and social implications of the transfer for the employee; and (iv) the measures envisaged in relation to the employees. Where the employer does not recognize employee representatives, the employer is obliged to put in place arrangements for the selection of employees' representatives.[800]

V. The Non-recognizing Employer and the Industrial Relations (Amendment) Acts 2001–2004

280. The Industrial Relations (Amendment) Acts 2001–2004 were introduced in order to deal with the problem of employers who neither recognize trade unions, nor participate in the State's dispute resolution machinery. In describing the objective of the legislation Geoghegan J in *Ryanair* v. *Labour Court* said that that:

> there is an obvious danger in a non-unionized company … that employees may be exploited and may have to submit to what most reasonable people would consider to be grossly unfair terms and conditions of employment. With a view to curing this possible mischief the Industrial Relations Acts 2001 and 2004 were enacted.

The scheme in the 1990 Act operates in combination with the Industrial Relations Act 1990 (Enhanced Code of Practice on Voluntary Dispute Resolution) (Declaration) Order 2004.[801] The 1990 Code provides that, in the case of a trade dispute involving an employer who refuses to recognize a trade union, one of the parties may refer the matter to the Industrial Relations Commission. The other party must respond to the reference within two weeks (para. 3). The dispute resolution process is subject to a six weeks' maximum. In the event of matters remaining unresolved the process will be deemed to have been exhausted (paragraph 7).

It is when an employer refuses to participate in dispute resolution, that the Industrial Relations Acts 2001–2004 come into operation. Section 2(1) provides that where (i) either the employer has failed to observe a provision of the Code of Practice on Voluntary Dispute Resolution 'specifying the period of time for the doing of anything' (such as the two weeks allowed by paragraph 3 to respond to a reference), or the dispute having been referred to the Labour Relations Commission for resolution in accordance with the provisions of such code, no further efforts on the

---

799. SI No. 131/2003.
800. European Communities (Safeguarding of Employees Rights on Transfer of Undertakings) (Amendment) Regulations, 2000 (SI No. I, 487).
801. SI No. 276 of 2004.

part of the Commission will, in the opinion of the Commission, advance the resolution of the dispute; (ii) it is not the practice of the employer to 'engage in collective bargaining negotiations in respect of the grade, group or category of workers who are party to the trade dispute';[802] (iii) the trade union has not acted in a manner which has frustrated the employer from complying with the code; (iv) the trade union has not had recourse to industrial action after the dispute was referred to the Commission, the matter may be referred by the trade union to the Labour Court.[803] The Labour Court may make a recommendation. If that recommendation is not implemented, the Labour Court may a binding determination.[804] If the employer fails to comply with the terms of a determination within the time specified in the determination, the Circuit Court may, on the application of the trade union, make an order directing the employer to carry out the determination or review in accordance with its terms or findings, as appropriate (section 10). Failure to observe the terms of a Circuit Court order will constitute a contempt of court.

VI. The Right of Disassociation in Irish Constitutional Law

281. Irish law recognizes, as a constitutional principle, an individual's entitlement to desist from joining a trade union – the right of disassociation. The leading decision is *Educational Company of Ireland* v. *Fitzpatrick*.[805] In *Fitzpatrick*'s case the Supreme Court identified three separate sources for the existence of the constitutional right of disassociation: the right of freedom of expression (a right whose exercise would be compromised were an individual forced to join a trade union with principles inconsistent with the individual's convictions); from the constitutional right to personal property (which would be infringed were an individual forced to join a union with power to deduct membership fees); and from the right to form unions, a right premised on the voluntary nature of freedom of association.

The right of disassociation may be invoked against private parties, as well as against the state. Therefore, the dismissal of an employee for failure to join a trade union has been held to be an actionable breach of constitutional rights.[806] Furthermore, a trade union exposes itself to a series of liabilities where it engages in industrial activity which has, as its objective, the compelling of an individual to join a trade union against his will. The various immunities from responsibility for civil liability incurred in the course of industrial action, which are given by the Industrial Relations Act 1990, are restricted to cases where the union is involved in a 'trade

---

802. This term was considered in *Ryanair* v. *Labour Court* [2007] IESC 7, [2007]4 IR 199. In that case the employer maintained a scheme of Employee Representative Committees for consulting with pilots. The pilots withdrew from the internal company scheme and then argued that, as a result, no arrangements were in place.. The Supreme Court held that the Labour Court jurisdiction under the 2001 and 2004 acts could only be invoked where 'collective bargaining arrangements were not in place'. 'Arrangement' meant 'institution'; here the institution remained in place. Its existence was not affected by the unilateral withdrawal of the employees.
803. There were four referrals to the Labour Court in 2011 *Labour Court Annual Report 2011* (Dublin 2012), p. 32.
804. S. 6(1).
805. [1961] IR 345.
806. *Meskell* v. *CIE* [1973] IR 121.

dispute'. However, the courts have held that trade dispute means legitimate trade dispute. Where a trade union is involved in action which has, as its objective, the compelling of another to give up a constitutional right, the union is not involved in a legitimate 'trade dispute'.[807] The union loses its immunity from vicarious responsibility for the acts of its officials, and its funds may be seized.[808] This principle has been applied in cases where it has been alleged that the objective underlying industrial action has been to compel an employer to discipline employees who decline to join a trade union: *Nolan Transport* v. *Halligan*.[809]

---

807. *Educational Company of Ireland* v. *Fitzpatrick* [1961] IR 345.
808. *Nolan Transport* v. *Halligan* [1995] ELR 1; [1998] ELR 177.
809. See above.

Chapter 2. The Law Regulating Trade Unions

§1. Registration and Licensing of Trade Unions

282. Trade unions may first be distinguished according to whether they are Irish trade unions or non-Irish trade unions. The difference does not, in practice, significantly affect the legal characteristic of the union. Currently 44 unions hold negotiating licences.[810]

Irish trade unions may be conveniently described as quasi-corporate bodies which have been registered under the Trade Union Act 1871, and licensed to operate under the Trade Union Act 1941. The licence requirement derives from the Trade Union Act 1941 which makes it illegal 'for any body of persons, not being an excepted body' to enter into negotiations about terms and conditions without a negotiation licence.[811] The quasi-corporate status of trade unions is, in Irish law,[812] a legal incident of the act of registration under the Trade Union Act 1871. This status is explained in greater detail below. The central point, however, is that although a trade union is not formally granted the status of a corporation, registration confers so many of the essential characteristics of incorporation as to make it virtually a corporation; in other words, a quasi-corporation. Since registration is a legal condition to the obtaining of a negotiation licence under the Trade Union Act, 1941, all unions who hold a negotiation licence will also be quasi-corporations.

A second species of trade union is the foreign trade union. A non-Irish based trade union will also require a negotiation licence under the Trade Union Act 1941. It is not a condition of obtaining a negotiation licence that the foreign union be registered under the Trade Union Act 1871. However, since most foreign-based trade unions in Ireland are English, and are, in fact, usually registered under the Trade Union Act 1871, they too are quasi-corporate bodies.[813]

I. The Registration of Trade Unions: the Trade Union Act 1871

283. At common law the property of an unincorporated body is held between all of the members equally. This creates great practical difficulties in transactions dealing with property: in principle, the consent of all of the members is required as a condition to the legality of any property transaction. Section 8 of the Trade Union Act 1871 deals with this conveyancing difficulty by providing that the real and personal estate of a registered union is vested in the union trustees. These trustees may purchase or sell buildings in the name of the union. Trustees of a registered trade union may bring or defend any action concerning the property, or claim to property of the trade union.

---

810. *Report of the Register of Friendly Societies 2010* (Dublin 2011), 18.
811. S. 6 Trade Union Act 1941.
812. *R. (Irish Union of Distributive Workers and Clerks)* v. *Rathmines UDC* [1928] IR 260.
813. *Taff Vale Railway Company* v. *Amalgamated Society of Railway Servants* [1901] AC 426.

In *Taff Vale Railway Co. Ltd* v. *Amalgamated Society of Railway Servants*[814] the House of Lords characterized a trade union registered under the Trade Union Act 1871, as a quasi-corporate body. Although not formally incorporated, a registered trade union shared some of the leading characteristics of an incorporated body: it could litigate in its own name; it could hold property in its own name. This analysis of the legal character of a registered trade union was endorsed in Ireland in *R. (IUDWC)* v. *Rathmines UDC.*[815]

Registration under the Trade Union Acts 1871–1990 is administered by the Register of Friendly Societies.[816] The application for registration must be made by no fewer than seven persons. subscribing their names to a constitution, which must not have an unlawful objective.[817] The constitution must contain the particulars required under the First Schedule of the Trade Union Act 1871.

II. The Negotiation Licence

284. Distinct from the registration condition is the requirement to be licensed. The licence requirement derives from the Trade Union Act 1941 which makes it illegal 'for any body of persons, not being an excepted body' to enter into negotiations about terms and conditions without holding a negotiation licence.[818]

In the case of an Irish-based union, the conditions required in order to obtain a negotiation licence are: (i) that the union have been registered under the Trade Union Act 1871; (ii) That the union have deposited the legally appropriate sum in the High Court. The appropriate sum is €25,394.76 in the case of a union whose membership does not exceed 2000. The amount of the deposit increases according to the size of the membership.[819] (iii) The applicant union must notify the Minister for Jobs, Enterprise and Innovation, the Irish Congress of Trade Unions, as well as any trade unions, of which any members of the proposed union are members of its intention to make the application.[820] (iv) The applicant must publish in a daily newspaper notice of its intention to make an application.[821] (v) The applicant must demonstrate to the satisfaction of the Minister for Enterprise that, both at the date of the application, and not less than eighteen months before the date of the application, it has not less than 1,000 members resident in the state.[822] (This, in practice, is the most effective deterrent against proliferation of trade unions.) (vi) The rules of the

---

814. [1901] AC 426.
815. [1928] IR 260.
816. S. 17 of the Trade Union Act 1871.
817. S. 6 Trade Union act 1871.
818. S. 6.
819. The amounts are detailed in the Third Schedule, Industrial Relations Act 1990.
820. S. 2(1)(1) of the Trade Union Act 1971.
821. S. 2(I)(iii) of the Trade Union Act 1971. Trade Union Act, 1971 (Notice of Intention to apply for Negotiation Licence) Regulations, 1972 (SI 158 of 1972).
822. S. 2(2)(6) of the Trade Union Act 1971, as amended by S. 21(2) of the Industrial Relations Act 1990.

proposed new union must contain provision for the secret balloting of its members prior to engaging in industrial action.[823]

An 'excepted body' is excluded from the requirement of possessing a negotiation licence. A long list of excepted bodies is set out in section 6(2) of the Trade Union Act 1941 and section 3 of the Trade Union Act 1942. The more important of this catalogue include (in section 6(3)(a)) a body 'which carries on negotiations for the fixing of the wages or other conditions of employment of its own (but no other) employees'. This section makes an employer an 'excepted body' and thereby immunizes an employer from requiring a licence. Section 6(2)(c) includes 'a civil service staff association recognized by the Minister for Finance'. Section 6(2)(d) includes 'an organization of teachers recognized by the Minister for Education'. An excepted body includes (in section 6(3)(h) of the Trade Union Act 1941 (as amended by the Trade Union Act 1942) a 'a body all the members of which are employed by the same employer and which carries on negotiations for the fixing of wages or other conditions of employment of its own members (but no other employees)'. 'The purpose of the 1942 Amendment was to deal with a situation where both an employer and employees in a small firm wanted to negotiate terms and conditions.'[824] This exception was necessary since otherwise such employees would be acting illegally for not having a negotiation licence.

III. The Grant of a Negotiation Licence Where the Union Has Less than the Required Minimum Membership

285. Under section 3 of the Trade Union Act 1971, where an applicant for a negotiation licence has less than the required minimum membership of 1,000, the High Court may, none the less – where it considers it not inconsistent with the public interest – grant a negotiation licence. The applicant must be registered under the Trade Union Act 1871, and must have lodged the necessary deposit. Section 3(2) provides that:

the High Court, after hearing any evidence adduced by the applicant, the Minister, the Congress and any other trade union, may at its discretion declare that the granting of a negotiation licence would not be against the public interest.

It has been held that this machinery is to be relied upon only as a last resort and that unions should explore all possible avenues compatible with the legislative policy of reducing the number of trade unions before applying to the High Court.[825]

IV. Obligations Imposed on Trade Unions Holding a Negotiation Licence

286. A union which has been granted a negotiation licence also incurs a series of statutory obligations. Failure to observe these obligations may result either in criminal sanction, or in the withdrawal of the licence. An authorized trade union

---

823. S. 16 (3) Industrial Relations Act 1990.
824. *Ryanair* v. *Labour Court* [2007] IESC 7.
825. *Irish Aviation Executive Staff Association* v. *Minister for Labour* [1981] ILRM 350.

must include in its rules provisions specifying the conditions of entry into, and membership of the union.[826] The union must also maintain at its office a register of its members, which may be consulted by the Minister for Jobs, Enterprise, and Innovation, or by any person interested in the funds of the union.[827] Failure to comply with these provisions may result in prosecution and a small fine. A union must also include provision in its rules for the holding, prior to engaging in industrial action, of a secret ballot. Here the sanction is more series: the union may have its negotiation licence revoked.[828]

V. Foreign-based Trade Unions

287. The other species of trade union is the foreign-based union. The essential legal characteristics of a foreign-based union are similar to those of a local trade union: it is a quasi-corporate body licensed under the Trade Union Act 1941. Foreign-based unions, like Irish-based unions, must obtain a negotiation licence if they are legally to carry out the negotiation of terms and conditions of workers in Ireland. Infringement of the negotiation licence requirement will result in the same criminal sanctions.[829]

The conditions to the grant of a negotiation licence in the case of a foreign-based union are: (i) that it be a trade union under the law of another country;[830] (ii) that it lodge the appropriate deposit; (iii) that the union maintain an office within the state;[831] (iv) that the union has a controlling authority, every member of which is resident in the state, and which is empowered by the rules of the union to take decisions in matters of an industrial or political nature; (v) that the union maintains within the state a register of its members; (vi) that the union contain within its constitution rules regulating the conditions of entry into membership;[832] (vii) that the union promulgate rules providing[833] for the holding of a secret ballot prior to engaging in industrial action;[834] (ix) that the union give notice of changes in its constitution, of changes in the composition of its board of management, and of its principal officers.

Where an organization operates without a negotiation licence it will commit a criminal offence, and will, furthermore, be disqualified from the immunities from civil liability which the Industrial Relations Act 1990 provides to trade unions engaged in industrial action.

---

826. S. 12 of the Trade Union Act 1941.
827. *Ibid.*
828. Industrial Relations Act 1990, s. 16.
829. S. 6 of the Trade Union Act 1941.
830. S. 7(1)(a) of the Trade Union Act 1941.
831. S. 13(1)(6) of the Trade Union Act 1941.
832. S. 13(1)(4) of the Trade Union Act 1941.
833. S. 7(I)(6) of the Trade Union Act 1941.
834. S. 16 of the Industrial Relations Act 1990.

VI. Employers' Associations

288. The Trade Union Act 1941 does not distinguish between trade unions and employers' organizations. Section 6 of the 1941 Act provides that it is an offence for any body of persons to carry on negotiations for the fixing of wages or any other conditions of employment unless the body is the holder of a negotiation licence. Therefore, like workers' trade unions, employers' organizations must register under the Trade Union Act 1871, and obtain a negotiation licence under the Trade Union Act 1941.[835]

IBEC (the Irish Business and Employers' Confederation) is the largest employer representative, and holds a negotiation license under the Trade Union Act 1941. IBEC is a central component in the tripartite social partnership and has been a party to all of the modern national agreements. Twelve other employer representative bodies are licensed under the Trade Union Act 1941 of which the largest are the Construction Industry Federation; The Irish Pharmaceutical Union; the Irish Hotels Federation; and the Licensed Vintners Association.

VII. Trade Unions and the Political Fund

289. The basic elements of the trade union constitution are detailed in the Trade Union Act 1871. The 1871 Act requires that as a condition of registration every trade union rule book must contain provisions dealing with each of the following matters:

(1) the name and place of meeting for business of the trade union;
(2) the objects for which the trade union is to be established, the purposes for which the funds thereof shall be applicable, and the conditions under which any members may become entitled to any benefit assured thereby and the fines and forfeitures imposed on any member;
(3) the manner of making, altering and rescinding any rules;
(4) provision for the appointment and removal of a general committee of management, of a trustee or trustees, treasurer and other officers;
(5) provision for the investment of funds, and for an annual or periodical audit of accounts;
(6) inspection of books and names of members of the trade union by every person having an interest in union funds;
(7) provision for dissolution;
(8) provision for a secret ballot prior to engaging in a strike or other industrial action;
(9) a description of the rules governing the entry into and cesser of membership.[836]

---

835. Currently there are 11 employer associations registered under the Trade Union Act 1871 (*Report of the Register of Friendly Societies 2010* (Dublin 2011), 18).
836. First Schedule Trade Union Act 1871.

Section 3 of the Trade Union Act 1913 lays down the conditions which must be in place if a union is to establish a political fund.[837] The conditions, which are described in section 3, require the addition to the constitution of the trade union of a provision which contains the following safeguards:

> The funds of a trade union shall not be applied … in the furtherance of the political objects to which this section applies, unless the furtherance of those objects has been approved as an object of the trade union by a resolution for the time being in force passed on a ballot of the members of the union taken in accordance with this act for the purpose by a majority of the members voting; and where such a resolution is in force, unless rules, to be approved, whether the union is registered or not, by the Registrar of Friendly Societies, are in force providing –
>
> (a) That any payments in the furtherance of those objects are to be made out of a separate fund (in this act referred to as the political fund of the union); and for the exemption in accordance with this Act of any member of the union from any obligation to contribute to such a fund if he gives notice in accordance with this Act that he objects to contribute; and
> (b) That a member who is exempt from the obligation to contribute to the political fund of the union shall not be excluded from any benefits of the union, or placed in any respect either directly or indirectly under any disability or at any disadvantage as compared with other members of the trade union (except in relation to the control or management of the political fund) by reason of his being so exempt, and that contribution to the political fund shall not be made a condition for admission to the union.

The effect of the 1913 Act, therefore, is that in the case of a trade union which wishes to establish a political fund, rules must be put in place detailing: (i) the secret ballot prior to establishing a political fund; (ii) that any payment is to be made out of a separate fund; (iii) that any member may be exempted from the obligation to contribute; (iv) and that no disability may be imposed upon any member who chooses not to contribute.

VIII. The Juridical Nature of the Union–Member Relationship

290. The relationship between the union and the member may be analysed as founded in contract.[838] Maladministration by a union is controlled either by the member seeking a declaration that the union is acting *ultra vires* or by an action for damages for breach of contract. The union is expected to comply with the procedural conditions prescribed in the union's constitution. In addition to the express provisions contained in the contract, there is an implied obligation on a trade union

---

837. Just four trade unions administer a political fund (*Report of the Register of Friendly Societies 2010* (Dublin 2011), 20.
838. *Lee* v. *Showmen's Guild of Great Britain* [1952] 2 QB 329.

to observe fair procedures in its dealings with its members.[839] Failure to observe the express or implicit terms in the contract of membership may be restrained by injunction; alternatively, the fact that there has been an infringement may be judicially confirmed by a declaration.[840]

---

839. *Doyle* v. *Croke*, High Court, 6 May 1988.
840. For an early instance see: *O'Neill* v. *Irish Transport & General Workers Union* [1934] IR 633.

Chapter 3. Worker Participation in Ireland

§1. WORKER PARTICIPATION IN IRISH LAW

291. Institutionalized collaboration between employers and workers in Irish employment law may be broken down into the following divisions. (i) Worker participation as directors on the boards of public bodies: here the source of the legal obligation is statutory, and the duty is compulsory. (ii) Works councils in public commercial bodies: here again, the legal source is statutory and compulsory. (iii) Works councils in community-wide organizations: here again, the source of the duty is legislative. (iv) Safety committees, where the range of application extends to private as well as public bodies. The institution has its origin in legislation. (v) Works councils in private undertakings. Here, the source of the institution is the voluntary agreement of unions and employers.

I. Worker Directors in Public Commercial Bodies

292. A legal right of worker participation on company boards was first introduced in the Worker Participation (State Enterprises) Acts 1977–2001. The organizations which are subject to the duty to accept worker directors are described as 'designated bodies'. These corporations are named in Parts I and II of the First Schedule to the Worker Participation (State Enterprises) Act 1977, as amended by the Worker Participation (State Enterprises) Act 1988. The number of companies which are deemed designated companies is fairly limited. It includes An Post; Bord Na Móna; Nitrigin Éireann; and the National Rehabilitation Board. There is also power permitting the Minister to extend the provisions of the legislation to subsidiaries of the designated companies (section 9 of the Worker Participation (State Enterprises) Act 1988). In pursuance of this statutory authority the Minister has designated Irish Fertilizer Industries Ltd as subsidiaries to which the Act applies.[841]

The number of worker directors is established by the Minister for Jobs, Enterprise, and innovation.[842] In the case of Bord Na Móna, the Electricity Supply Board and the National Rehabilitation Board, worker directors are to make up one-third of the members of the board. In the case of the other designated companies, the number of worker directors must be not less than two nor more than one-third of the total board.[843]

There is no right of personal nomination. Nomination to the position of worker director is controlled by trade unions, or qualified bodies who are recognized for the purpose of collective bargaining by the designated body. The electoral college for the purpose of these elections is all employees of not less than 18 years, who have been employed for a period of not less than one year before the taking of the poll.[844]

---

841. The Worker Participation (Irish Fertiliser Industries Ltd) Order 1990.
842. S. 23 of the Worker Participation (State Enterprise) Act, 1977–2001.
843. *Ibid.*
844. S. 10 of the Worker Participation (State Enterprise) Act, 1977–2001.

The legislation does not, however, describe the duties of worker directors, or expand the content of directors' duties to the company's employees. Worker directors function as ordinary company directors subject to the usual fiduciary duties of company directors, with the primary function of safeguarding shareholders' interests.

II. Works Councils in State Enterprises

293. The model under the Worker Participation (State Enterprise) Act, 1977 provides for employee membership of boards. However, employee participation at board level was not complemented by general employee rights of participation. However, in 1988 with the contract of the Worker Participation (State Enterprises) Act 1988, provision was made for works councils – though in public commercial bodies only.

Section 6 of the Worker Participation (State Enterprises) Act 1988 provides that the representatives of employers and employees of 'a specified body' may enter into 'arrangements' dealing with: (i) the exchange of views and reliable information; (ii) the giving by the specified body in good time of information which is liable to have a significant effect on the interests of employee of the specified body. The range of bodies for which these arrangements may be established is wider than the collection of bodes in which formal board-level participation applies: originally 39 semi-state companies were designated as specified companies.[845]

The establishment of worker consultation arrangements is initiated by the employees of the body. Consultation arrangements may be activated either at the request of the trade union recognized by the company or, in a case where a majority of the employees vote in favour of consultative arrangements.[846]

III. Works Councils in Community-scale Undertakings

294. The Transnational Information and Consultation of Employees Act 1996 implements Directive 94/45/EC on the establishment of European Works Councils into Irish law. The 1996 Act applies to Irish Community-wide enterprises. The threshold requirement to the application of the Act is that the enterprise have 1,000 employees and at least 150 employees in two Member States. Where these conditions apply, the company qualifies as a Community-scale undertaking. Employee numbers, for the purpose of the application of the definition, are, as Article 2(2) of the directive requires, calculated by reference to both full-time and part-time employees. In determining whether the number of employees meets the relevant workforce threshold, the average number of employees in the undertaking during the two years before the date that a request is made is calculated.[847] The management of the establishment or group undertaking in which the greatest number of

---

845. S. 1, and the First Schedule of the Worker Participation (State Enterprises) Act 1988.
846. S. 4 of the Worker Participation (State Enterprises) Act 1988.
847. S. 5(1) of the Transnational Information and Consultation of Employees Act 1996.

employees are employed in any one Member State is required to assume the responsibility for enabling informational and consultative rights.[848]

Although section 3 provides that an employee has a right to information and consultation, that right is a conditional one. It is conditional on the written request of at least ten per cent of employees. If the workforce remains inert the facility will not be activated. Where a request is made the parties must, within six months, agree to establish either (a) an information and consultation arrangement,[849] or (b), an agreement in accordance with the Standard Rules.[850] However, an employer is not obliged to construct either of these institutions if there is already a 'pre-existing agreement' dealing with information and consultation in place in the undertaking. This pre-existing arrangement must have been approved by the employees, signed by the employer and applicable to all employees.[851]

The first model is the information and consultation agreement. Section 8 prescribes the procedure for establishing information and consultation arrangements. It does not, however, prescribe the subject matter of that information and consultation. The subject matter is left for negotiation by the parties. The nature of the forum is also left to the parties: it may be in the form of a general assembly of employees; or it may be a smaller model involving the employer and employee representatives.[852] The agreement must be (a) in writing and dated; (b) be signed by the employer; (c) be approved by the employees; (d) be applicable to all employees to whom the agreement relates; and (e) be available for inspection by those persons.[853] The agreement must (section 8(5) provide information as to duration; the subjects for information and consultation; and the method by which information and consultation is to be provided (whether directly with employees or through employees representatives).

The second model – the Standard Rules – may be adopted in three cases: (i) where the parties voluntarily agree to adopt this model; (ii) where an employer refuses to enter into negotiations within three months of receiving a request, or (iii) where the parties cannot agree to an information and consultation arrangement within the six months allowed.[854] The contents of the Standard Rules includes information and consultation about 'recent and probable development of the undertaking's activities and economic situation'; on the situation and probable development of employment within undertaking'; on decisions likely to lead to 'substantial changes in work organization'.[855]

Currently there are 57 Irish-based undertakings with various forms of European Works Council arrangements.[856]

---

848. S. 9 (1) of the 1996 Act.
849. S. 8 of the Transnational Information and Consultation of Employees Act 1996.
850. S. 10 of the Transnational Information and Consultation of Employees Act 1996.
851. Ss. 9 (2) and (3) of the Transnational Information and Consultation of Employees Act 1996.
852. S. 8(5)(c) and (d) of the Transnational Information and Consultation of Employees Act 1996.
853. S. 8(2) of the Transnational Information and Consultation of Employees Act 1996.
854. S. 10 (1).
855. Schedule 1, para. 1 (a).
856. EWCdb.eu.

Disputes between the employer concerned with negotiations prior to the establishment of one of the mechanisms, or the interpretation of the contents of a pre-existing agreement or the Standard Rules may be submitted to the Labour Court. Access to the Labour Court is heavily restricted by the requirement that the parties have first had recourse to internal resolution procedure in the place of employment, and that the Labour Relations Commission has issued a certificate confirming that no 'further efforts on its part will advance the resolution of the dispute.[857] So far no dispute has been referred to the Commission.

IV. Worker Involvement Consequent on the Establishment of a European Company

295. Directive 2001/86/EC on worker involvement consequent on the establishment of a European Company has been implemented in Irish law by the European Communities (European Public Limited-Liability Company) (Employee Involvement) Regulations 2006.[858] This set of consultative duties apply to every SE – a company established under Council Regulation 2157/2001/EC on the Statute for a European Company – which is registered in the state.[859]

Regulation 4 (1) requires that when the competent organs of participating companies draw up plans for the establishment of a Societas Europaea 'they shall take the necessary steps to start negotiations with the representatives of the companies' employees in the SE'. The process of agreeing the arrangements for the involvement of companies begins with the establishment of 'a special negotiating body'. The composition of this pan-European Special Negotiating Body is determined on the principle of one seat where the number of employees in that Member State equals ten per cent or a fraction of the total workforce.[860] The remit of the Special Negotiating Body' is to negotiate with the competent organs of the participating companies arrangements for the involvement of employees within the Societas Europaea: Regulation 8(1), and the form of the 'representative body' which will negotiate with the competent organ of the Societas Europaea. A period of six months is given to finalize that agreement; (in default, the Standard Rules will operate). The final agreement must specify (a) the scope of the agreement; (b) the composition of the representative body; (c) where the parties agree to establish arrangements for participation, the contents of that arrangement.[861]

---

857. S. 15(2).
858. SI 623/2006.
859. Regulation 2 of the European Communities (European Public Limited-Liability Company) (Employee Involvement) Regulations 2006.
860. Regulation 5(4) of the European Communities (European Public Limited-Liability Company) (Employee Involvement) Regulations 2006.
861. Regulation 13 of the European Communities (European Public Limited-Liability Company) (Employee Involvement) Regulations 2006.

V. European Communities (Cross-Border Mergers) Regulations 2008

296. Council Directive 2005/56/EC is implemented in Irish law by the European Communities (Cross-Border Mergers) Regulations.[862] This imposes various employee informative and consultative duties on merging companies in a cross-border merger, ie a merger involving at least one Irish company and at least one EEA company.[863]

The directors' explanatory report shall be made available to the representatives of the employees, or where there are no representatives, to the employees directly.[864] This report must inter alia explain the implications of the cross-border merger for employees.[865] In addition, as soon as possible after the publication of the draft terms of a cross-border merger, the management or administrative organ of each merging company shall take the necessary steps to start negotiations with the representatives of the employees of that company on arrangements for the involvement of those employees in the successor company'.[866] An institution known as a special negotiating body must be established for the purpose of making these arrangements. There are complex rules regulating the composition of the special negotiating body. However, the basic rule is prescribed in Regulation 25(3): one seat for each portion of employees in a Member State which equals 10 per cent, or a fraction thereof of the total number of employees. The function of the Special Negotiating Body is to determine arrangements for the involvement of employees within the successor body.[867] The agreement must specify the substance of any agreement for employee participation that, in the course of negotiations, the parties decide to establish'.[868]

The Standard Rules apply where (i) the parties agree; or (ii) no agreement is concluded within the six months permitted by Regulation 34 and the management or administrative organs decide to accept the application of the Standard Rules, and, on that basis, to continue with the merger. The Standard Rules require the establishment of a Representative Body. That Representative Body has the right to be informed 'on the progress of the business of the successor company and its prospects';[869] to be informed of exceptional circumstances affecting employees' interests; to meet with the competent organ of the post-merger body; where the competent organ decides not to act in accordance with the views of the Representative Body, to request a further meeting with a view to seeking agreement.[870]

Disputes relating to the composition of the Special Negotiating Body, or to the interpretation of an agreement, or to the interpretation of the Standard Rules, may,

---

862. SI No. 157/2008.
863. Regulation 2 of the the European Communities (Cross-Border Mergers) Regulations.
864. Regulation 6(1) (b) of the European Communities (Cross-Border Mergers) Regulations.
865. Regulation 6(2) (a) of the European Communities (Cross-Border Mergers) Regulations.
866. Regulation 24(1) of the European Communities (Cross-Border Mergers) Regulations.
867. Regulation 28(1) of the European Communities (Cross-Border Mergers) Regulations.
868. Regulation 33 (1) of the European Communities (Cross-Border Mergers) Regulations.
869. Schedule 1, Part 2, Regulation 11 (2) of the European Communities (Cross-Border Mergers) Regulations.
870. Schedule 1, Part 2, Regulation 12 (3) of the European Communities (Cross-Border Mergers) Regulations.

subject to exhaustion of alternative processes, be referred to the Labour Court.[871] An appeal lies from the Labour Court to the High Court on a point of law.

§2. EMPLOYEE SHARE OWNERSHIP

297. About 6 per cent of employees are covered by share ownership schemes.[872] Irish revenue law now encourages the development of employee share-holding schemes. Tax incentives have been put in place the purpose of which is to encourage companies to put in place share ownership trusts; and to encourage employees to take remuneration in the form of shares.

There exist two financial participation models: the profit sharing schemes;[873] and the approved share option scheme.

I. Approved Profit-sharing Scheme

298. Under the approved profit sharing scheme[874] – first established in 1982 – profits are distributed in the form of shares which are conveyed to a trust acting on behalf of participating employees. The employee is not liable to income tax in respect of the right to receive the shares. This supersedes the common law position in *Abbot* v. *Philbin*[875] where it was held that the grant of a share option represented a perquisite or profit of office, and was therefore subject to income tax. Where the employee allows the trust to retain the shares for three years, he may then acquire the shares (and the power to dispose of these shares) without any liability to income taxation (although capital gains tax will be payable on the profits of sale of the shares).[876] The trust most commonly used for the holding of these shares is the employee share ownership trusts established by the Finance Act 1997.[877] These arrangements are used most commonly in public or semi-public companies.

II. Approved Share-option Scheme

299. Under the approved share option scheme introduced by the Finance Act 2001,[878] options to purchase shares in the employer's company may be acquired at a reduced price below market price. No liability to income tax is incurred by reason of the receipt of the right to the shares. If those options are then exercised, the

---

871. Regulation 40 of the European Communities (Cross-Border Mergers) Regulations.
872. Employee Involvement Regulations 2007 (SI 259 of 2007).
873. Chapter 1, Part 17 of the Income Tax Act, 1997.
874. Taxes Consolidation Act 1997, s 510; Schedule 11.
875. [1961] AC 352.
876. S. 510; s. 512.
877. S. 51 Taxes Consolidation Act 1997.
878. S. 15. Taxes Consolidation Act 1997

employee will be relieved of the liability to income tax – though he or she may still be amenable to capital gains tax on profits from sale of the shares.[879] That exemption is lost where the right is exercised within three years. Related to the share option scheme is the savings-related share option scheme constituted under the Finance Act 1999.[880] This is a mechanism which may be used by employees to save the money for the purchase of shares. The employee enters into a savings contract in which contributions will be made in order to facilitate the exercise of the option.

879. S. 519D Income Tax Act 1997 (inserted by s. 15 of the Finance Act 2001).
880. S. 519A Tax Consolidation Act 1997.

Chapter 4. The Law Governing Strikes and Industrial Action

§1. The Wages and Dismissal of Employees Involved in Industrial
Action

I. Wages and Industrial Action

300. Those who engage in industrial activity may incur a series of civil sanctions. These range from disentitlement to wages; liability to dismissal; to liability in damages for the economic torts committed by persons who engage in industrial action. Furthermore, criminal liability is incurred by persons who engage in an industrial picket.

The consideration for wages is willingness and ability to work. Therefore, an employee engaged in a strike is not entitled to wages: he will not have satisfied the first condition to the recovery of wages, willingness to work.[881]

At common law, the view has also been taken that conduct short of a complete withdrawal of labour (a go-slow or a work ban) is indistinguishable from a full withdrawal of labour. A work ban, or go-slow, is analysed as a repudiation of the contract which entitles the employer to decline to pay wages.[882] The entitlement not to pay wages is, however, conditional on the employer making it clear that he will not accept reduced service.[883] If, however, the employer accepts reduced provision of work without protest, he will be obliged to pay for that reduced service.[884] Where the employer accepts reduced service, the accepted legal analysis is that the employees are offering a new contract of service, which the employer, by not protesting, is deemed to accept. Having accepted that revised offer he is obliged to pay a reasonable sum by way of wages, Where, on the other hand, the employer makes it clear that he will not accept reduced service he cannot be taken as accepting any new offer. In *Wiluszyski* v. *Tower Hamlets Borough Council*[885] local authority housing officers, as part of a campaign of industrial action, implemented a ban on answering queries submitted by political representatives on behalf of constituents. The Borough Council wrote to the officials saying that it regarded the ban as a serious dereliction of duty and informed them that they need not attend work if they were not prepared to work as normal. They were advised that if they did attend, their work would be regarded as purely voluntary and that they could not expect to be paid. ('You will not be allowed to pick and choose which duties you perform and if you are not prepared to work normally, you will be sent off the premises. You will only be paid your salary if you continue to work normally in accordance with the requirements of your contract.') The workers did attend and claimed remuneration for the work that they did perform. The Court of Appeal held that they were not entitled to any payment. Here, unlike the *Miles* case, the employees' offer of reduced work had

---

881. *Henthorn* v. *Central Electricity Generating Board* [1980] IRLR 361.
882. *Wiluszyinski* v. *Tower Hamlets Borough Council* [1989] IRLR 259; *Miles* v. *Wakefield* [1987] AC 549; *Carr* v. *Limerick VEC* (Supreme Court, 23 November 2000).
883. *Wiluszynski* v. *Tower Hamlets LBC* [1989] IRLR 259.
884. *Miles* v. *Wakefield* [1987] AC 549.
885. [1989] ICR 493.

not been implicitly accepted by the employers. The employers were not required to physically eject the employees; it was enough that they were given a genuine warning. There was no new contract and the employees were entitled to nothing.

Section 5 of the Payment of Wages Act 1991 (which imposes on an employer the obligation, prior to making a deduction from wages, to comply with a series of procedural pre-conditions prior to making a deduction on account of an act of the employee) does not apply in a case where 'the act' is the employee's participation in industrial activity. Where wages are not payable by reason of participation in industrial action, the deduction may be made without the need to adhere to the procedural steps prescribed in section 5.

II. Dismissal for Participation in a Strike or Other Industrial Action

301. Dismissal on account of participation in strike activity will be unlawful in two circumstances: (i) where strike notice has been given; and (ii) where the dismissal is a selective dismissal contrary to section 5(2) of the Unfair Dismissals Acts 1977–2007.

According to the legal theory underlying strike notice, there is implied into all contracts of employment the right to suspend the contract of employment by giving strike notice.[886] The effect is that an employee, who is engaged in industrial action, having given strike notice, is relieved of the ordinary duty of obedience and cooperation. The employer will, therefore, have no grounds for dismissal. The right to take leave in order to pursue industrial activity is contingent upon the giving of adequate strike notice: strike notice is lawful only when the notice is of the same duration as the notice required of an employer to lawfully resign. (There are important limits to the strike notice doctrine. The principal weaknesses are that the contractual right to suspend the contract may be overridden by an express contrary term in the contract of employment.[887] Secondly, it is not clear, either, whether the entitlement applies in the case of lesser forms of industrial action short of an actual strike.)

Section 5(2) of the Unfair Dismissals Act 1977 deems a dismissal to be unfair where (i) one or more employees are reinstated following a strike on their original terms and conditions, but the dismissed employee is reinstated on inferior terms and conditions; (ii) if the employee is dismissed, but one or more employees of the employer who took part in the strike were not dismissed; (iii) if the dismissal of some of the employees who took part in the strike is revoked, but is maintained in the case of the claimant. In *Tuite* v. *Caoilte Éireann*[888] the dismissal of some, though not all the employees who had participated in an industrial dispute was held to constitute unfair dismissal of those who were not re-engaged.

---

886. *Becton Dickenson* v. *Lee* [1973] IR 1; *Bates* v. *Model Bakery* [1993] ILRM 22.
887. *Ibid.*
888. [1998] ELR 324.

There are, however, limits to the protection against dismissal for participation in industrial activity under section 5 of the Unfair Dismissals Act 1977. The protection against dismissal given by section 5 of the Unfair Dismissals Act 1977, only applies in the case of employees who have worked for more than fifty two weeks. Secondly, the prohibition against dismissal only operates in the event of selective dismissal. Non-selective dismissal is not covered. There is, as yet no case law on whether, and, if so, the conditions under which, non-selective dismissal might be regarded as illegitimate. Thirdly and somewhat curiously, industrial action is defined as 'lawful action taken in the course of a trade dispute'. However, since most industrial action is contractually unlawful, section 5 would not seem to apply in such cases.

§2. Torts Committed by Persons Engaged in Industrial Action

I. The Tort of Inducement of Breach of Contract

302. Participation in industrial activity, inevitably, involves the commission of a series of torts. The most important of these are the torts of *direct* inducement of breach of contract, and the tort of *indirect* inducement of contract. *Direct* inducement occurs where the defendant's acts are the immediate cause of the breach of some other contract. *Indirect* inducement occurs where the defendant's acts cause some other agent to breach the contract. A union organizer directly induces a breach of contract of employment where he prevails upon employees to come working. An employee whose participation in industrial action precipitates a breach of a commercial contract directly induces a breach of a commercial contract also commits the tort of direct inducement of breach of contract.[889] An organizer who, by directly inducing workers to break their contracts of employment, indirectly induces the collapse of dependent commercial contracts, commits the tort of indirect inducement of breach of contract.[890]

The components of the tort are: (i) the fact that the defendant is aware of, or is reckless to, the existence of the contract which is being breached; (ii) the existence of an intention to induce the breach of the contract;[891] (iii) the fact that the cause of the breach of contract was the unlawful (rather than lawful) conduct of the defendant; thus, where the defendant is doing a lawful act (being absent from work following the giving of notice) no cause of action is available; (iv) the existence of a causative connection between the breach of contract and the inducement (thus, the wrong is not committed where the breach of content results from the spontaneous action of the contract-breaker, rather from any act of persuasion or inducement);[892] (v) the absence of justification. In certain, very exceptional circumstances, the fact

---

889. *Lumley* v. *Gye* (1853) 2 EB 216; 118 ER 749, *Temperton* v. *Russell* [1893] 1 KB 715.
890. *Sherrif* v. *McMullen* [1950] IR 236.
891. *Ibid.*
892. *Iarnrod Éireann* v. *Holbroke*, High Court, 14 April 2000.

that employees are being seriously mistreated may provide a justification for inducing others to withdraw business from an abusive employer.[893]

A. The History of the Tort of Direct Inducement of Breach of Contract

303. The foundation case at common law is *Lumley* v. *Gye*.[894] Here, the defendant, a rival of the plaintiff, was a music hall impresario. He persuaded a popular opera singer, Johanna Wagner, who had been engaged to play at the plaintiff's concert rooms (the Queen's Theatre), to break her engagement and perform for the defendant at his theatre in Covent Garden. The Court of Queen's Bench held that an action lay for the intentional and malicious inducement of a breach of contract of personal service. Earle J. said:

> The authorities are numerous and uniform that an action will lie by a master against a person who procures that a servant should unlawfully leave his service. The right of action in the master arises from the wrongful act of the defendant in putting an end to the relation of master and servant … He who procures the non-delivery of goods or services according to contract may inflict an injury, the same as he who procures abstraction of goods after delivery; and both on the same ground ought to be made responsible.[895]

The court rejected the argument that an action in breach of contract against the contract breaker was sufficient to compensate the injured party: 'the remedy on the contact may be inadequate where the measure of damages [in contract] is restricted'.[896]

The tort was soon translated into the arena of industrial disputes. In *Temperton* v. *Russell*[897] the plaintiff was a builders' supplier in Hull who had a valuable contract for the supply of building materials with a third party, a builder, Bentrano. The defendant persuaded Bentrano (by threatening him with a strike) to refuse to take further supplies from the builders' suppliers. Bentrano complied and so broke his contract with Temperton. The defendant was successfully sued for inducing a breach of the contract between the builder and the builders' suppliers.

The act is a persuasion by the defendant of a third party to breach a contract existing between such third person and the plaintiff. It cannot be maintained that it is not a natural and probable consequence of the act of persuasion that the third person will break the contract.

An inducement of breach of contract may be brought about by physical means (such as the employees not being available to work) as well as by persuasive pressure. In *Thomson* v. *Deakin*[898] Jenkins LJ said:

---

893. *Brimelow* v. *Casson* [1924] 1 Ch. 302.
894. (1853) 3 E&B 114; 118 E.R. 749.
895. 118 ER 749, at p. 755.
896. *Ibid.*, at p. 756
897. [1893] 1 QB 715.
898. [1952] Ch. 646.

> I see no difference in principle between persuading a man to break his contract with another, preventing him by physical restraint from performing it, making his performance of it impossible by taking away or damaging his tools or machinery, and making the performance of it impossible by depriving him, in breach of their contracts, of the services of his employees.[899]

Industrial life is based on a long chain of interdependent contracts. Where one contract is interfered with, another contractual relationship which is dependent on that contract may also be affected. Where a defendant persuades a party to breach a contract he *directly* induces its breach. Where that breach impairs another, dependent contract, he may *indirectly* induce the breach of that second, dependent contract. This extension of the tort – to include indirect inducement of breach of contract – arrived on the scene in Ireland and in England almost contemporaneously in the early 1950s.

In *Sheriff* v. *McMullen*[900] the plaintiff who owned a timber business was in dispute with the Irish Transport and General Workers Union over alleged refusal to recognize trade unions. The timber business had a valuable contract for the supply by instalments of wood to Irish Shoe Supplies Ltd. The defendant, the General Secretary of the ITGWU, induced workers at a shoe factory not to work on the timber supplied by the plaintiff. This made production at the shoe factory impossible, and, in order to survive, the factory owner was forced, in breach of his contract with the timber supplier, to refuse supplies, and to seek materials elsewhere.

Here the defendant had *directly* induced breach of the full performance of the employees' contracts of employment (persuading the employees not to fulfil all of their contractual duties). The indirect result was to force the premature breach/ repudiation of a commercial contract (the timber contract from Sheriff). By directly inducing the workers to black the timber the organizers had indirectly induced breach of the contract between the Sheriff and Irish Shoe Supplies.

A parallel English example is *Thomson* v. *Deakin*.[901] Bowaters, a paper manufacturer, had a commercial contract with Thomson & Co. Ltd, a newspaper and magazine publisher. Since the General Strike of 1926, Thomson had a policy of not employing persons who were members of trade unions. In pursuance of this policy, Thomson dismissed one of its members who had joined a union. A campaign was initiated by the Trade Union Congress for union recognition in Thomson's plants. Influenced by the campaign, Bowaters' drivers, who were members of the TGWU intimated to Bowaters that they would not deliver paper to Thomson. Bowaters did not instruct the workers to take the delivery, but wrote to Thomson regretting that in the light of the union difficulties it would be unable to complete the order.

The Court of Appeal held that the tort of procurement of breach of contract was not confined to direct intervention. Here the contracts whose breach was induced were at one remove from the breach of contract complained of'. Nevertheless, there was no reason why there should not be liability where the inducement was not

---

899. *Ibid.*, at p. 696
900. [1952] IR 236.
901. [1952] Ch. 646.

applied directly to one of the contractors, but was applied to some entity on whom the contractor was dependent:

> An actionable interference with contractual relations may be committed by a third party, who with knowledge of a contract between two persons, and with the intention of causing its breach, or of preventing its performance, persuades, induces or procures the servants of one of those parties, on whose service he relies for the performance of his contract, to break their contracts of employment with him, either by leaving him without notice or by refusing to do what is necessary for the performance of his contract, provided the breach of contract between the two parties intended to be brought about by the third party does, in fact, ensue as a necessary consequence of the third party's wrongful interference.[902]

The elements of the tort of indirect inducement may be defined as follows:

(i) The defendant must use unlawful means.
(ii) The defendant must have knowledge, actual or constructive, of the contract broken.
(iii) The defendant must intend, or have the objective of breaking the contract in question.
(iv) There is no justification for the defendant's acts.
(v) The breach of contract must have resulted from the defendant's acts, and not from any alternative cause.

B. The Means Must Be Unlawful

304. It would obviously be oppressive to make persons civilly liable for the consequences of their *lawful acts.* For example, an employee may, by lawfully taking holidays, prevent his employee from completing a commercial contract; or an employee may refuse to work overtime and thereby frustrate completion of a commercial contract. Liability would be inconsistent with the existence of the contractual right to take holiday leave, or to refuse overtime. Likewise, a person who persuades an employee to exercise an entitlement, even if the exercise of that entitlement causes contractual inconvenience to the employer, should not be liable for the economic loss caused.

Where an employee exercises his right to give strike notice, notice of an intention to engage in strike activity, which is of the same length as is required to give legal notice of resignation, the contract is regarded as being in a state of lawful suspension. The employee's obligation to attend work is in suspension, while the employer's obligation to pay wages is also, in suspension. The doctrine of strike notice was originated by Denning LJ in *Morgan* v. *Fry:*[903]

---

902. Per Jenkins LJ at p. 696.
903. [1968] 2 QB 710.

The truth is that neither employer nor worker wish to take the drastic action of termination if it can be avoided. The men do not wish to leave their work forever. The employers do not wish to scatter their labour force to the four winds. Each side is, therefore, content to accept a strike notice of appropriate length as lawful. It is an implication read into the contract by the modern law as to trade disputes. If a strike takes place, the contract of employment is not terminated. It is suspended during the strike; and revives again when the strike is over.

In *Becton Dickenson* v. *Lee*[904] the Supreme Court held that there was implied into every contract of employment an implied term that employees might lawfully give strike notice, and that such strike notice would suspend the mutual obligations of the parties. Walsh J. said:

> there is to be read into every contract of employment an implied term that the service of strike notice, the length of which is not shorter than would be necessary to terminate the contract of employment, would suspend the contract, and strike activity would not break the contract. Such an implied term, of course, could not be read into a contract when there is an express provision in the contract to the contrary.[905]

The strike notice doctrine relieves from liability union officials, who might, otherwise, be regarded as inducing breaches of employees' contracts of employment. There is nothing unlawful about persuading a person to do something which is lawful. Therefore, the trade unionist who persuades an employee to serve strike notice is not guilty of indirectly inducing a breach of any contracts which are indirectly affected by his/her action. The trade unionist has not used unlawful means.

However, the strike notice doctrine is, in a number of respects, fragile. The principle is merely an implied term. Therefore, it may be displaced by a contrary term in the contract of employment. Second, the legality of strike notice is dependent on the giving of notice of the same length as is required to terminate the relationship.[906] Accordingly, there may be practical difficulties in operating the procedure where the required notice period is very long.

C. The Defendant Must Be Aware of the Contract

305. It is *not* necessary that the wrongdoer have actual, positive knowledge that his conduct is inducing breach of a specific contract, the contents of which he has been apprised. A pragmatic view is taken. If a reasonable person would have thought it obvious that the defendant's conduct is imperilling the terms of some contractual arrangement, the defendant will be deemed to have constructive

---

904. [1973] IR 1.
905. At p. 14
906. *Becton Dickenson* v. *Lee* [1973] IR 1.

knowledge. In *McMahon* v. *Dunne*[907] the defendant, the general Secretary of the Marine Port and General Union, had placed an embargo on the unloading of cargo in Dublin port. The defendants claimed that they were unaware that there was a specific contract between the freight carrier and the plaintiff. The High Court rejected the suggestion that there was any requirement for actual, positive knowledge:

> In many instances in modern life it must be obvious to the ordinary onlooker that some transaction is taking place on foot of some contract, particularly where matters of payment and delivery are concerned … If some term is clearly discernible in the particular circumstances is there any reason for exempting him merely because he did not know who the other party was, or of the existence of any particular form of contract or its exact conditions?[908]

D. There Must Be Intention to Interfere with the Contract

306. The defendant is only liable when his object is to interfere with the contract.[909] This important limiting principle[910] means that the defendant is not liable for all of those contracts incidentally broken as a result of the industrial action. Otherwise the liability for a private wrong would be limitless. The essence of the requirement is that only those contracts whose interference forms part of the strategy adopted by the strikers may be the subject of an action for the tort of inducement of breach of contract. To take a hypothetical example: building workers may be engaged in a housing construction project. Their employer may be in a contractual relationship with a development company. As part of an industrial strategy the strikers may withdraw their labour with the intention of hurting their employer. Here the organizers may be liable for indirectly inducing breach of the construction contract. The development company may have sold housing to private customers. These contracts may be breached. These purchasers may have entered into contracts for the sale of their own homes. These contracts may be breached. The strikers should not be liable to the long list of consequentially affected parties. The principle is that the strikers not desiring to interfere with these contracts cannot be held liable for the tort, otherwise liability would be endless.

E. Absence of Justification

307. Circumstances of extreme abuse or oppression may provide a justification for a campaign of industrial excommunication against an employer, and furnish a defence to the tort of inducement of breach of contract. This defence has succeeded

---

907. (1965) ILTR 45.

908. At p. 53

909. This is made clear in *Lumley* v. *Gye* 118 ER 749, AT P. 756; *Thomson* v. *Deakin* [1952] Ch. 646 at p. 696; *Sheriff* v. *McMullen* [1952] IR 236, at p. 257 and *Timeplan Educaton Group* v. *NUT* [1997] IRLR 457.

910. The principle is explicitly rationalized as a principle designed to limit liability in *Thomson* v. *Deakin* [1952] Ch. 646.

only once: in *Brimelow* v. *Casson*[911] where the underpayment of chorus girls employed by the plaintiff was so severe as to force them into prostitution. The employer's behaviour was held to justify a campaign undertaken by the actors' association, whereby theatre owners were induced into withdrawing from contracts with the employer:

> the only way they could achieve their objective [of remedying the exploitative treatment] is by inducing the proprietors of theatres not to allow persons like the plaintiff the use of their theatres, either by breaking contracts already made or by refusing to enter into contracts ... No general rule can be laid down as a general rule in such cases, but I confess that if justification does not exist here I can hardly conceive of a case where it does exist.

But it will only be in the most extreme cases that the courts will hold a defendant justified in attempting to economically destroy a business.[912]

F. The Defendant's Actions Must Be the Cause of the Breach of Contract

308. The defendant's acts, and not the acts of some other agent, must cause the breach of contract. Therefore, organizers will not be capable of being sued for spontaneous supportive conduct which has not been induced by the organizers. In *Iarnród Éireann* v. *Holbrooke*[913] officials of a train drivers' union were sued for inducing breaches of train drivers' contracts of employment, resulting in stoppages on the Athlone and Westport routes. The strike followed the refusal of the employers to treat with the union leader, Brendan Ogle. The High Court found that the strike was the result of the spontaneous action of the drivers, supporters of Brendan Ogle, who were upset at the manner of his treatment. The union officials had not caused the breaches of contract.

II. The Tort of Unlawful Interference with Trade

309. The second major tort committed by persons engaged in industrial action is the tort of unlawful interference with trade. The components of the tort are: (i) the use of unlawful means; (ii) an intention to cause economic harm to the plaintiff; (iii) the fact that the defendant's activity has caused economic loss to the plaintiff. There is no necessity that the plaintiff's conduct has caused a breach of contract. It is sufficient that the effect of the industrial action has caused economic loss by preventing the employer from entering into future contracts.[914] The primary strategic

---

911. [1924] 1 Ch. 302.
912. The fact that the acts were carried out sincerely in the interests of the union's membership will not alone constitute justification: *Read* v. *Friendly Society of Stonemasons* [1902] 2 KB 88.
913. High Court, 14 April 2000.
914. *Barretts and Bairds* v. *Institute of Public Servants* [1987] IRLR 3: *Hadmor Productions* v. *Hamilton* [1982] IRLR 103.

advantage of this tort is that it is not necessary to prove that the loss was caused through the breach of an existing contract. All that is required is economic loss. Where a defendant's unlawful conduct prevents a business *entering into a contract* the defendant may not be sued for inducing breach of contract. There is no contract in existence. However, the trade union may be liable for the tort of intentionally interfering with trade. Here all that is required is: illegality; intention to financially injure the defendant; and, the fact of the defendant having suffered economic loss. In *Hadmor Productions* v. *Hamilton*[915] the plaintiff was a programme-making company. Thames TV had acquired a licence to show a series of programmes made by the plaintiff but had not yet entered into any contractual commitment to show the programme. Under pressure from the television production workers union, ACTT, Thames TV decided to cease business relations with the plaintiff. The House of Lords held that the tort was committed: there was the presence of unlawful means (the tort of intimidation); there was an intention to injure Hadmor in its business; and, there was an interference with Hadmor's business:

> The tort upon which Hadmor relies is interference with its trade by unlawful means; and the unlawful means relied upon consisted of the acts of [the trade union officials] in threatening that they would induce other persons, *viz.* ACTT members employed by Thames to break their contracts of employment with Thames. Such an act is capable of constituting unlawful means, and its effect is to cause damage to someone even though he is not a party to the contract, by interfering with the third party's trade or business.

The important point was that the tort of indirectly inducing breach of contract would not have succeeded. Hadmor had no contractual right to have the programmes shown. The most that Hadmor had was a 'commercial expectation that the programmes would be transmitted and its reputation as a newcomer in the field enhanced and its prospects greatly improved'.

The elements of the tort were described by Henry J in *Barretts & Bairds* v. *Institute of Public Servants*:[916] (i) that there should be an interference with the plaintiff's trade or business; (ii) that there must be unlawful means; (iii) that there must be intention to injure the plaintiffs; (iv) that the actions should, in fact, injure the plaintiffs.

III.   The Tort of Intimidation

310. A third industrial action-related tort is that of intimidation. The tort of intimidation is committed where a wrongdoer threatens another party with some civil, or criminal illegality unless the other complies with that demand. If, on complying, the person against whom the threat is directed, or some other party, suffers economic loss, the victim will have a cause of action in intimidation. The tort has

---

915. [1982] IRLR 103.
916. [1987] IRLR 3.

been recognized in the context of industrial disputes. In *Riordan* v. *Butler*[917] the defendants threatened the employer that they would take unlawful strike unless the plaintiff was dismissed. The employer complied, and the plaintiff was dismissed. The plaintiff was held to have an action for intimidation against the union organizers.

§3. STRIKE ACTIVITY AND INFRINGEMENT OF CONSTITUTIONAL RIGHTS

311. An infringement of the constitutional rights of others may also provide a further ground of liability. This is a product of two principles. First, Irish constitutional law recognizes as constitutionally protected the property interests of business affected by industrial action. Secondly, Irish constitutional law recognizes that constitutional rights can be injured by the acts of private parties, as well as public bodies, and requires private parties, as well as of public bodies, to respect the constitutional entitlement of others. These principles were applied in *Talbot (Ireland) Ltd* v. *ICTU, Merigan and others*.[918] Here the Supreme Court rationalized, in constitutional terms, the interests of parties affected by a strike at a car manufacturing plant. The contractual entitlements of car dealers and of motorists, which were damaged by the strike, were regarded as constitutional property rights. Trade unions, it was held, must operate within the constitutional framework and constitutional guarantees of Article 40(3) of the Constitution:

> a body of persons must operate within the constitutional framework and the constitutional guarantees in Article 40, and it would have to be borne in mind that innocent persons could to be damnified – and when he spoke of innocent persons he was not referring to the union or the company but to persons such as dealers who had no dispute with anybody, or the owners of vehicles who had no dispute with anybody but who, because of this embargo, could not get their vehicles serviced – a service they were entitled to under their contract.

On the other hand, the Supreme Court implied that the personal rights of individuals must be balanced against the legitimate entitlement of others to engage in industrial action. The court appeared to recognize a competing constitutional right to take industrial action. The Supreme Court implied that abuse of industrial action would exceed the legitimate entitlement to engage in industrial action, and would be capable of infringing the constitutional rights of others. The court stressed the particularly destructive, nature of the strike action involved in this case. Henchy J emphasized that 'what had happened went far beyond any picket; far beyond any strike; far beyond legitimate industrial action'.

---

917. [1940] IR 347.
918. Supreme Court, 1 May 1981.

§4. ILLEGALITIES COMMITTED BY PERSONS ENGAGED IN A PICKET

312. Distinct from the torts associated with taking industrial action, are a series of torts associated with engaging in a picket.

I. Private Nuisance

313. Private nuisance consists of unlawful interference with a person's ordinary use or enjoyment of his land:

> The generic conception involved in private nuisance may really be found in the fact that liability in nuisance flows from an act or omission whereby a person is annoyed, prejudiced or disturbed in the enjoyment of land or with his health, comfort or convenience as occupier of such land.[919]

A component of the right to the enjoyment of land is the right to be let alone without unreasonable interference. Towards the end of the 19th century, and into the early years of the 20th century, the courts debated the question whether a purely peaceful picket could amount to an *unreasonable* interference with this right.

In the earlier of these cases, *Lyons* v. *Wilkins*[920] the courts endorsed the view that even a purely peaceful picket might be illegal. There, the organizers placed a few men outside the plaintiff's works to distribute cards to persons entering or leaving the premises. The pickets had not used violence, threats or intimidation. The court held, none the less, that the fact that the picket was being undertaken to compel the plaintiffs to abstain from acting as they were entitled to behave was enough to make the picket unlawful. The land ownership interest which the court stressed was the employer's liberty to conduct his trade as he wished. The picketers' coercive intrusion upon this liberty was held to be an annoyance of 'a serious character' and 'of such a degree as to interfere with the ordinary comforts of life'.

On the other hand, in a later decision, *Ward Lock* v. *OPAS*[921] held that a peaceful picket of business premises did not amount to an unreasonable interference with the right to enjoyment of personal property. Again, the picket was entirely peaceful. The aim of the picket was to compel the employer to employ union labour, and for that purpose a picket, conducted in two shifts of three pickets each, was assembled. Again, there was no violence, molestation, or obstruction. The plaintiff, relying on *Lyons*, alleged nuisance on the basis that this 'watching and besetting was done with the purpose of compelling the plaintiffs in accordance with the wishes of the defendant society'. However, this time the Court of Appeal found that the conduct did not constitute nuisance: merely to have the objective of compelling the plaintiffs in the administration of their business was not a nuisance:

---

919. *Salmond and Heuston on the Law of Torts* (18th edn, London, 1981) at p. 48.
920. [1896] 1 Ch. 81.
921. (1906) 22 TLR 327.

Both cases involved compulsion of exactly the same type. In the *Ward Lock* case the court considered that picketing was an ordinary incident of the use of property for commercial reasons. By contrast, the court in *Lyons* considered that picketing was always an unacceptable intrusion upon the property owner's freedom to conduct business.

The more conservative *Lyons* view of peaceful picketing has proved the more enduring and has, on several occasions, been endorsed in Irish law. In *Educational Company of Ireland* v. *Fitzpatrick* Kingsmill Moore J. stated:

> Picketing is a murderous weapon and even if carried out with scrupulous avoidance of any expressed threats its inevitable effect is to cause such a conditioned effect in all trade unionists as inevitably to interfere with the business of the party picketed and with the ordinary user and enjoyment of his property.[922]

II. Harassment

314. The tort of harassment was developed in the English miners' strike of the mid-1980s. *Thomas* v. *NUM*[923] involved a claim by working miners in South Wales for an injunction restraining mass picketing as they were being bussed into work. The High Court could find no assault (the plaintiffs suffered no apprehension of immediate personal violence);[924] nor could the plaintiffs sue for nuisance (the only person who may sue for nuisance is a landowner). However, the court identified a new civil wrong: the tort of 'unreasonable harassment'. The court held that as an extension of, and by analogy with, the tort of nuisance which protected private property, the right of persons to use the highway should also be protected. An unreasonable interference with this right would constitute a tort: 'The tort might be described as a species of private nuisance, namely unreasonable interference with the victim's rights to use the highway'.[925]

III. Pickets and Section 11(1) of the Industrial Relations Act 1990

315. With common law almost entirely outlawing picketing, the right to picket has been given statutory licence. This was originally provided by section 2 of the

---

922. [1961] IR 365, *Lyons* v. *Wilkins* was also endorsed in *Larkin* v. *Belfast Harbour Commissioners* [1908] 2 IR 214, at p. 223.
923. [1985] 2 All ER 1.
924. 'Assault is defined in Clark & Lindsell on Torts, 15th edn, paragraph 14/10 as 'an overt act indicating an immediate intention to commit a battery, coupled with the capacity to carry that intention into effect'. The tort of assault is not, in my view, committed, unless the capacity in question is present at the time the overt act is committed. Since the working miners are in vehicles and the pickets are held back from the vehicles, I do not understand how even the most violent of threats or gestures could be said to constitute an assault" (at p. 20).
925. At p. 22.

Trade Disputes Act 1906. Subsection 1 of section 11 of the Industrial Relations Act 1990 now provides the statutory immunity from civil liability for the torts described above:

> It shall be lawful for one or more persons, acting on their own behalf or on behalf of a trade union, in contemplation of a trade dispute, to attend at, or where that is not practicable, at the approaches to a place where their employer works or carries on business.

The four opening words of section 11, subsection 1, 'it shall be lawful', mean that no action may be taken by employers against picketers for: private nuisance, public nuisance, harassment, or indirect inducement of breach of contract. However, the immunity only applies in a case where the conditions described in section 11 are meticulously complied with.

A. The Persons Who May Picket

316. Section 9(1) provides that the immunity in section 11 shall only apply to authorized trade unions and the members and officials thereof.[926] Accordingly non-union members are not entitled to the immunity laid down in section 11. In *Penny's Ltd v. Kerrigan*, High Court, 7 February 1977, a dismissed worker was joined by her father and sister-in-law. The father and sister-in-law were removed from the picket on the grounds that they were non-union members.

In addition the picketers must be acting 'on their own behalf'. This requires that picketers be engaged in pursuit of their own interests. Therefore, union members are disqualified from sympathetic picketing, or from joining a picket in support of other workers, where their own personal interests are not at stake. However, the range of persons permitted to picket is expanded by subsection (4) which provides that it shall be lawful for a trade union official, defined[927] as any paid official or any officer of a union or branch elected in accordance of the union, to accompany any member of his trade union.

B. The Picketing Must Be Peaceful

317. The section 11 immunity is confined to peaceful picketing. This may be infringed by physical violence. It may, also, be breached by language which is defamatory. In *Ryan v. Cooke*[928] picketers carried posters outside the plaintiff's shop, stating, untruthfully, that she refused to employ trade union labour. She was granted

---

926. '9(1) Sections 11, 12 and 13 shall apply only in relation to authorized trade unions which for the time being are holders of negotiation licences under the Trade Union Act, 1941, and the members and officials of such trade unions, and not otherwise.'
927. S. 11(5).
928. [1938] IR 512.

an injunction to restrain the picket, the High Court holding that that the dissemination of a falsehood could never be described as a 'peaceful' way of 'communicating information'. The use of abusive language may also take the action outside the statutory immunity. In *E.I. Co Ltd* v. *Kennedy*[929] Walsh J. stated:

> The use of words such as 'scab' or 'blackleg' are historically so associated with social ostracism and physical violence as to be far beyond anything which might be described as mere rudeness or impoliteness and go beyond what is permitted by law ... Excessive numbers in pickets may also go beyond what is reasonably permissible for the communication of information or for the obtaining of information and may amount to obstruction or nuisance or give rise to a reasonable apprehension of a breach of the peace.

Excessive numbers may be intrinsically intimidating, thereby making the picket non- peaceful, and thereby taking it outside the protection given by section 11. There must be a reasonable relationship between the size of the picket and the nature of the premises. In *Brendan Dunne Ltd* v. *Fitzpatrick*[930] 60 picketers were congregating outside the plaintiff's premises in central Dublin. Budd J. held that there must be a reasonable proportion between the size of the picket and the premises targeted.

C. The Location of the Picket

318. A picket may only be held at the place where the employer works or carries on business.[931] The accent in section 11 is on 'at'. 'At' does not mean *in* or *within*. A picket which gathers within the employer's premises is not protected. In *Larkin* v. *Belfast Harbour Commissioners*[932] a picket within the docks complex owned by the Harbour Commissioners was not protected. Similarly, in *Ryanair* v. *Members of SIPTU* a picket which assembled within the runway area of Dublin airport was held not protected by section 11, and an injunction was granted dispersing it.[933]

D. The Object of the Picket May Only Be either the Communication of Information, or Persuasion Not to Work

319. Pickets which are motivated by objects other than the two objectives of neutral communication of information, or the persuasion of workers not to attend

---

929. [1969] IR 69.
930. [1958] IR 29.
931. It does not include a place where an employer previously worked: *Dublin City Council* v. *National Engineering and Electrical Union* [2010] IEHC 289.
932. [1908] IR 214.
933. *Irish Times*, 12 March 1998. A picket at an employer's home is, obviously, also, unprotected. In *Tidey* v. *Burke, Irish Times*, 20 November 2001, an employer was granted an interlocutory injunction restraining the carrying out of picketing outside his home in County Dublin.

for work, fall outside the strict words of section 11. Picketing may only be carried on for legitimate objectives. Therefore, pickets which have as their objective the persuasion of customers not to do business with the targeted business are not covered by section 11. Here, the objective is to persuade persons to do something other than not attend for work. In *Ryan* v. *Cooke*[934] a picket was organized outside a retail creamery, the Monument Creamery, on Henry Street. The picketers carried placards which read 'This firm refuses to employ trade union labour. Support fair traders'. The High Court held that the tactic was persuasive, and went beyond the mere provision of information. On the other hand, it fell outside the one type of legitimate persuasion recognized by the legislation: the persuasion of workers not to work. Here, the persuasion was targeted at customers.

Similarly, persuading workers of another business not to complete deliveries, or not to collect products is not protected. Here again, the motivation is to persuade others to do something other than the only legitimate purpose for which persuasion may be used: the persuasion not to attend for work. Therefore, the picket is being used for an improper reason and is not covered by section 11. In *Newbridge Industries* v. *Bateson*[935] the plaintiff had ceased production, and former employees in a dispute over redundancy pay had mounted a picket outside the premises. Waterford Carpets, a customer, had a contract to collect a delivery of industrial fibre manufactured by the plaintiffs; when the driver sent by the customer arrived, he was approached by the picketers, and asked to turn back. This measure was held to be unprotected by section 11: 'the picket was not put in place for the purpose of peacefully obtaining or communicating information or of peacefully persuading any person to work or cease working. It was put on to prevent the material in the factory being taken out of [the factory'.

E. On Worker Disputes Where Agreed Grievance Procedures Have Not Been Exhausted

320.   Section 9(2) of the Industrial Relations Act 1990 provides that in the case of a one worker dispute, where there are agreed procedures availed of by custom or in practice in the employment concerned, or provided for in a collective agreement, for the resolution of individual grievances, then section 11 shall only apply where these procedures have been exhausted.[936] In *Iarnród Éireann* v. *Derby*[937] a bus

---

934. [1938] IR 512.
935. High Court, 15 July 1978; also reported in (1988) 7 *Journal of the Irish Society for Labour Law* 190.
936. S. 9(2)-(4) provides: 'Where in relation to the employment or non-employment or the terms or conditions of or affecting the employment of one individual worker, there are agreed procedures availed of by custom or in practice in the employment concerned, or provided for in a collective agreement, for the resolution of individual grievances, including dismissals, sections 10, 11 and 12 shall apply only where those procedures have been resorted to and exhausted. (3) Procedures shall be deemed to be exhausted if at any stage an employer fails or refuses to comply with them. (4) The procedures referred to in subsection (2) may include resort to such persons or bodies as a rights commissioner, the Labour Relations Commission, the Labour Court, an equality officer and the Employment Appeals Tribunal but shall not include an appeal to a court.'
937. *The Irish Times*, 23 March 1991.

driver had been suspended for refusing to undergo a medical examination. Pickets were mounted at bus and railway stations and within a few hours the entire public transport system had ceased operating. An injunction was granted restraining the picket on the ground that the dispute was a one-person dispute, and that internal procedures within the organization had not been exhausted. By contrast in *Bus Éireann* v. *SIPTU, The Irish Times* 17 June 1993 there had been a long-running dispute arising out of the reorganization of Bus Eireann, with the company seeking to change drivers duties and to introduce productivity measures. These measures were bitterly resented by the workers. At Sligo bus station one of these drivers refused to undertake a new roster, and was suspended. Pickets were placed at the entrance to the station and at other transport centres. This time the High Court refused to grant an injunction, holding that this was not, in reality a one-person dispute. The dispute over the dismissed worker had merely ignited the wider, ongoing dispute.

F. Actions Contrary to the Outcome of a Secret Ballot

321. While it is not a condition to the legality of a picket that a secret ballot have been held
(though failure to hold a secret ballot will make an injunction inevitable) a picket contrary to the outcome of a secret ballot will render the action unprotected by section 11. Section 17(1) provides that section 11 shall not apply in respect of industrial action 'in disregard of, or contrary to the outcome of a secret ballot relating to the issue of or issues involved'.

G. Secondary Picketing

322. Secondary picketing is distinct from ordinary or primary picketing in that it is carried on outside the premises of some party other than the strikers' employer. The strategy can be very destructive in that innocent employers, who happen to be customers or suppliers or customers of the targeted employer, may find themselves the subject of a picket if they do not withdraw contact from the targeted business. Section 11, subsection 2, severely limits the right to engage in secondary picketing, allowing it only where the secondary employer is acting for the purpose of frustrating the industrial action. This provides that secondary picketing is only lawful where

> it is reasonable for those who are so attending to believe at the commencement of their attendance and throughout the continuance of their attendance that that employer has directly assisted their employer who is a party to the trade dispute for the purpose of frustrating the strike or other industrial action, provided that such attendance is merely for the purpose of peacefully obtaining or communicating information or of peacefully persuading any person to work or abstain from working.

The word *purpose* in the phrase 'for the purpose of frustrating the strike' is crucially important here. The phrase 'purpose of frustrating' suggests object or desire. However, a secondary party may make a strike virtually ineffective, and effectively frustrate a strike without having this as his objective.[938] For example, a besieged employer may sub-delegate his orders to a third party. This third party may enable the employer to survive the strike; but it cannot be said that the third party's objective is to frustrate the strike. Indeed, he may wish the strike to continue. Only those secondary employers who are ideologically committed to breaking the strike, or employers who are associated with the primary employers business, will be likely to have the defeat of the primary employer as an objective or purpose.

The proposition that assistance without intention to frustrate will not justify the imposition of a secondary picket is illustrated in *Ryanair* v. *Members and Officials of SIPTU*.[939] Here, Ryanair workers had assembled outside the services assess point of Gategourmet, the supplier of in-flight services to Ryanair. Gategourment was a secondary employer, and, since there was no evidence that it was acting in order to frustrate the strike, the picketers were not protected by section 11(2).

The limited right to engage in secondary picketing does not apply in a case where the employer is a health service and the supportive action is taken to maintain life support services. Subsection (3) of section 11 qualifies the entitlement to undertake secondary picketing in the case where a secondary party is providing assistance by providing that:

> For the avoidance of doubt any action taken by an employer in the health services to maintain life-reserving services during a strike or other industrial action shall not constitute assistance or the purpose of subsection (2).

For example, if the technicians in a hospital pathology laboratory were to engage in industrial action, and were the provision of the service to be handed over to a private laboratory, it would not be possible to mount a secondary picket on the private laboratory, since the laboratory is providing life-preserving functions, and may not, in any circumstances, be picketed.

§5. REMEDIES AGAINST PERSONS ENGAGED IN WITHDRAWAL OF LABOUR OR PICKETING

323. The last two sections have described the wrongs which may be committed by persons involved in a withdrawal of labour or in picketing. This section described the principal remedies which may be awarded where these torts have been committed.

---

938. In *Nolan's Transport* v. *Halligan,* unreported, 20 December 1994 Barron J. said that s. 11 only permitted secondary picketing where the person being picketed had acted outside the ordinary course of business and solely for the purpose of making the primary picket ineffective.
939. *The Irish Times,* 12 March 1998.

I. Damages, Trade Unions and Vicarious Responsibility

324. Damages may be recovered for the various torts committed by persons who organize, or engage in, picketing or withdrawal of labour. The quantum of damages will be the economic loss which can be demonstrated to have been caused by the industrial action, calculated by comparing the business' anticipated turnover with actual turnover following the strike or other industrial action (where the difference can be shown to have been caused by the industrial action).[940]

This sum may be very extensive, and may exceed the financial means of the parties involved. May damages be recovered from the trade union on the basis that it is vicariously responsible for the wrongs committed by its officers?

In *Taff Vale* v. *Amalgamated Society of Railway Servants*[941] it was held that a trade union was a quasi-corporate body, and was therefore subject to one of the responsibilities of corporations: responsibility for the torts of its agents or servants committed in the course of their employment. This potential vicarious responsibility is, however, drastically curtailed by section 13 of the Industrial Relations Act 1990 which provides that:

> An action against a trade union, whether of workers or employers, or its trustees or against any members or officials thereof on behalf of themselves and all other members of the trade union in respect of say tortious act committed by or on behalf of the trade union in contemplation or furthermore of a trade dispute, shall not be entertained by any court. (2) in an action against a trade union … in respect of any tortious act alleged or found to have been committed by or on behalf of a trade union it shall be a defence that the act was done in the reasonable belief that it was done I contemplation or furtherance of a trade dispute.

'Trade dispute' is defined as 'any dispute between employers and workers which is connected with the employment or non-employment of the terms or conditions of or affecting the employment of any person'.[942]

This immunity is from vicarious responsibility only. It does not affect the personal responsibility of the union officials or members. Secondly, this immunity only applies where the act is committed in the *course of a trade dispute*. Where a wrong is committed outside the context of a trade dispute the immunity will not arise.

The phrase 'furtherance of a trade dispute' is moderated by the provision in subsection 2 that the defence still will apply where the defendant acts 'in the reasonable belief' that the act was in contemplation or furtherance of a trade dispute. This problem arises where action is objectively ineffective. According to one school of thought, objectively ineffective action is objectively not '*in furtherance* of a trade dispute'.[943] Subsection 2 is designed to block this interpretation; objectively

---

940. *Nolan Transport* v. *Halligan* [1995] 6 ELR 1.
941. [1901] AC 426.
942. S. 8 of the Industrial Relations Act 1990.
943. *Express Newspapers Ltd* v. *McShane* [1980] AC 672.

ineffective action is still protected so long as it is done in reasonable belief that it is in contemplation of a trade dispute.[944]

The definition of 'trade dispute' does not encompass a dispute which has the objective of depriving another person of a constitutional right.[945] Therefore, a dispute which has, as its purpose, the compelling of another person to join a trade union against their will, or to prevent the employment of women, will not be regarded as a trade dispute, and will not be protected by section 13.

II. The Interlocutory Injunction

325. In practice the most common remedy against industrial action is the interlocutory injunction against the organisers. The interlocutory injunction is a prohibitory order directing the wrongdoers to cease, pending the full trial, their committing the illegalities alleged against them. In the context of an industrial dispute, such an order will be directed against the organizers and will direct them to cease committing the economic torts (inducing breaches of contracts of employment, unlawfully causing economic loss, intimidation) which it is alleged their acts constitute.

In order to obtain an injunction, the plaintiff must first establish a fair case that the defendant is committing an illegality. It used to be the law that the plaintiff had to demonstrate on the balance of probability that the defendant was committing an illegality. In *Educational Company of Ireland* v. *Fitzpatrick*[946] the Supreme Court held that it would only grant an injunction restraining a picket where it was satisfied that the defendants actions were *probably* illegal or where there was a reasonable prospect of succeeding. However, in the mid-1970s the courts in England lowered the burden resting on plaintiffs. The courts were tired of the inefficiency of reviewing the same question twice: at the motion for the injunction, and later at the trial. It was more efficient to postpone the resolution of the merits to the trial. Accordingly, in *American Cyanamid* v. *Ethicon*[947] the House of Lords held that a fair question was established once the plaintiff could establish some possibility that the defendant was behaving unlawfully. The new test was more pro-plaintiff. There is a great difference between having to prove that something is merely possible and having to prove that something is *probable*. It is almost always feasible to prove that there exists a possibility that an illegality has been committed. A defendant could only resist an injunction where he could show that the defendant 'had no real prospect of succeeding in his claim'. The *American Cyanamid* test was intended to be of general application. However, in the context of labour disputes the *American Cyanamid* test favours the plaintiff employer. The *American Cyanamid* test was soon followed in Ireland: *Irish Shell* v. *Elm Motors*[948] and *Campus Oil* v. *Minister*

---

944. *Dublin City Council* v. *Technical Engineering and Electrical Trade Union* [2010] IEHC 288.
945. *Educational Company of Ireland* v. *Fitzpatrick (No. 2)* [1961] IR 345; *Murtagh Properties* v. *Cleary* [1972] IR 330.
946. [1960] I.R. 323.
947. [1975] 1 All E.R. 504.
948. [1984] 1 I.L.R.M. 595.

for Industry and Energy.[949] The effect is that the court must grant an injunction so long as the case is arguable even if it is weak.[950]

The second of the necessary conditions to an injunction at common law is that the plaintiff should establish that the balance of convenience favours the grant of an injunction. The balance of convenience involves the making of a cost/benefit analysis. An injunction will only be granted where the advantage to the plaintiff in granting an injunction outweighs the cost to the defendant in granting an injunction. Applied to applications to restrain allegedly unlawful industrial action the cost/benefit analysis will almost always benefit the employer. The advantage to the employer in granting an injunction is that he may be spared economic devastation of further agitation. (2) On the other hand, if an injunction is granted the only loss suffered by the strikers, it is said, is the temporary suspension of their campaign of disruption. *Bayzana* v. *Galligan*[951] is a good example of this reasoning in Irish law. The company stood to lose £3.5 million in EEC aid unless the picket was lifted. The Supreme Court weighed the huge economic loss to the plaintiffs against the purely temporary loss of the right to picket which would be suffered by the picketers until the matter went to trial if an injunction was granted.[952]

The ease with which these principles facilitated the grant of an injunction was objected to by the trade union movement (and even by sections of judicial opinion).[953]

A. Section 19 of the Industrial Relations Act 1990

326. Section 19 of the Industrial Relations Act, 1996, drastically restricts the capacity of employers to obtain injunctions. Section 19 provides that where (a) a secret ballot has been held in accordance with section 14; (b) the ballot favours industrial action; (c) the union has given not less than one week's notice of its intention to engage in industrial action, and (d) the defendant union establishes a fair case that they have been acting in furtherance or contemplation of a trade dispute, no injunction may be granted. Section 19, in effect, shuts down the court's ordinary power to grant an interlocutory injunction.

---

949. One subsequent authority has suggested that the court at interlocutory stage may assess the weight of the argument on an interlocutory injunction. This exception would arise only in cases involving a pure point of law (rather than a difficult issue of fact which would require a full trial): 'in a marginal case involving little or no conflicting evidence, and concerned with a net issue of law, there is nothing in principle wrong with a judge bringing his critical and analytical skills to bear with respect to the strength or otherwise of the plaintiff's case and taking that into account in the consideration of whether or not there is a fair issue to be tried' *Chieftan Construction* v. *Ryan* [2008] IEHC 147.

950. [1983] IR 88.

951. [1987] IR 241.

952. The application of the balance of convenience was rationalized in the same way in *Malincross* v. *BATU* [2002] 13 ELR 78; *DARU Blocklaying* v. *Building and Allied Trade Union* [2003] 14 LR 244.

953. See the comments by McCarthy J. in 'To do a Great Harm Do a Little Wrong' (1986) 6 *JISSL* 1, at pp. 6,7

Prior to the passing of the Industrial Relations Act 1990 employers could obtain interlocutory injunctions with great ease. The low burden of proof, combined with the ease of establishing that the balance of convenience, made injunctions easily obtainable. Section 19 of the Industrial Relations Act 1990 is one of the most valuable statutory privileges ever granted to trade unions in Ireland. Section 19 shuts down the courts' power to grant injunctions where the trade union can show that it has given the employer one week's notice, has obtained the approval of those have been called upon to engage in the action, and can demonstrate that it was acting in the course of a trade dispute. Section 19(2) provides:

> Where a secret ballot has been held in accordance with the rules of a trade union as provided for in *section 14* , the outcome of which or, in the case of an aggregation of ballots, the outcome of the aggregated ballots, favours a strike or other industrial action and the trade union before engaging in the strike or other industrial action gives notice of not less than one week to the employer concerned of its intention to do so, a court shall not grant an injunction restraining the strike or other industrial action where the respondent establishes a fair case that he was acting in contemplation or furtherance of a trade dispute.

One point must be stressed. Compliance with section 19 does not necessarily immunize participants from liability in damages for torts committed during industrial action. It does not render action *lawful*. It merely cancels the court's power to grant an injunction. It does not affect the court's power to award damages or any other remedy, bar an injunction.

B. The Conditions of Entitlement to the Protection of Section 19

327.   In order to qualify for the protection under section 19 a defendant must be able to establish compliance with the requirements in section 14 (the secret ballot provision). In *Nolans Transport* v. *Halligan*,[954] Keane J, while noting that the objective underlying the measure was to relieve unions from the abuse of the injunctions, described, also, the corresponding responsibilities imposed:

> Whilst [section 19] does afford an important protection to trade unions, there is also a specific and very important requirement that the subsection only comes into place, as it were, where there has been a secret ballot held in accordance with the rules of the trade union, as provided for in section 14 of the Industrial Relations Act 1990. The other factor which the Oireachtas clearly took into account is that the protection of this section should only be available to trade unions who ensure that the action undertaken has the support of union members and that it has their support as demonstrated in a secret ballot. That is, of course, important because it is not simply the employer and the employer's business which is very often affected by picketing, the employees themselves may not approve and may not even have been consulted in relation to

---

954. High Court, 24 March 1994.

the action being taken, and that particularly applied in times gone by to unofficial strikes, or 'wild cat' strikes, as they were called. That seems to me to be the background to this legislation and it is important that the courts should give effect to the objective of the Oireachtas in enacting the legislation.

The onus of proof of compliance with sections 14 and 19 is carried by the defendant. Five points are of particular importance.[955] First, a secret ballot must have been held in accordance with the rules of the trade union.[956] Second, entitlement to vote in the secret ballot must have been conferred on all persons whom it is reasonable to expect will be called upon to engage in the strike, or other industrial action.[957]

Third, the union must have taken reasonable steps to ensure that every member is given a 'fair' opportunity of voting. In *G&T Crampton* v. *BATU*[958] the ballot papers simply asked the membership to approve 'strike or other industrial action'. The Supreme Court held that implicit in the requirement that each individual be given 'a fair opportunity' of voting was a further requirement: that every member likely to be called upon to participate be informed of the exact nature of the action in which they were being asked to participate. This had not been done in this case; therefore, section 19 did not apply. Accordingly, the courts were free again to apply the simple fair case/balance of convenience tests, and an injunction was granted.

The fourth requirement is that as soon as practicable after the conduct of the secret ballot the trade union should take reasonable steps to make known to its members entitled to vote in the ballot, the number of papers issued; the number of votes cast; the number of votes in favour of the proposal; the number of votes against and the number of votes against. In *Nolan Transport* v. *Halligan*[959] there had not been full compliance with the requirement that the voting details be disclosed. It followed the High Court was liberated from the prohibition on granting injunctions imposed by section 19. The matter could be treated as it was in pre-1990 days: was there a possibility that the defendant was acting illegally? Did the balance of convenience favour the employer?

Fifth, the authority initially given by a ballot may have to be renewed where the circumstances change. The union must hold a further ballot when the conditions envisaged in the original proposal have altered. In *Malincross* v. *BATU*[960] the original ballot authorized a picket at a building site which was described as the company's site. The company then ceased to use the premises. The High Court held that this transformed the situation: industrial action at a place in which the employer had

---

955. *Dublin City Council* v. *Technical Engineering and Electrical Trade Union* [2010] IEHC 288.
956. S. 19(2) of the Industrial Relations Act 1990.
957. This condition was not complied with in *DARU Blocklaying* v. *Building and Allied Trade Union* [2003] 14 LR 244: the only persons who were called upon to participate in the ballot were the three persons involved in the immediate dispute. The High Court held that there was a difference between the persons involved in the dispute and the persons who might be called upon to engage in the dispute; the second category was wider and the category captured by the Act.
958. [1998] 1 ILRM 430.
959. High Court, 22 March 1994.
960. [2002] 13 ELR 78.

no connection (and which injured third parties) was fundamentally different to industrial action at a place which the employer occupied.[961]

III. The Remedy of Specific Performance

328. An order directing the strikers to return to work (an order of specific performance) has never been made by the Irish courts. This is a consequence of the general doctrine that an order of specific performance may never be made in order to compel a worker to work with an employer with whom there has been a breakdown of trust.[962]

§6. Strikes, Industrial Action and the Criminal Law

329. Persons employed in essential services who engage in industrial activity also run the risk of incurring criminal liability. Section 4 of the Conspiracy and Protection of Property Act 1875 (as amended by section 110 of the Electricity Supply Act 1927) is targeted at workers in public utilities. Section 4 provides that it is a criminal offence for any person employed by an undertaking upon whom is imposed by Act of Parliament the duty of supplying gas, water or electricity, to wilfully and maliciously break a contract of employment with that undertaking, knowing or having reasonable cause to believe that a probable consequence of his so doing will be deprive the inhabitants of that city or borough or place of their supply of water, gas or electricity.

The offence of endangerment created by the Non-Fatal Offences against the Person Act 1997 may also be used against persons participating in strikes in emergency services. Section 13 provides that it is an offence for a person to engage in conduct which intentionally or recklessly creates a substantial risk of death or serious personal harm to another. The offence, which has, in other jurisdictions been used against strikers in the essential services,[963] may be punished by fine or by imprisonment of up to seven years.

Along similar lines, section 5 of the Conspiracy and Protection of Property Act, 1875 incriminates the act of wilfully and maliciously breaking a contract of employment, knowing or having reasonable cause to believe that the probable consequences of so doing will be to endanger human life, or to expose valuable property to destruction or serious injury.

---

961. A rival view is that the High Court should not be excessively strict in limiting the terms of authorization. In *Dublin City Council* v. *Engineering and Electrical Union* [2010] IEHC 288 the ballot authorized the placing at pickets on the company's premises' authorized the placing of pickets after the employer had left the premises.
962. *De Francesco* v. *Barnum* (1890) 45 Ch. R. 430; *Gillis* v. *McGhee* (1863) 13 Ir. Ch. Rep. 48.
963. See the New York case *People* v. *Vizzini* 359 NYS 2d 143 (1974) where New York fire fighters who engaged in a five and a half hour stoppage were convicted of the offence of reckless endangerment.

Chapter 5. Settlement of Industrial Disputes

§1. Dispute Resolution Machinery

330. The machinery for the investigation and resolution of industrial disputes – itself a declining phenomenon[964] – is made up of the combination of two institutions: the Labour Court and the Labour Relations Commission.

I. The Labour Relations Commission

331. The Labour Relations Commission was established by the Industrial Relations Act 1990. The Commission's conciliation functions are activated by the occurrence of a 'trade dispute'. A 'trade dispute' is defined as 'any dispute between employers and workers which is connected with the employment, or non-employment, or the terms or conditions of, or affecting, the employment of any person'.[965] The Labour Relations Commission may, at the request of one or more of the parties to a trade dispute, or at its own initiative, offer the parties its appropriate services with a view to bringing about a settlement of the dispute.[966] Industrial Relations Officers are appointed to the Commission for the purpose of carrying out these conciliation services. In 2011, 1700 disputes were referred to the Commission's Conciliation Service. The conciliation service is effective: in 2011 it had an 84 per cent success rate.[967]

II. The Labour Court

332. Above the Labour Relations Commission sits the Labour Court, the more senior institution established by the Industrial Relations Act 1946. The Labour Court is conceived of as an institution of last resort, with jurisdiction to adjudicate only where applications to the Labour Relations Commission have failed. Prior to 1990 the Labour Court performed the conciliation functions now performed by the Labour Relations Commission. In 1990 – by the Industrial Relations Act 1990 – that conciliation function was withdrawn, and the Labour Court re-cast as a tribunal of last resort.

Under the new arrangements, the Labour Court is restricted in its capacity to intervene to five cases only: (i) where the Labour Relations Commission have failed to resolve a dispute, and the parties to the dispute request the Labour Court to investigate the matter; (ii) where the Labour Relations Commission decides to waive its conciliatory role, and the parties request the Labour Court to investigate; (iii) where the Labour Court, following consultation with the Commission, considers that there

---

964. In 2011 just 3695 days were lost due to industrial disputes. The number of disputes was eight. This is the lowest figure in modern times. Labour Court Annual Report 2011 (Dublin 2012).
965. S. 8 of the Industrial Relations Act 1990.
966. S. 25(2) of the Industrial Relations Act 1990.
967. *Labour Relations Commission Annual Report 2011* (Dublin 2012), 18.

are exceptional circumstances justifying its intervention.[968] (iv) In addition, the Minister for Enterprise, Trade and Employment may, where he considers that a trade dispute, actual or apprehended, affects the public interest, refer the matter to the Labour Court.[969] (v) The Labour Court may also hear a dispute where the workers concerned in a dispute request the Labour Court to investigate the dispute and undertake to accept the recommendation of the Court.[970]

In 2011, 180 cases were referred to the Labour Court by the Labour Relations Commission on the ground of the Commission's inability to resolve the dispute (section 26(1)(a)).[971] In the same year, 131 cases were referred directly to the Labour Court by a union or workers who had undertaken to accept the Labour Court's recommendation in advance. Six disputes were referred on the undertaking of both parties to accept the Court's recommendation.[972]

The Labour Court's investigative function is defined in section 68 of the Industrial Relations Act 1946: 'The Court having investigated a trade dispute may make a recommendation setting forth its opinion on the merits of the dispute, and the terms on which it shall be settled.' The Labour Court does not (except in a case where the parties invite the court to investigate the dispute, and undertake to accept the recommendation of the Labour Court) have power to bind the parties.[973] The Labour Court's function is simply to make recommendations. The Labour Court has been judicially described as 'a highly responsible board of conciliation [which] investigates a trade dispute with a view to making not an order but a recommendation. The objective is to bring about peace by persuasion, instead of submission by coercion'.[974]

Generally, the Labour Court is not obliged to investigate a trade dispute. The jurisdiction under Section 68 of the Industrial Relations Act 1946 is a discretionary one. The only cases in which the Labour Court must investigate a trade dispute arises either where the parties request the Court to investigate the dispute, and undertake to accept the recommendation of the Court[975] or where the Minister directs the Labour Court to investigate the dispute.[976]

---

968. Ss. 26(1), (3) and (5).
969. S. 38(1) Industrial Relations Act 1990.
970. S. 20(1) and 20(2) of the Industrial Relations Act, 1969.
971. *Labour Relations Commission Annual Report 2011* (Dublin 2012), 25.
972. S. 20(1) of the Industrial Relations Act, 1969.
973. S. 20 of the Industrial Relations Act, 1969.
974. Per Gavin Duffy J. in *McElroy* v. *Mortished*, unreported, High Court, 17 June 1949.
975. S. 20 of the Industrial Relations Act 1969.
976. S. 38(1) of the Industrial Relations Act 1990.

Selected Bibliography

TEXTBOOKS ON IRISH EMPLOYMENT LAW

Arthur Cox Employment Law Yearbook (continuing annual publication)
Cox, N., V. Corbett and D. Ryan, *Employment Law in Ireland* (Clarus Press, 2009)
Daly, B. and M. Doherty, *Principles of Irish Employment Law* (Clarus Press, 2010)
Forde, M., A.P. Byrne, *Employment Law* (Dublin 2009)
Kerr, A., *Irish Employment Legislation* (Dublin 1998, continuing)
Meenan, F., *Employment Law* (Dublin 2014)
Regan, M. (ed.), *Employment Law* (Tolley, 2014)

THE LAW OF DISCIPLINE AND DISMISSAL

Kerr, T., *Termination of Employment Statutes* (Dublin 2007)
Mills, S., J.P. McDowell, E. Burke and A. Ryan, *Disciplinary Proceedings in Statutory Professions* (Dublin 2011)
Redmond, M., *Dismissal Law in Ireland* (Dublin, 2007)
Stewart, E. and N. Dunleavy, *Compensation on Dismissal* (Dublin 2007)

PUBLIC SECTOR EMPLOYEES

Gallagher, B. and C Maguire, Civil Service Regulation (Dublin, 2011)
Hogan, G. and D Morgan, *Administrative Law in Ireland* (Dublin 2010)

EMPLOYMENT EQUALITY

Bolger, M., C. Bruton and C. Kimber, *Employment Equality Law* (Dublin 2011)
Kerr, A., *Employment Equality Legislation* (Dublin 2013)

TRANSFER OF UNDERTAKINGS

Houston, E., *Transfer of Undertakings in Ireland* (Dublin 2011)
McMullen, J., *Business Transfers and Employee Rights* (1988- continuing)

Selected Bibliography

THE LAW OF INDUSTRIAL ACTION

Kerr, Anthony, *The Industrial Relations Act 1990-20 Years On* (Dublin 2010)
Maguire, C., *Trade Union Membership and the Law* (Dublin, 1999)
Redmond, M., T. Mallon, Strikes; An Essential Guide to Industrial Action and the
  Law (Dublin, 2011)

Index

Numbers given refer to paragraphs.

Index

Index